SWANENDAEL
IN NEW NETHERLAND

WILLIAM J. COHEN

SWANENDAEL
IN NEW NETHERLAND

THE EARLY HISTORY
OF
DELAWARE'S OLDEST SETTLEMENT AT LEWES

WILLIAM J. COHEN

Lewes Historical Society
Lewes, Delaware

Cedar Tree Books
Wilmington, Delaware
2004

First Edition

Published by
Cedar Tree Books, Ltd.
Nine Germay Drive, Wilmington, DE 19804
and
The Lewes Historical Society
110 Shipcarpenter Street, Lewes, DE 19958

ISBN: 1–892142–24–4

Title: Swanendael in New Netherland
Author: William J. Cohen
Book Design: Angela Werner, Michael Höhne Design

Copyright:© 2004 Lewes Historical Society

Library of Congress Cataloging-in-Publication Data
Cohen, William J.
Swanendael in New Netherland : the early history of Delaware's oldest
 settlement at Lewes / William J. Cohen.-- 1st ed.
    p. cm.
Includes bibliographical references and index.
ISBN 1-892142-24-4 (hardcover : alk. paper)
  1. Lewes (Del.)--History. 2. Delaware--History--Colonial period, ca.
1600-1775. I. Title.

F174.L6C64 2004
975.1'02--dc22

                                          2004013456

Printed in the United States of America on 60# archival, acid-free paper meeting
the requirements of the American Standard for Permanence of Paper for printed
Library Materials.

To the people of the past,
The first Indians who lived here and the settlers who came here;

To the people of the present,
The citizens who make this place their home;

To the people of the future,
For they will know what we do today.

Table of Contents

*This book was made possible
by the financial assistance of the
Delaware Heritage Commission
and the
Delaware River & Bay Authority.*

Forward

Though small in area and population Lewes has been the focal point of many events of historical significance. The 1631 Dutch whaling post at Hoernkill (Lewes) provided a pivotal legal point in the settlement of the Penn/Calvert dispute for control of the peninsula. The location of Cape Henlopen played a role in defining the boundary between Delaware and Maryland. Several Lewes citizens had contributing roles in both the Revolutionary War and the War of 1812. Lewes was also the location of the first social experiment in communal living in the new world. The story includes armed raids by neighboring colonists from the south, raids by pirates and sunken treasure ships off the coast.

Many facets of Lewes's history are unique and perhaps none more so than the so-called "Warner Grant." Visitors and newcomers to Lewes are often taken aback to learn that a significant part of the town is owned "in common" and residents and businesses lease residential and commercial lots from the city. The history of this unusual arrangement is worthy of a volume all its own. As a result of meticulous research and access to sources not readily available, a complete story of the evolution of the common lands is presented. It is a story that began over three hundred years ago: at times it pits citizen activists against city, state or local governments; it includes individual citizens claiming undeeded land; there are calls for certain lands to be set aside for common use in perpetuity; there is litigation and threat of litigation.

Controversial land-use issues are prevalent in current headlines and seemed destined to be topical in the foreseeable future. This scholarly and thoroughly documented account of the Warner Grant will be the starting point for anyone interested in understanding many of the issues.

This history has been recorded by numerous authors in many publications. General histories of the town have been included in larger state and regional volumes. Specific events in the town's past have been researched and published in historical periodicals. Swanendael in New Netherland tells the story in one volume and provides a continuity not found elsewhere. The author has produced a history worthy of the First Town in the First State and the extensive list of source material is a valuable asset for future researchers and others interested in Lewes's history.

Preface

The History of Swanendael in New Netherland
1968 - 2003

1

This book has been a long time in the making – thirty-five years to be exact. What started out as one research element in a state government community planning project accelerated into a wonderful intellectual adventure becoming, at times, a time consuming drive to uncover the story of the early history of a small coastal community in Delaware. What has intrigued me most about this experience is that Lewes has also captivated the interest and passion of many people, ranging from those who have the intellectual curiosity for historical research; to those who have committed to preserving older homes and other buildings; to those who trace their own family histories in this community back many generations; and finally to those who have chosen Lewes as their year round or summer home.

It is expected that in a publication of this sort, the author will write a brief preface or introduction that sets the stage for the remainder of the text. These preliminaries would, of course, be followed by acknowledgements. However, when Michael DiPaolo, The Lewes Historical Society's first Executive Director, suggested that a "history of the history" would be an informative and interesting inclusion, I concurred.

As I thought about the structure that such a piece should take it became clear that as I set about constructing the "history of the history" I could be very clever about the effort and have it also serve as something akin to an ethnographic narrative. As such, it could reveal the chronology of people and events that have contributed to this publication. In this sense it would serve as both an introduction and an acknowledgment to the many people who have contributed their ideas, advice, support, and critical reviews over the last thirty-five years. So, that is what I have done, and that is what follows.

2

I had not been to Lewes before the early part of 1968. In that year I was appointed the project coordinator for the town's first comprehensive planning program being conducted by the Delaware State Planning Office. For the next two years I would be enmeshed in field work, research, attending many meetings, and finally the writing that would produce eight background studies (released between October 1968 and July 1969), the town's first comprehensive development plan in December 1970, followed by recommendations concerning zoning, subdivision regulations, and capital budgeting.

From the beginning of the program it was expected that I must learn about every aspect of the community and develop a close working relationship with town officials. In the case of the latter, it would be indispensable to the success of the planning program that the planning commission directly participate and be willing to contribute both their leadership and their knowledge. The planning commission, chaired by Dr. James Beebe, Jr., met both of those criteria over the next two years.

In addition to Dr. Beebe, the commission included F. Robert Mercer as Vice Chairman, Mrs. Emory B. (Hazel) Brittingham as Secretary, and the following members: Mrs. D. Anthony (Helene) Potter, William T. Manning, Frederick D. Thomas, Howard Seymour, Mrs. Jesse F. Jones, and William S. Ingram, Jr. Lewes' first city manager, Ronald Donovan, became not only my guide to understanding every aspect of the community, but my friend. A key person was the mayor, Alfred A. Stango, who at times could be controversial, but consistently supported sound community planning.

The background studies provided a crucial learning experience for my planning assignment in Lewes since I had to examine a number of characteristics about the community, including, but not limited to the demographic composition and changes over time; the pattern of land use and development; the level of community services; and the adequacy of the infrastructure such as the transportation system and public utilities.

When I began the field work and research for the final background study, that was ultimately called, "History, Historic Sites, and Buildings," I found that getting started was not very difficult. Many historical accounts were easily available. One day as I was checking what our office library had, I stumbled across copies of two 1963 publications of the Delaware State Planning Office that established the planning parameters for what would become the Cape Henlopen State Park. One of the documents was titled, *Information Supplement To A Plan for the Public Utilization of Cape Henlopen, Delaware,* and relied on material from a variety of sources. One in particular was mentioned — "Mr. Houston Wilson, Esquire's report, 'Cape Henlopen.'" The *Information Supplement* contained an extensive series of "Historical Notes on Cape Henlopen" that provided "…some important details which are significant to the disposition of the land on which the Fort Miles military installation is situated." Not only did this information peak my curiosity but I decided that I must seek out the author.

I drove from Dover to Georgetown on a cool spring day in 1969 to make a scheduled meeting with Houston Wilson, a well known and highly regarded attorney. He had completed a "report" in 1942 as part of the condemnation litigation when the United States acquired a vast amount of land on Cape Henlopen to construct Fort Miles. Wilson knew the purpose of my visit from my initial telephone conversation. He welcomed me with a firm handshake and few preliminaries. We got right into the subject of the history of an evolving concept of setting aside certain lands to be used as a public commons in and around Cape Henlopen since colonial times. At last, he walked across the room and retrieved from his book shelf the document that I was anxious to see.

I moved my chair close to his desk as he carefully explained the organization of his typewritten two volume "report." It did not take long to realize that I would need a fair amount of time to go over all of his findings, analysis, and exhibits. The breadth of Wilson's research was very impressive. I asked if I could make a photo copy of the treatise, since he had made me aware that very few copies of it existed. He consented and I assured him that I would personally return all of his materials as soon as possible, which I did. What I have cited as the Wilson Report has never been published and is not generally known. Because of its thoroughness of historical documentation I have relied on it to be the essential framework of Chapter 7.

Back in Lewes I found that three members of the planning commission took a special effort to advance my understanding of the community, principally its history and traditions. As my research proceeded I found ample information about the dominant ethnic and cultural traditions of the community, primarily the Dutch and the English. I would learn about the Indians, who lived on the Delmarva Peninsula before the Europeans, initially by examining archeological records. Yet, it was Frederick Thomas, a local school principal, who opened my awareness to what he called, "the other Lewes." This was the tightly knit black community that Thomas was a member of and originally formed by African slaves brought here by the English in the eighteenth century. His insightful and empathetic portrayal gave me an added understanding and appreciation for Lewes.

When I first embarked on learning about Lewes' history (in the fall of 1968) Hazel Brittingham immediately offered assistance in finding historic materials. She gave me a copy of Virginia Cullen's very popular, History of Lewes, that had been published in 1956 by the Colonel David Hall Chapter of the Daughters of the American Revolution. Helene Potter was a member of that chapter and she likewise took a personal interest and extended my research pursuit to identify historic homes and buildings. Both Hazel and Helene became invaluable sources of information and strong allies in my work. One day I was asked, "Have you met Dr. Marvil?" I responded. "No," and added, "Do you think I should?"

3

It was on one of the many visits to Lewes in 1968 that an appointment had previously been arranged with the Lewes Historical Society's founding president and prominent Sussex County physician, Dr. James E. Marvil. A man of slight build he exuded a gentle demeanor coupled with a firm and uncompromising dedication to preserving Lewes' past — both its history and its buildings. That first meeting would be the beginning of an evolving friendship. We would spend many hours together and keep in touch by correspondence over many years as I became more engaged in researching the history of Lewes. In a very personal way Dr. Marvil (as I always addressed him) would become my hero in Lewes.

I walked just about every street, road, and alleyway in Lewes with Dr. Marvil as he pointed out the various buildings that were the visual representation of the history of the town. He was particularly pleased with the "Historical Enclave," a square block at Third and Shipcarpenter Streets that became the location of rescued and restored buildings. The Historical Enclave has secured its place as a living example of Lewes' historic past. Back at his home on Gills Neck Road, a home built in 1760 that he and Mrs. Marvil had meticulously restored with superb architectural integrity, he showed me books, documents, and art work that provided additional impetus to my research on the history of Lewes. His passion for Lewes was obvious, and his passion to preserve the history of Lewes was even greater.

Dr. Marvil took great pride in the "Doctor's Office," a former dilapidated cypress shingle dwelling that he had moved to 324 W. Third Street, that served as his office. He personally designed and carefully supervised the restoration and interior layout of what is today one of many beautifully restored buildings in Lewes. In one of our conversations I mentioned that I would like to contact George Fletcher Bennett, a nationally known historic architect whose classic work, *Early Architecture of Delaware,* was first published in 1932. Dr. Marvil liked the idea, since he was familiar with the work, but had never met the man.

I invited Bennett to come to Lewes and provide a commentary on historic architecture. On May 23, 1969 I picked him up at his home near Dover and during the drive to Lewes tape-recorded our conversation, which I later transcribed (an excerpt is cited in Chapter 6). By prearrangement I drove to Dr. Marvil's office for a tour of the "Doctor's Office." After viewing every nook and cranny inside and out, from all perspectives, Bennett proclaimed that no architect could have done a more responsible, accurate, and sensitive restoration than this. Dr. Marvil beamed and I became convinced that his doctor's office should serve as a prototype for future individual restoration projects, which it has.

4

Within a few weeks after the "History, Historic Sites, and Buildings" study had been presented to the planning commission it immediately hit a chorus of interest. Dr. Marvil's close friend, journalist and historian Emerson Wilson, wrote a very favorable article that appeared in the Wilmington Evening Journal on July 29, 1969. A companion article on the same page by Alan Poland, a Sussex County reporter, was titled, "Lewes Out to Grow, Preserve Heritage." Within the week an editorial appeared on August 4th in the Wilmington Morning News written by Anthony Higgins, Associate Editor of the Editorial Page, and captioned, "Old Lewes and the Future." In part Higgins wrote

> It is good to see the old salty town of Lewes made the subject of a special backward-looking study of the state government, this time by the State Planning Office. Sometimes a backward look is necessary in wisely looking forward.

Not realizing it at the time, but the fate of my modest study was now sealed, since it had received state-wide publicity, approbation from many citizens in the community, and most important, unequivocal approval from Dr. Marvil. I don't remember exactly when, but sometime soon after the newspaper coverage, Dr. Marvil suggested that if I was interested the Lewes Historical Society could publish the work, and distribute it to a wider audience. I responded casually that if that would happen then I ought to do some additional research to examine in depth various aspects of the study that, during the planning project, could only be addressed in a cursory way. Dr. Marvil agreed and I agreed to begin the research. Now the real intellectual adventure would begin and extend well into the next decade.

5

In December 1970 Lewes' first Comprehensive Development Plan was published and my work in the community in a professional planning capacity effectively came to an end. I was assigned other duties in the Delaware State Planning Office. The director, David R. Keifer, and my supervisor, Nick Fisfis both knew of my continued interest to do further research in Lewes in anticipation of a publication, as long as I did it on my own time. Well, there were times that took me away from the office, during "working hours" to go to the state archives (the Hall of Records), the University of Delaware library, or even visit Dr. Marvil in Lewes. Dave and Nick never reprimanded me and for their support (or for not looking) I was very grateful.

Now after all of these years I can finally admit that I over extended my time out of the office on more than one occasion. The more I dug into sources of information that would open up new vistas of knowledge about the early history of Lewes, the more dedicated I became that no avenue should be left unexplored. I spent many hours (well beyond lunch time) at the state archives, and one day I met Michael L. Richards, a Research Associate, who took a genuine interest in my "project." Mike helped me locate information that was not easily accessible, especially the fascinating collection of maps. The rare maps and other irreplaceable documents were judicially guarded by the State Archivist, Leon de Valinger, and access to them, to an outsider, was forbidden. When I discovered references that would depict the Lewes area on seventeenth and eighteenth century maps, I simply had to look at them.

Mike agreed to help me, but I would have to come back to the archives when de Valinger and the senior staff were at lunch. When everyone was gone my co-conspirator would cautiously open the door to the musty inner sanctum of the rare map collection and allow me to view the maps and make a list of those that would be relevant to my search. Mike would also photocopy source materials that I would later utilize when writing the manuscript that I would call, *Swanendael in New Netherland.* It is significant to point out that he completed the first transcription of the logs of *HMS Roebuck,* the British man-of-war that harassed the Town of Lewes during the Revolution in 1776 (as discussed in Chapter 5).

While the experience at the state archives proved that oftentimes, in order to gather historic information, one has to resort to being a surreptitious researcher, that was not the case when I needed archeological records. Another state agency, that was then known as the Delaware

Archeological Board, was very generous and open about, not only forwarding information about the archeological investigations in the Lewes vicinity, but reviewing the draft manuscript as well. The State Archeologist, Ronald A. Thomas, was especially helpful. I had many conversations with Ron, and he always followed through in getting me accurate records and the latest information and data.

6

One of the great surprises during the preparation of the manuscript was the interest taken in my work by C.A. Weslager, the renowned historian, archeologist, and ethnographer, who had written a voluminous number of books and journal articles about the early Indian, Dutch, and English settlements. His *Dutch Explorers, Traders and Settlers in the Delaware Valley 1609 – 1664* was published by the University of Pennsylvania Press in 1961, and after reading it, I embraced it as the model that I would use for the preparation of my own work. Because of his erudition Weslager would have a significant influence on this publication as exemplified by my citation of fourteen books or articles that he authored and one article that he co-authored with Professor A.R. Dunlap.

I discussed with Dr. Marvil my thoughts about contacting Weslager to see if he would be interested in reviewing my drafts that were now beginning to be completed. On February 8, 1970, I wrote to Dr. Marvil.

> I met Weslager on Saturday, and we talked for almost three hours. I am really quite pleased with the way things developed. He was very interested and receptive to the project, and offered any assistance....
>
> Weslager loaned me his entire working file he used subsequent to writing *Dutch Explorers, Traders,* etc. which contains correspondence with various persons concerning the Lewes settlement, as well as information

about the attempt to have the [Swanendael] fort site
made a national landmark. He granted me permission
to copy anything I needed.

Weslager was a loquacious man, with a sparkling wit and engaging personality. He immediately took a genuine interest in what I was doing. Within the next few months I began to submit the first chapters for his review detailing the archeological and historic recorded evidence pertaining to the Indians (as presented in Chapter 1), as well as the first Dutch and later the English and Plockhoy settlements (Chapters 2, 3, and 4). He would make his notations and return the draft. By January 1971 he had reviewed the first draft of the entire manuscript.

Over the next few years I would stay in contact with Weslager both by telephone and through a few visits to his home in Yorklyn, Delaware, where he had a study crammed with books, a wide assortment of documents, and archeological finds from his many explorations during the 1930s and 1940s. On one occasion I received a correspondence from him as he traveled to Europe to do his own research. It contained a succinct revelation written on a post card from Paris, dated June 7, 1973. "Visited Dr. Simon Hart [author of *The Prehistory of the New Netherland Company,* 1959] in Amsterdam last Monday, and learned about new, exciting, untranslated Mss data pertaining to Dutch settlements on the Delaware." We did not pursue the matter further.

Weslager was more than just helpful in his support and enthusiasm. He gladly provided many critical suggestions and corrections and openly shared much of his own resource materials. He was to me an important inspiration.

7

There would be a number of drafts that preceded the final version between 1969 and 1971. With each iteration the new draft had to be reconciled with the previous draft. I determined that the process required that one person read to another. In this way I would be assured that unfamiliar Dutch nomenclature and the obsolete rendition of seventeenth and eighteenth English spelling was correctly transferred from one draft to the next. My wife, Sally, was the quintessential proofreading partner. She helped me enormously. One summer, while vacationing in Fenwick Island we would sit on the sand, as our young son Josh played nearby, reading to each other from one draft to the next. It seemed laborious, especially when one is on vacation, but that was part of the adventure.

By September 1971 all of Weslager's changes to the draft manuscript had been incorporated. Hoping that this latest draft would be at least the penultimate effort, I began to mail chapters to Dr. Marvil. On November 24th he sent me the following. "I have received the last chapter of your history of Lewes and wish to congratulate you for such a fine work." My optimism was at its apex.

Now that it was "done" I felt that a total "fresh eye" reading should be conducted. I approached one of my colleagues in the State Planning Office to see if he would do a full editorial review. Kenneth C. Haas and I had been graduate students at the University of Delaware and by 1971 we worked together in Dover. I knew Ken as a bright and careful researcher, who later would earn a Ph.D from Rutgers University. I trusted him more than anyone else to give the manuscript a comprehensive reading. Ken's review was completed in March 1972 and I then decided that after I had made his corrections the first *Swanendael in New Netherland: Delaware's Oldest Settlement at Lewes* manuscript was now completed.

Everything should fall into place to get the manuscript to publication, or so I thought. Dr. Marvil began to be concerned that the Historical Society would not have sufficient funds to publish the work, and it seemed that the momentum was beginning to wane. I am not certain what was transpiring but the prospect of finally seeing a book grew dimmer and dimmer. We did discuss options and alternative publishing possibilities, but nothing was finalized. For the next few years despite good intentions and a modest effort on my part to secure a publisher, plans to make *Swanendael in New Netherland* a reality practically came to a halt. However, in 1973 one event did offer hope that the manuscript would get published.

Kenneth Douty who had retired to Lewes and become active in the Historical Society, seemed to pick up the torch to promote the publication. About the same time he was arranging for me to make a presentation to the Lewes Historical Society on October 19, 1973, to speak about "Preservation by the Historic District Zoning Concept," he expressed interest in the manuscript. I sent Douty a complete version of the work, but that was the last I heard. I was starting to harbor thoughts that Swanendael in New Netherland might simply become a lost fragment of history.

8

Sometime during 1974 through mutual friends, I was introduced to George Nocito, Professor of Art at the University of Delaware, and a member of the American Association of Environmental Artists. George and I had an immediate rapport and shared a deep concern for the environment, especially how certain changes over time affect the design of the built environment. As a friendship developed we realized that we also had a mutual interest in Lewes. George was interested in Lewes' history as it depicted changing attitudes and the visual design consequences of land use. I was interested in Lewes' history from the perspective of understanding how human associations and institutions develop and change over time. Over the next few months we would casually talk about how we could merge my manuscript and extensive historic documentation with the photographic documentation George had done in Lewes to illustrate the changes in the built environment.

While my manuscript still lay dormant, George was fashioning a symposium, that was held in Lewes on May 28, 1975 under the sponsorship of the Lewes Historical Society (with funding from the Delaware Humanities Forum). The purpose was to examine "some local laws in the context of environmental potential, traditions, economic factors and the humanistic aesthetic requirements for the man-made environment." The symposium provided somewhat of a structure to subsequent conversations George and I had that would culminate in a joint venture: we would combine our previous work — my history and his photographs — for a new publication.

My original manuscript would not, at least not yet, fall through the cracks and be completely forgotten in Lewes. The day before the symposium was held Hazel Brittingham wrote me on May 27, 1975 the following:

> I have been thinking about the work you did toward a publication about Lewes history. Where does it stand? I would feel it unfortunate that those who are interested could not somehow, sometime, benefit. I feel we are having, and will have, an influx of publications and I worry about the quality. I would not worry about the quality of yours and am interested in its status.

On December 5, 1975, I tape recorded a conversation that George and I had as the beginning effort to formally establish the parameters for our joint venture. George proposed a hypothesis that would guide the framing of our work. Simply stated (by George): "There are certain periods of time in the history of the country when there were rapid changes taking place, and these changes tend to have a visual character in many places. A [tentative] conclusion is that in times of great economic activity there seems to be less concern for order and aesthetic quality." George also proposed that the new title for our mutual undertaking be, "Urban Design and the Changing Environment: A History of People and Events." I think that it captured what we were up to.

This then would be the new direction and by March 1976 we were pondering two alternative "outlines" for the work and a newly written "introduction," and "table of contents" that George prepared for my review. I needed to feel comfortable with this new and rather enterprising approach to modify a work that I had spent so much time with. So, I suppose it was a cathartic endeavor that influenced my suggestion that we co-author a brief article that would, to some degree, serve as a first cut approach to our joint venture. I prepared an essay, that George reviewed, and then submitted it to the *Delaware Conservationist,* a highly regarded periodical published by the State Department of Natural Resources and Environmental Control. The article appeared in the Summer 1977 issue under the title, "The Changing Lewes and Rehoboth Canal." Shortly afterward, my friend George Nocito died, and that would bring to a close any further contemplation to modify *Swanendael in New Netherland.*

9

Between 1979 and 1981 the flame of interest to get the manuscript to a publication stage was not entirely extinguished, yet it was burning at a fairly low level. Even though Weslager kept encouraging me to keep the flame burning, nothing developed.

Hazel Brittingham and I had occasional correspondence for a number of years, underscored by her dedication to preserve the history of Lewes. She, more than anyone else, has shared with me from the beginning the challenges and frustrations in trying to arrange the publication of Swanendael in New Netherland. So, I was not surprised when she wrote me on February 10, 1981.

> Re-reading your draft of table of contents and introduction this morning absolutely makes chills run up and down my spine. Your writing covers the period of history about which there is so much misinformation. Hopefully some day it will be freely available to anyone interested.

Despite her continued support and encouragement, Hazel's genuinely sincere and kind words did not motivate me to continue searching for a publication avenue. I had other adventures to pursue. One morning in 1981 I carefully packed all of my materials including notes, various drafts, copies of many documents and maps, and correspondence over the years, and stored them. All of my work would now rest quietly. It would be a hiatus that lasted for the next twenty years.

10

In late October 2001 I received a telephone call. "Are you the Bill Cohen who many years ago, wrote a 'history' of Lewes?" "Yes, I answered." It turned out that the manuscript had been found among Dr. Marvil's papers that came into the possession of The Lewes Historical Society after his death. E. Michael DiPaolo, the Society's Executive Director, indicated that there was a sincere renewed interest in having the work published by The Lewes Historical Society. I welcomed the opportunity to open up a door that had been closed for so long.

On November 5th Mike, along with George Elliott, the current president of the Historical Society and Dr. Marvil's son-in-law, and Hazel Brittingham, who I had not seen in many years, traveled from Lewes to my home in Wilmington. In preparing for that meeting I retrieved the boxes that contained all of the archival material I had packed away two decades before. In order to reconstruct the saga of the *Swanendael in New Netherland* manuscript, to serve as both a refresher for me and to be the focus of the discussion with Mike, George, and Hazel, I prepared a listing of contents of what I termed the "Swanendael Archives," and what I would later revise as "The Swanendael Manuscript Archives 1968 – 2003. This includes all of the documents and correspondence that I retained in preparing the manuscript, and as of this writing are still in my possession.

There was an air of excitement and a non-stop exhilaration that did not end during a meeting that lasted over three hours on that early November day. George was very clear and direct when he said that the Historical Society wanted to finally publish the manuscript. Without hesitation, Mike and Hazel offered their assistance to put the final touches on the manuscript for publication. When we had examined all of the options to proceed, the strategy to make the publication a reality was firmly in place. We all concurred that the first step would be for me to brush off the cobwebs and read it once again, to see what changes needed to be made.

Mike arranged to have the old typewritten final draft transferred to electronic disk, that would facilitate the inclusion of any modifications. He would also take the lead to design a dust cover, search for photographs, and locate appropriate graphics to make the publication more visually interesting. Hazel would do a complete proof read and edit, and Mike would be the final "set of eyes" to review the manuscript. So now, I had two partners to share the path to publication with.

By February 2002 I had moved to Maine and with relocation and other personal and professional commitments I did not have much time until the following year to attend to what I was now sure would be my *absolute final* re-working of the manuscript. When I did turn back to the manuscript once again, between May and July 2003, it was intended to be for a fresh look. As it turned out I found that some reorganization would make the narrative easier to follow.

I did not feel that further research was required, even though, for example, I recognized that during the last several decades additional archeological investigations were undertaken that might add some new information to what I presented in Chapter 1. Therefore, I decided to add a slight, yet important, qualifier to the title— the *Early History* — and only address "first" rather than successive findings or events. It is my hope that this will exonerate me from any accusations of being derelict in not incorporating new findings or research since the final draft was completed in March 1972.

My latest involvement in re-editing the manuscript was finished by the middle of July 2003. In early August Hazel's review comments had been incorporated, and the finished work was sent down to Lewes.

This book will have been a long time in the making as this "history of the history" attests. What must rank as the highest personal reward is that countless hours, days, and months of research, writing, and re-writing will now be finished. Critical events in the early history of Lewes can now be documented and made available in one source, as Hazel Brittingham had always wanted. And, in a very tangible way, the dream of Dr. Marvil will be realized.

William J. Cohen
Summer 2003
Mount Desert Island, Maine

Abbreviations Used in Footnotes

Archeolog   *The Archeolog,* The Sussex Society of Archaeology and History (Mimeographed).

Bulletin, ASD   *Bulletin,* The Archaeological Society of Delaware (Wilmington).

Duke of York   *Original Land Titles in Delaware: The Duke of York Record* (Wilmington, 1903).

Dunlap, 1956   A.R. Dunlap, *Dutch and Swedish Place-Names in Delaware* (Newark: University of Delaware Press, 1956).

Hall of Records   Delaware Public Archives, Department of State, Dover, Delaware.

Narratives, A.C. Myers, ed., *Narratives of Early Pennsylvania, West New*
Myers   *Jersey and Delaware, 1630-1707* (New York, 1909).

N.Y. Colonial   E.B. O'Callaghan, ed., *Documents Relative to the*
Documents Colonial History of the State of New York, vols. 1 and 2 (Albany, 1856).
    B. Fernow, ed., *Documents Relating to the Dutch and Swedish Settlements on the Delaware River,* vol. 12 (Albany, 1877).

Pa. Magazine   *The Pennsylvania Magazine of History and Biography* (Philadelphia, the Historical Society of Pennsylvania).

Papers, HSD   *Historical and Biographical Papers* (Wilmington, Historical Society of Delaware).

Scharf, 1888   J. Thomas Scharf, *History of Delaware,* 1609-1888, 2 Vols., (Philadelphia, 1888).

Turner, 1909   C.H.B. Turner, *Some Records of Sussex County, Delaware* (Philadelphia, 1909).

VRB   A.J.F. Van Laer, ed., *Van Renneslaer Bowier Manuscripts* (Albany, 1908).

Weslager, 1961   C.A. Weslager in collaboration with A.R. Dunlap, *Dutch Explorers, Traders and Settlers in the Delaware Valley 1609-1664* (Philadelphia: University of Pennsylvania Press, 1961).

Weslager, 1968   C.A. Weslager, *Delaware's Buried Past,* rev. ed. (New Brunswick: Rutgers University Press, 1968).

Chapter 1

The Indians of Lewes

The dawn of history unfolded thousands of years ago. The exploration of the phenomenal origin of our species, and how we became what we are today, has always been the subject of intellectual and spiritual pursuit. There has existed the constant urge to unravel the mystery of the growth and evolvement of man, the development of tribes and human associations, and, of course, unique patterns of cultural affinity. For generations, those who have been interested or concerned about our human heritage have delved into the examination of historical perspective, either as a method of understanding ways of life, or as a means of appreciating philosophical ideas.

There is a curious manifestation of our "humanness"—we tend to learn history, but not the lessons of history. Too often we tend to rationalize our existing actions as unique relationships, devoid of any antecedent. We are, in no small measure, the product of our past, and if we are to survive as a species, we must be aware of the history we write today for those who will follow.

Let us turn now to a story about a piece of our early history—the fascinating story surrounding Delaware's oldest settlement at Lewes.

In the beginning and throughout much of time, this was a land not yet spoiled by the touch of man, a seemingly everlasting bliss of incomparable beauty. Here the elements of water, earth, and sky coalesced in an inexplicable primeval harmony. And it was here that creatures of an ancient heritage lived, compelled only by their instinct for life. This is as it was for eons.

When our first human ancestors came to these shores, we, of course, cannot be certain. But whoever was the first to behold the relentless pounding surf, the solitude of quiet bays, and great stretches of sandy beach surrounding a hinterland of bush and thickets must have thought this was surely a new world.

The Beginning of Delaware Archeology 1865 – 1879

The original residents of what is now Lewes, and its environs, nestled within Cape Henlopen on the western side of lower Delaware Bay have been called by archeologists prehistoric Indians, since they lived here long before the first Europeans arrived on these shores. Where they came from and how and when they reached this area are questions that archaeologists have long been trying to answer. One explanation is that this immediate region may have been occupied when the Paleo-Indian pursued mammoths and mastodons in the east from 8,000 to 10,000 years ago. The only record we have of the prehistoric Indians at Lewes before their inevitable contact with the early Europeans is found on the sites they occupied in the form of stone, bone and shell artifacts; pottery vessels; in sub-surface features, such as storage pits, hearths and post molds; and in the skeletal remains of the people themselves.

It was quite by accident that the Lewes area Indians began to be investigated through archaeological pursuits one day in 1865—it marked the beginning of Delaware archaeology. Dr. Joseph Leidy, a noted scientist of his day, a professor of medicine and the founder of American parasitology, became curiously attracted to the ancient and shifting sand dunes of Cape Henlopen while vacationing aboard a yacht anchored in Lewes Harbor. Upon investigating the dunes, Leidy discovered shell heaps, which he determined were original kitchen middens, or Indian refuse dumps. He also found pieces of clay pottery of aboriginal (Indian) design and human bones, which by purpose or accident, had been mixed with the refuse.[1]

In reporting his findings at a meeting of the Academy of Natural Sciences in Philadelphia on June 20, 1865, Leidy admitted that he had only one hour to examine the find, and thus it was done rather quickly.[2] With his interest aroused, Dr. Leidy set out for Cape Henlopen the following summer to make a further study. Along with three interested associates he noticed that the shell accumulation extended from just below Lewes for about the distance of a mile or more to the base of a large sand dune between the bay shore and the Cape Henlopen Lighthouse. The group inspected several heaps in which were found pottery fragments, chips of jasper and stone arrowheads.[3] Although Leidy never returned to Lewes to excavate the shell heaps he had only superficially exposed, the story of Delaware archaeology can be said to have had its beginning with his cursory investigations of 1865 and 1866.

The shell heaps attracted no further attention until 1879 when Francis Jordan, a member of the Numismatic and Antiquarian Society of Philadelphia, explored the shell heaps, which he found to be more extensive then Leidy had reported. Beginning at Lewes, and following the bed of a dried-up waterway, Jordan traced a continuous series of shell deposits all the way to the Cape. He was told by one local resident that fifty years before the shell heaps had reached a height of twenty feet, and that their bold whiteness could be seen by ships far out to sea. Jordan found no European objects in the soil – only crude native Indian-made artifacts, which brought him to the conclusion that this area must have been occupied prior to 1600.[4]

---

[1] See Weslager, 1968, 10-14.

[2] *Proceedings of the Academy of Natural Sciences,* (Philadelphia, April, May, and June 1865), 95.

[3] See Ibid. On October 23, 1866 the Academy of Natural Sciences received Leidy's report on his second visit to the Lewes shell heaps titled "Report on Kitchen Middens at Cape Henlopen" (1866).

[4] Weslager, 1968, 26-29. Jordan's two reports regarding this find are "Remains of an Aboriginal Encampment at Rehoboth, Delaware" (1880) and "Aboriginal Fishing Stations on the Coast of the Middle Atlantic States" (1906).

Archeological Investigation 1938 - 1939

In either 1867 or 1868, a little known incident occurred when a shallow cut was made between Madison Avenue in Lewes and the southwestern bank of Lewes Creek (now the Lewes and Rehoboth Canal) during the construction of the Junction and Breakwater Railroad, which today is part of the ConRail system. A local physician, Dr. David Mustard, was asked to examine several human skeletons which were uncovered during the work. He did and pronounced them to be Indian. Unfortunately, no artifacts were found, and the site was ultimately destroyed by the railway cut.[5]

In October 1938, a skeleton was uncovered along the Lewes and Rehoboth Canal on lands owned by Jacob Moore. This skeleton was reported to have been "buried in an extended position with the head facing the southeast."[6] The Archaeological Society of Delaware (organized in 1933), which had already completed its first archaeological investigation in Sussex County at the Slaughter Creek site immediately expressed interest in this new find. A committee was formed to investigate and conduct preliminary work at the Moore shell heaps (as the find was called) during the summer and fall of 1939.

The observations and discoveries made during this inquiry have been recorded by C.A. Weslager, the well known Delaware Valley historian and archaeologist, who took part in the investigation. One spring day while the committee was busily digging in the shell heaps and Jake Moore was plowing in one of the adjacent fields, a heavy downpour interrupted their work. When the weather cleared, the group, unable to

---

[5] "Archaeological Site Survey Report," Delaware Archaeological Board, site no. 7-S-D12 (1867). See also Helene C. Potter "Facts vs. Fiction," Archeolog 4 (November 1952), unpaged. Recording of archeological sites is on United States Geological Survey maps. The code (7-S-D12) is interpreted as follows: (7) refers to Delaware, (8) Sussex County, (D) the block location, and (12) the twelfth site reported.

[6] C.A. Weslager, "An Aboriginal Shell Heap Near Lewes, Delaware," *Bulletin, ASD* 3 (October 1939): 4.

*C.A. Weslager, a prominent Delaware historian.
Courtesy of the Archives of The Lewes Historical Society.*

continue digging because of the wet soil, hastened to see if the plowing had uncovered anything worthwhile. The rain had come down with such force that the tracks of the tractor and the plow furrows had been completely erased. Scattered over the muddy field were approximately fifty circular areas where the earth was stained deep red in color. Each of these areas measured six feet in diameter, and they spread over the field in no particular pattern. Investigating one of the red areas, the group found the soil to be permeated with ashes, charcoal, aged animal and fish bones, burnt shells, and stones long since cracked and broken from intense heat, which had been plowed out of the soil before the storm. For a few moments the members of the group were puzzled, but quickly became aware that they were viewing the remains of ancient campfires. The ideal combination of freshly upturned earth and the driving rain had been responsible for making the rare observation possible. Later, after additional test diggings, the discoveries confirmed that this had, indeed, been a major place of occupation – a village of Indians who had been responsible for the nearby shell heaps. The group further found a number of post molds (the remains of decayed posts) which were once the upright corner poles of Indian huts.[7]

---

[7] Weslager, 1968, 75-76.

Although the investigating group limited their digging to a confined area, they further discovered several artifacts, including axes, a stone hoe, bone implements, and a large quantity of potsherds. There was easily enough evidence to conclude that this area, sometime before 1600, had been "a community of prehistoric fisherman and farmers developed on a plateau that is now the Moore form."[8]

The Sussex Society for Archaeology and History 1947

In September 1947, two citizens from Lewes discovered an Indian site 2 ½ miles southwest from the center of Town. News of their find spread quickly and preliminary investigations showed that the site was of fairly good size containing numerous Indian artifacts. Very often when such discoveries are made, many unassuming people, excited by their innate curiosity, avail themselves to have a look. As a result the remains of a long buried past may be hastily uncovered with little regard to intelligent inquiry.

It was fortunate that Kenneth Givan and H. Geiger Omwake were among those who had made the initial investigations. Their knowledge of archeology, coupled with their appreciation for keeping accurate records of objects found at such sites and particularly at this new site, led to the formation on January 8, 1948 of the Sussex Archaeological Association with Givan elected as first president. The name was later changed to the Sussex Society for Archaeology and History.

The Townsend Sites 1948 – 1953

One of the first acts of the Society was to obtain permission to dig from the owner of the land, Julian Townsend, of Georgetown. During 1948, after digging rules and record forms were developed, the society began its excavation of the area that was designated Townsend Site #1.

The site produced outstanding data all of which were meticulously recorded and examined. There were enough potsherds, skeletal

---

[8] Ibid., 76-77.

Road scraper used in first excavations at DeVries Site; general view looking northwest towards Delaware Bay. May, 1952.
Courtesy of the Archives of The Lewes Historical Society.

remains, as well as other materials to indicate "a settled occupation of a stable local culture."[9] The general interpretation of the artifacts made by Margaret C. Blaker, who analyzed the aboriginal ceramics found at the site, noted that "the pottery of the Townsend series [the various pits excavated at the site] belongs to a Late Woodland cultural horizon and is part of a late prehistoric shell-tempered pottery tradition of the Atlantic Coastal area which in characteristics other than temper, retains the classic features of earliest Woodland pottery."[10]

John Witthoft from the Pennsylvania Historical and Museum Commission concluded after making his analysis of the artifacts, that, "this culture had a long pre-history in the immediate region. Strong relationships with Algonkian peoples to the north and south are indi-

---

[9] H. Geiger Omwake and T.D. Stewart, eds., "The Townsend Site Near Lewes, Delaware," *Archeolog* 15 (1963): 68. See also the report on the examination of the material excavated from the site by the Smithsonian Institution reprinted in *Archeolog* 6 (June 1954): 4-5. Also see Margaret C. Blaker, "Pottery Types from the Townsend Site; Lewes, Delaware," *Eastern States Archaeological Federation Bulletin,* No. 9 (July 1950): 11.

[10] Ibid., 29-30.

cated, with very little evidence of cultural relationships or stylistic resemblances to the people of the interim. Cultures and physical types of the region show continuity and gradual internal change through long time intervals. This suggests that the region in pre-historic times was a refuge area, well buffered and quite insolated from social upheavals, movements of people, or strong intercommunications with other regions."[11] During 1953, four small refuse pits were found on the east side of Kings Highway just north of Murray's Corner and named Townsend Site #2. The find here consisted mainly of bone tools and pottery; no burials were uncovered.[12]

The Lewes School Site 1948 - 1951

In 1948 during grading operations as part of the laying out of a new athletic field for the Lewes School (now part of the Cape Henlopen School District) a number of refuse pits were unearthed.[13] Unfortunately, the machinery used for this work cut through a small knoll, slicing through the pits, which scattered the contents over a wide area and practically destroyed any aboriginal material. Among a group of interested archaeologists who first viewed this find was Orville H. Peets, who gathered enough shards to restore a large vessel. A brief description was made of the various artifacts that the group had been able to recover, and it was indicated that they bore a marked similarity to the pottery being excavated from the investigations then underway at the Townsend Site.

---

[11] Ibid., 68.

[12] See "Archaeological Site Survey Report," Delaware Archaeological Board, site 7-S-D1 (1955). There was also a report filed at the Zwaanendael Museum in Lewes.

[13] The first find at the Lewes School site took place in 1931 when the playground was being graded for a tennis court. A horse-drawn scoop unearthed a single human interment along with oyster and clam shells. Irvin Kepner, a teacher at the school, salvaged the remains and sent them to Omwake who suggested that it had been an Indian burial. The remains were not identified until 1948 by the United States National Museum. See H. Geiger Omwake, "For the Record," *Archeolog* 1 (September 1948): 6.

South line looking SE towards Lewes Dairy with C.A. Bonine mapping postmolds.
Courtesy of the Archives of The Lewes Historical Society.

In the spring of 1950, further grading work was started in con-junction with a program of physical expansion of the school building. When a refuse pit was subsequently discovered, several persons pro-ceeded at once to investigate. Their discovery included a considerable quantity of pottery, a nearly complete elbow-type clay pipe and two pipe stems of Indian origin, several bone implements, and a perforated gorget (flat tablets of stone used as ornaments).

The chronology of the discovery of Indian sites near the Lewes School was completed in 1951 when four additional refuse pits were found during the first stage of still another building expansion. James A. Moore performed the investigations from which were uncovered finds similar to the previous discoveries.

The most significant evidence found at the Lewes School site was the pottery, particularly the restored vessels, which were systematically examined and compared with the pottery found at the Townsend Site. The analysis brought Peets to the conclusion "that the pottery recovered from the school ground represents merely an extension of the culture complex revealed at the Townsend Site."[14]

The Miller-Toms Site 1949 - 1954

In 1949 a large tract of land owned by Stanley Miller directly behind the Lewes School was extensively graded for residential development. During these operations, several small refuse pits and postmolds were observed. In October, H. Geiger Omwake investigated a refuse pit on the crest of a knoll at the western end of the same tract. Subsequent investigations of a larger area, including property owned by Mrs. Gladys Toms north of the Miller property, disclosed a number of other pits. The entire area, which became known as the Miller-Toms Site, did not become further investigated until the fall of 1951 and the following winter and spring.

In 1954 after recovering sufficient data from the site to make an analysis, Omwake drew the following conclusions: "The people inhabiting the Miller-Toms Site depended for the most part on the sea for their food. They ate large quantities of oysters and clams and somewhat fewer numbers of conch and mussels. These mollusks could be gathered without the use of any weapons."

Omwake continued that the life of the people who inhabited the area "was apparently so ordered that they were called upon to use little initiative and to expend little effort in order to survive. In general it may be said that the cultural pattern disclosed in the refuse pits of the Miller-Toms Site varied little, if at all from that revealed at other sites in the Lewes area."[15]

---

[14] O.H. Peets, ed., "Aboriginal Evidence from the Grounds of the Lewes School," *Archeolog* 3 (May 1951): 4.

The Wolfe's Neck Site 1951 - 1966

In the early 1950s, a large shell-tempered cord marked caldron was found near the canal on a spit of high ground that penetrated into the surrounding marsh that was known as Wolfe's Neck. The find was made just above the Moore shell heaps.[16] Subsequent investigations conducted in this vicinity disclosed a large shell deposit. Later work conducted here disclosed a large shell deposit. "There is evidence," said the finding report, "that this nameless branch of Lewes Creek was a much larger stream 400 years ago and navigable for canoes to the shell deposit....There is also evidence of five other shell deposits and extensive indications of Indian occupation in this area of Wolfe's Neck between Pot Hook Creek on the northwest, the nameless stream on the southeast, the [Moore] farm house site on the southwest and the bank of Lewes Creek on the northeast."[17]

The Derrickson Site 1951

In the fall of 1951, James Parsons uncovered a cache of twenty-five conch shells as well as other materials from a refuse pit on the Derrickson Farm near New Road. The shells ranged from very small to medium in size and had all been deposited in one depression of the pit. Of special interest was the fact that each shell had had its spiral ends trimmed, which led to a preliminary conclusion that they had

---

[15] H. Geiger Omwake, "A Report on the Miller-Toms Site, Lewes, Delaware," *Archeolog* 6 (June 1954): 8.

[16] O.H. Peets, "The Caldron," *Archeolog* 3 (May 1951): 2.

[17] David Marine, et al, "Preliminary Report on a Shell Deposit in the Wolfe's Neck Archaeological Complex," *Archeolog* 17 (1965): 1, 5, and 14-15. Additional references on the Wolfe's Neck Site area include O.H. Peets, "Site 7-S-D10 Should Be Restudied," *Archeolog* 13 (October 1961): 14-16; and D. Marine, S. Bryn, R.R. Bell, "Further Work on a Shell Deposit in the Wolfe's Neck Archaeology Complex (7-S-D10)," *Archeolog* 18 (1966): 8-20.

John Ludlow of Delaware Archaeological Society (wearing cap), measuring and recording postmold No. 191.
Courtesy of the Archives of The Lewes Historical Society.

been used either as an object of utility or as an ornament. The find was described by Orville Peets:

> The shells themselves lead one to conjecture what purpose impelled the Indians to remove a section of the Column [the spiral end]. Was it the conch shell itself which was to serve some useful purpose or was it the length of the spiral stem? It is easily conceivable that shells of this variety served admirably as drinking cups or as ladles but for either of these uses shells of considerable size would appear to have been more acceptable whereas all of those found in the cache were of relatively small size. For either purpose, the full length of column would have been desirable.[18]

---

[18] O.H. Peets, ed., "The Derrickson Site 'Worked Conchs,'" *Archeolog* 4 (February 1952): 9.

Peets continued that, "The alternate implication suggested by these intentionally altered conch shells is the possibility that the sections of column were removed as a preliminary step in the manufacture of beads."[19] Although columnar beads had not before nor since been found in refuse pits in the Lewes area, Peets' conclusion that these shells represent the discarded material of an ancient Indian bead maker must await further inquiry.[20]

The Ritter Sites 1951 - 1952

During the fall of 1951 and extending into 1952, an investigation was carried out on a small site near New Road abutting Black Oak Gut (a branch of Mill Creek). The site became known as Ritter Site #2 since it was the second site that was located on the farm lands of Messrs. William and Lynn Ritter and portions of land owned by Ira Brittingham. The Ritter Site #1 – located north of Site #2 and near Canary Creek – had first been investigated in 1950, but the arrival of the planting season brought work to a halt. A detailed account of the findings at Ritter Site #1 had not been documented, yet it seems reasonable to assume that this site is merely an extension of the Ritter Site #2. Even though the relationship between the two sites had not yet been determined, they were treated as individual sites particularly by Omwake, in light of the fact that Ritter Site #2 at the time of discovery "represented a small archaeological concentration seemingly contained within its own restricted limits."[21]

The initial inspection of the Ritter Site #2 revealed the presence of eleven small refuse pits of which ten were uncovered. There were no substantial finds and "cultural objects were limited almost exclusively,

---

[19] Ibid.

[20] Weslager points out, however, that a bead of this type had been found at the Mispillion Site. See Weslager, 1968, 178.

[21] H. Geiger Omwake, "A Report of the Excavations at the Ritter Site #2 near Lewes, Delaware," *Archeolog* 6 (December 1954): 4.

to pot sherds. One broke[n], triangular, brown jasper arrowpoint having a concave base, a chipped jasper shell, two pipe stem fragments, and a small fragment of a pipe bowl comprised the non-pottery objects found in the pits. No bone or antler tools were found."[22] Moreover, the rather scarce amount of cultural material found at the site indicated that it was either occupied by a small band of people or occupied for only a short period of time. The conclusion based on a detailed examination of the finds indicated that Ritter Site #2 should be regarded as another manifestation of the cultural pattern as characterized by the Townsend Sites.

There was one interesting aspect, however, of the Ritter Site #2 which did not escape Omwake's eye. He observed that between Ritter Site #1 and the Russell Site (discussed below) – which were about a mile apart – there extended a range of land topographically slightly higher than the surrounding area. Ritter Site #2 is on the highest part of this elevation. Omwake surmised that, "It seems possible that a path connecting Ritter Site #1 with the Russell Site must have followed this slightly elevated range because a route to the south of it would have led through low swamp areas or would have entailed a long detour to the south to circumvent them."[23] Moreover, continued Omwake, if there was such a pathway between the two encampments, then some kind of footbridge or crossing over Canary Creek must have existed when the sites were occupied.

The Russell Site 1951

From February to December, 1951, an area of just less than one acre consisting of clear and brush land was investigated by members of the Sussex Society for Archaeology and History. It was located about

---

[22] Ibid., 10. Cf., H. Geiger Omwake, "A Report of the Archaeological Investigation of the Ritter Site #2 Near Lewes, Delaware," *Bulletin*, ASD 6 (April 1954) unpaged; and H. Geiger Omwake, "Preliminary Comments on the Ritter Site near Lewes, Delaware," *Archeolog* 4 (July 1951): 7-8.

[23] Ibid., 12.

one mile south-southwest of the deVries Monument on Pilottown Road and about 900 feet northwest of New Road on a farm owned by Samuel Russell. A total of nineteen shell refuse pits were discovered and excavated in addition to two areas designated as "features." One such feature was described as an equine (horse) burial, and the other "an exploratory trench at the edge of the marsh where a bend in Pagan (Canary) Creek comes within 50 feet of high ground.[24] The investigators dug a trench two feet wide and one foot deep beginning at the junction of the marsh and the firm ground and extended it twelve feet in a northeasterly direction toward the field. Several artifacts were gathered from the trench including a lump of bog iron weighing about five pounds.

In referring to the whole site, the archaeological report concluded, "it is our opinion that this encampment was recent (probably within the historic period), temporary or seasonal and of short duration."[25] On December 9, 1951, a closer examination was made of the second feature and, as a result, David Marine later reported that this crossing of Canary Creek had been a dike or causeway originally constructed by the Dutch to facilitate trade between themselves and the Indians. He cited a survey of the Rowland property between Lewes Creek and Canary Creek drawn by John Shankland on July 26, 1773, which showed a dike or causeway being used as part of a roadway that extended from Pilottown southwestward into the "backcountry."[26]

Useful Indian Path 1955 - 1958

After reading David Marine's (at the time unpublished) report on the Russell Site, Omwake was more certain about his theory regard-

---

[24] David Marine, "Report on the Russell Site," *Archeolog* 9 (May 1967): 1.

[25] Ibid., 6.

[26] See David Marine, "Examination of the Pagan Creek Dike," *Archeolog* 7 (June 1955): 1. A copy of the Shankland Survey may be found in *Archeolog* 4 (November 1952): unpaged. Cf., David Marine, "The Woolbank (Wiltbank) Grant and the Russell Site," *Archeolog* 4 (July 1951): 6-7.

An unidentified workparty at the DeVries Site.
Courtesy of the Archives of The Lewes Historical Society.

ing a crossing of Canary Creek, which would have facilitated contact between the inhabitants of the Ritter Site #1 and the Russell Site. However, upon further evaluation, based on additional archaeological work, he proposed that the dike, as well as a causeway—also crossing the Creek to the northwest was originally of Indian construction, not Dutch, and built as part of a travel route among the several pre-European contact sites in the Lewes vicinity. Omwake carefully theorized about such a route and course the pathway followed: [27]

Discussing the problem of mapping the Ritter Site #1 during its exploration, the author [Omwake] stated that the problem was complicated by the discovery of seven refuse pits a thousand feet, more or less, removed from the area of concentrated occupation. It is appropriate here to note that at the time of the investigation of the Ritter Site #1, the existence of the Ritter Site #2 was not even suspected and the discovery of the cluster of seven shell refuse pits at such a distance from the larger habitation area seemed an inexplicablephenomenon. It now

---

[27] See H. Geiger Omwake, "A Report of the Archeological Excavations at the Ritter Site #2."

appears legitimate to presume that these pits must have been associated with one or more houses which stood along side a pathway which traveled in a direct line slightly northeastward from the Ritter Site #1 to the Ritter Site #2. Elsewhere it has been suggested that the pits of the Ritter Site #2 were themselves associated with a few houses which may have stood along a pathway leading from the Ritter Site #1 to the Russell Site (via Derrickson).

Circumstantial evidence, the contemporaniety of the aboriginal occupations suggested by the absence of cultural distinctions, the locations of the prehistoric villages near the first sources of fresh water on the landward side of coastal tidal marshes, the extension of the marshes and swamplands inland for considerable distances beyond the occupied areas, the width of the marshes at those locales, the tremendous distances involved in canoe travel from village to village, the circuitous routes to be traversed over high land in order to effect intervisitation between villages which are in reality only a few hundred airline yards or so apart but separated by interweaving streams and their attendant marshes or swampy lowlands, the clustered refuse pits partway between Ritter Site #1 and Ritter Site #2, the very existence of Ritter Site #2 all suggest that a pathway directly connecting the known major villages was established by the Indians and that the strip of solid land crossing the marsh and the dike crossing the marsh thru which Canary Creek flows, were, in reality, land bridges artificially constructed by the Indians as parts of that pathway.[28]

Weslager has written—after citing *Duke of York* and other articles by Mayre—that "At least two important Indian trails connect-

---

[28] H. Geiger Omwake, "Did the Indians Construct the Dike Across Canary Creek and a Causeway Over One of Its Branches?" *Bulletin, ASD* 9 (March 1958): 19-20; William B. Mayre in a series of articles on "Indian Paths of the Del-Mar-Va Peninsula," *Bulletin, ASD* 2, Nos. 3-6 (March 1936 through June, 1938) referred to the "Old Indian Path to the Whorekill" as mentioned in the certificate of survey of "Unitie" in 1683. Unitie lies on the road between Berlin and Snow Hill, between Berlin and Ironshire in Maryland. See *Bulletin, ASD* 2 (June 1938): 4-5.

ed the Indian Village at Lewes with nearby points. One called the Useful Indian Path ran from Lewes to the Assateague Indian towns in Worcester County, Maryland. The second, the Whorekill or Wiccomiss Path, ran northwest from Lewes to the head of the Sassafrass River, probably intersecting the north-south Choptank Path."[29]

Hercules Company Property 1959 - 1960

During December, 1959, and February, 1960, Bert Salwen, from the Department of Anthropology at Columbia University, conducted an archaeological survey on a tract of approximately 812 acres owned by the Hercules Company. The land included the previously discovered Ritter Sites. Salwen's main objective was to locate additional shell pit sites which would give evidence of earlier cultural horizons of the area. He did uncover additional undisturbed shell deposits at Ritter Site #2, yet no new shell pit complexes were found. "One post-mold was exposed in a test pit adjacent to a shell deposit in one of the Ritter fields, but follow up work failed to reveal a pattern of molds.[30] However, a small collection of surface finds differed from the artifacts obtained from the shell pit excavation at the two Ritter sites. According to Salwen, "In the latter cases all of the points were triangular and all of the pottery was shell-tempered. Our surface collection contains 6 stemmed or notched points and only 5 triangles....This material would seem to indicate that there were one or more occupations on the Hercules properties before that of the shell pit users, by people with a somewhat different material culture. The evidence does not warrant a more definite conclusion."[31]

---

[29] C.A. Weslager, "The Indians of Lewes, Delaware and an Unpublished Indian Deed Dated June 7, 1659," *Bulletin, ASD,* 4 (January 1949): 9.

[30] Bert Salwen, "Archaeological Survey of the Hercules Powder Company Properties Near Lewes, Delaware," *Bulletin, ASD* 4, new ser. (Spring 1965): 15.

[31] Ibid., 31-33.

The Lighthouse Site 1965

This brief discussion of the first archaeological investigation in the Lewes area may be completed by mentioning one additional site that was discovered in the early 1960s when Clayton M. Hoff, a conservationist and naturalist, was exploring the sand dunes of Cape Henlopen. Walking across the dunes near where the lighthouse had once stood, he came upon a concentration of oyster and clam shells, along with numerous pottery sherds, which he recognized as being of Indian origin.

The site, subsequently excavated by Hoff and Weslager, proved to be a shell midden, and the sherds that were collected were analyzed by Dr. Clifford Evans of the Bureau of American Ethnology at the Smithsonian Institution. They were identified as belonging to the "Chickahominy Series of coastal and southeastern Virginia" and as being the same as Townsend Ware which was identified as being in the late Woodland period, representing the highest level of pottery development in Lower Delaware and at some sites in nearby Maryland Counties.[32] After additional analysis, Omwake wrote that "The inference is clear, the Cape Henlopen area of lower Delaware was host to at least two groups of people separated in time by many years, probably on the order of 2,000, and the clay-sherd tempered ware from the Lighthouse Site may be presumed to be representative of a stage of cultural development which occurred there during the Early Woodland or early in the Middle Woodland Period.[33]

---

[32] H. Geiger Omwake, "The Lighthouse Site, 7-S-D22, Cape Henlopen, Lewes, Delaware," *Bulletin, ASD* 4, new ser. (Spring 1965): 5.

[33] Ibid., 6.

The Early Archeological Results

Based on the artifacts, the pottery vessels, and the skeletal material that were uncovered during the first archeological investigations, it seems safe to conclude that the historic Indians who lived in Lewes and its environs were essentially of the same cultural horizon as those who occupied the eastern shore of Maryland and Virginia. To be specific, pottery, arrowheads, and other stone tools found on the Townsend Site are very similar to artifacts found on sites along the Nanticoke and Choptank Rivers in Maryland.

It would also seem, from a study of skeletal remains, that the makers of these artifacts were all of the same general physical type, but for the present time, conclusions must necessarily be tentative pending further excavations and comparative studies of the material. The similarity in what anthropologists term the "material culture" of these various prehistoric groups do not necessarily mean that their religious beliefs were the same, that they spoke identical languages, or that their traditions and social structures were alike. Answers to questions dealing with these broader technical aspects of the prehistoric Indian culture may never be accurately known since these earliest inhabitants did not leave written accounts for us to read.[34]

The Early Written Accounts

It is presumed that the prehistoric occupants of the Lewes area and other occupied areas on the Delmarva Peninsula were the forebears of the historic Indian tribes, although much yet remains to be learned about how these tribes were formed. We have already reviewed

---

[34] Many years after this manuscript had been completed C.A. Weslager wrote that there are "problems in reconstructing the geographical movements of migrating bands of Nanticokes. The full story may never be told, but by digging into the early records, scattered items of information can be found that permit reasonable conclusions." *The Nanticoke Indians—Past and Present* (Newark: University of Delaware Press, 1983), 18.

the archaeological work that has been done to help identify who the Indians were, and related aspects of their culture. Let us turn now to historic references to the earliest inhabitants of Lewes.

The first European explorers and settlers encountered a number of autonomous Indian communities on the Delmarva Peninsula, whose names were recorded as Assateagues, Pocomoke, Nanticokes, Wiccomiss, Choptank, Accomack, Accohannock, as well as others. There also lived on both sides of Delaware Bay and River some 30 or 40 separate and independent Indian communities whose occupants were given such names as Narraticons, Ockanickon, Mantes, Armewamex, Sankikons, Sweapoos, and Siconese, many of them taking their name from the stream on which their villages were located.

Although the Indians living along the tributaries of the Delaware River system were dispersed into small bands, each having its own chiefs, the term Lenape, or Lenni (Leni) Lenape, meaning "common people" came to be applied as a generic to all of them, and was later supplanted by the term Delaware Indians. Even though all of these groups spoke the Algonkian language, there were different dialects, just as in America today, different dialects of English are spoken in different parts of the country. From vocabularies that were recorded by early European scribes, it is evident that the Lenape dialects differed from those spoken by the Nanticoke and Choptank, as well as other Eastern Shore Indians.

Historical evaluations to identify of the various Indian tribes, including their common ancestry, that roamed the three-state region of the Delmarva Peninsula, has been the subject of much study. For example, several years ago Archibald Crozier wrote that the Nanticokes were "a tribe of the Algonkian family, who, if they were not actually an off shoot from the Lenni Lenape, or Delaware tribe, were connected linguistically, and ethnically with that tribe."[35] C.A. Weslager has said,

---

[35] Archibald Crozier, "The Nanticokes of the Delmarva Peninsula," *Bulletin, ASD* 1 (October 1934): 2. See also A.R. Dunlap, "A Bibliographical Discussion of the

"linguistically, the Nanticoke, Choptank, Assateague, and Conoy appear to have been all closely related to each other as well as to the Lenni Lenape."[36] Moreover, Weslager adds that both David Zeisberger (1721-1808) and John Heckewelder (1743-1823), two early Moravian Indian missionaries, have concluded that the language of the Nanticoke was similar to that of the Lenape. "Heckewelder added that the Nanticoke referred to the Lenape as "grandfathers", a term of respect and symbolic kinship presumably indicative of an earlier affiliation."[37]

Generally, there has been some controversy as to the actual settlement patterns of both the Nanticoke and Lenape bands, particularly regarding their penetration into Sussex County. For example, Dr. Frank G. Speck's sketch map of the Chesapeake Bay region clearly defines the Nanticoke territory to include all of the Eastern Shore of Maryland, part of Virginia, all of Sussex County, and most of Kent County as far north as Duck Creek.[38] However, later historical research has proven this to be somewhat exaggerated. As Weslager has pointed out, the Nanticokes lived in a restricted geographical area confined to the Nanticoke River and its tributaries, and nowhere else. On the other hand, the Lenape, or Delaware Indians, actually controlled land on the west side of the Delaware River extending from Philadelphia to Lewes.[39] Weslager has concluded that the Indians residing in the Lewes

---

Indian Language of the Delmarva Peninsula," *Bulletin, ASD* 4 (January 1942): 2-5.

[36] C.A. Weslager, *The Nanticoke Indians: A Refugee Tribal Group of Pennsylvania* (Harrisburg: The Pennsylvania Historical and Museum Commission, 1948), 115.

[37] Ibid. See also David Zeisberger, *History of the North American Indian*, A.B. Hulbert and W.N. Schwarze, eds. (Columbus, Ohio, 1910), 141; and John Heckewelder, *An Account of the History, Manners, etc.,* Historical Society of Pennsylvania Memoirs (Philadelphia, 1876), 122.

[38] See Frank G. Speck, "Indians of the Eastern Shore of Maryland," (Baltimore: Eastern Shore Society of Baltimore City, 1922), sketch facing p. 1.

[39] See C.A. Weslager, "The Anthropological Position of the Indian Tribes of the Delmarva Peninsula," *Bulletin, ASD* 4 (November 1947): 3-4. Weslager points out that the Lenape have been referred to by D.G. Britton, *The Lenape and*

area were Unalachtigo Delaware, who also are known to have existed across the river in southern New Jersey.[40]

Additional scattered archaeological finds have suggested that the Lewes area Indians may have been of a Nanticoke Indian physical type. However, some historical evidence has indicated otherwise. In 1970 the State Archeologist, Ronald A. Thomas, wrote that "All peoples living in the Delmarva at that time were considered homogeneous. This area corresponds remarkably well to the area in which the Nanticoke peoples, in the wider sense of the word, lived. No where in this area, including Lewes, have artifacts been found which can be identified with the Leni Lenape peoples." [41] Historian, C.A. Weslager took a different position when he wrote, "My own view, with which [Thomas] is not in agreement is that the historical evidence all points to a cultural affiliation between the Lenape and the Siconese of Lewes." [42]

When the report on the Townsend Site (the prehistoric Indian village discussed earlier in this chapter) was published in 1963, T.D. Stewart analyzed the human skeletal remains and reported that,

> The population sample recovered from the Townsend Site has demographic characteristics similar, especially in its youthfulness, to those from other

---

Their Legends, (1885) as three entities or sub-tribes as follows: Minsi, people of the stoney county; Unami, people down the river; and Unalachtigo, people who live near the ocean. Cited by C.A. Weslager in "Indian Tribes of the Delmarva Peninsula," *Bulletin, ASD* 3 (May 1942): 31.

[40] Ibid., 4. A close examination of source material corroborating this point has been done by William W. Newcomb, Jr., "The Culture and Acculturation of the Delaware Indians," *Anthropological Papers* No. 10 (Ann Arbor: University of Michigan, 1956), 5-10.

[41] Personal communication to the author October 22, 1970.

[42] Written comments provided to the author February 1971.

Late Woodland sites in the general area.[43] Likewise in physical characteristics, the Townsend sample appears to be similar to those from other nearby late sites. The type involved is undoubtedly the one which Hrdlicka described in 1916, and to which he gave the name Algonkian. The concept of this type has been expanded more recently by Neumann (1952), wherein the name 'otamid' is used to describe a variety of Indian which had a very wide distribution at one time but subsequently was pressed off into refuge areas, one of which was the northeastern part of North America."[44]

John Witthoft of the Pennsylvania Historical and Museum Commission, interpreted the cultural relationship of the Townsend Site as follows. "The Townsend Pottery Series occurs at a number of sites in the Delmarva Peninsula, being found almost entirely south of Wilmington, Delaware, and north of the Pocomoke Sound. It represents the latest native cultural horizon that has been recognized in this area, and seems to correspond in its distribution with the tribal area of the Nanticoke."[45] In reaching his conclusions, Witthoft held that "while there were many questions about the Townsend Site which we cannot answer, it seems clear that it was a typical Indian village of protohistoric date, probably of the Nanticoke."[46]

There are two pieces of historical evidence which show rather conclusively that the tribal affiliation of the Indians in the Lewes area was Lenape even though they were an independent band. In the first

---

[43] The Woodland peoples were the forebears of the Algonkian-speaking Indians who greeted the first European settlers; they therefore were, according to Weslager, a "prehistoric people" and probably occupied their villages between 1300 and 1600 A.D. See Weslager, 1968, 67 and 83.

[44] Omwake and Stewart, "The Townsend Site Near Lewes, Delaware," 53.

[45] Ibid., 61.

[46] Ibid., 68.

instance, we should examine the name or names of these Indians. The present City of Lewes and its environs was the location of either a single village or a group of related communities generally recorded in history as Siconese.[47] The earliest appearance of this identification is found on a manuscript Dutch map in the Library of Congress entitled, *Caerte vande Svydt River in Niew Nederland* (Map of the South [Delaware] River in New Netherland).

This map, drawn in 1629 (to be more fully discussed in Chapter 2), provides important information regarding ethno-history, since it marks Indian settlements on both sides of Delaware [Godyns] Bay. The legend appearing in script on the left of the map begins with the information that "the nations on the South River are Great Sironese [Siconese] on the Hoerenkil." This identifies the tribal group living in the area of Lewes. They were referred to as "Great" in contrast to one of the New Jersey shore groups called on the map "Kleyne [small] Sironese."[48] The Dutch word "kleyne" suggests the Siconese in New Jersey were either a smaller populated group or otherwise less important than their counterparts on the Delaware shore.[49] There was also an Indian village on the Eastern Shore of Virginia known as Chiconessex, which may be another variation of Siconese.[50]

---

[47] In their work *Indian Place-names in Delaware* (Wilmington: The Archaeological Society of Delaware, 1950), A.R. Dunlap and C.A. Weslager cite several recorded variations of "Siconese" e.g., Sickoneysincks, Siconece, Sikonesse, Ciconicing, Sekonnessinck, Checonesseck and Siconescinque, 38˙

[48] A.R. Dunlap and C.A. Weslager, "Toponymy of the Delaware Valley as Revealed by an Early Seventeenth-Century Dutch Map," *Bulletin,* The Archaeological Society of New Jersey Nos. 15-16 (November 1958): 3-4. Cf., C.A. Weslager's discussion of Robert Evelyn's treatment of the "Sikonesses" in New Jersey in "Robert Evelyn's Indian Tribes and Place-names of New Albion," *Bulletin,* Archaeological Society of New Jersey No. 9 (November 1954): 11-12.

[49] Ibid., 11.

[50] See Robert Beverly, *The History of Virginia* (reprinted from the London Edition of 1722 in 1855), 184.

Another documentary source confirms the "greatness" of the Delaware Siconese. In 1629 when the Dutch purchased from the Indians the land for their colony of Swanendael on the west side of Delaware Bay, a full council of "Ciconicins" were gathered along with "ye generation both young and old Inhabitants, out of their Villages compassed within ye Zouth corner of ye Baay of the Zouth river."[51]

In 1677 an incident occurred which also sheds more light on finding out who the Lewes Indians were. David Williams and his family, who had their home on the Wicomico River on Maryland's Eastern Shore, were killed by Indians. Two natives named Krawacom and Papomco were believed to have been guilty of the murders. Consequently, notice was sent by the proprietary officials to the King of the Choptank Indians, as well as to the rulers of the Assateague and Nanticoke Indians – all Eastern Shore tribes – demanding, under threat of war, the delivery of these two men if they were living within their domain. A meeting was arranged between several Indian chiefs and the colonial authorities at the New Town Court House in Maryland after the situation had been investigated. After examining documents in the Maryland Archives that recount the event, C.A. Weslager wrote that "The Indian found with the English clothing [of the Williams family], who had been surrendered by the [Indian] Emperor, had informed on two other Nanticokes, *Krawcom* and *Papomco* as the murderers. The Nanticoke delegation were asked if they knew the former. They replied he was an Indian belonging to the 'King of the *Checonesseck,* a Towne upon the Horekills.'"[52] Weslager concludes that "*Krawcom* being subject to the *King of Checonesseck* was described as being 'in no ways allied to the Nanticoke.'"[53]

---

[51] Ibid., 4 and A.R. Dunlap "Dutch and Swedish Land Records Relating to Delaware," *Delaware History* 6 (March 1954): 28. See also Weslager, 1961, 258-259.

[52] Weslager, *The Nanticoke Indians: A Refuge Tribal Group of Pennsylvania,* 1948, 39. "Horekills" refers to present-day Lewes.

Since the first coming of the Europeans and the eventual establishment of settlements and colonies, the identity of the native Indians was destined for either assimilation or oblivion. Even though surviving descendents still carry on cultural traditions, further knowledge about their ways, habits, and lifestyle await future discoveries through archeological investigations in the earth that they once lived on and cherished as their bounty.

As has happened in so much of American history, many of the early colonists who came to these shores have displaced the indigenous peoples under the aegis of bringing culture to the savage and establishing a self-righteous civilization. We take pride and admire those who ventured out to seek a new life here; we study their accomplishments and we preserve their buildings and sites that relate directly with them—they are now part of our culture. But so too should we recognize in much the same way those prehistoric cultures that preceded our forebears and lived on this land we now call ours—for they too are a part of our culture.

---

[53] Ibid. Weslager continues that this provides "evidence" that the Indians living in the Lewes area "were not of Nanticoke affiliation." Ibid. See Raphael Semmes, *Captains and Mariners of Early Maryland* (Baltimore: Johns Hopkins University Press, 1937), 347-348.

Chapter 2

Swanendael: The Founding of a Colony

Explorers and Traders Before Swanendael

In 1609 during his third voyage to the New World, Henry Hudson—an English seaman searching for a passage to China for the Dutch East India Company—diverted his route and sailed into Delaware Bay.[1] Information regarding this event must come from other sources since Hudson's own account remains unknown. When Johan de Laet wrote his history of the "New World" in 1625, he may have paraphrased Hudson's journal concerning the latter's discovery:

> Running thence to the northward they again discovered land in the latitude 38 degrees 9 minutes where there was a white sandy shore, and within it an abundance of green trees.[2] The direction of the coast was north-

---

[1] Hudson's mapping of his principal discoveries of the river that now bears his name as well as the vicinity of Manhattan Island may be referred to in I.N.P. Stokes, The Iconography of Manhattan Island, 6 vols. (New York: R.H. Dodd, 1915-1928), see especially 2: 41-61 and plates 21-22A. See also Weslager, 1961, 25-42.

[2] This describes the vicinity of the present- day Atlantic Coast of Maryland south of Ocean City.

northeast and south south-west...They continued to
run along the coast to the north, until they reached
a point from which the land stretched to the west-
northwest, and there was a bay into which several
rivers discharged. From this point land was seen to
the east-northeast, which they took to be an island;[3]
but it proved to be the mainland, and the second
point of the bay, in latitude 38 degrees 54 minutes.[4]
Standing upon a course north-west by north, they
found themselves embayed and encountering many
breakers, stood out again to the south-southeast.
They suspected that a large river discharged into the
bay, from the strength of the current that set out and
caused these sands and shoals.[5]

After the news of Hudson's discovery had reached Holland, private merchants, excited by the commercial opportunities that lay ahead,
became the first Dutch interest group to focus its attention on developing New Netherland, a massive coastal area that stretched from Cape
Cod to Delaware Bay. There awaited for these groups a great challenge,
and a great profit, in establishing a lucrative fur trade with the New
World natives. Several merchants formed groups specifically to turn
their attention to exploits in New Netherland. The wealthiest of these
groups was headed by Lambrecht (or Lambert) Van Tweenhuysen,
who had been an early participant in the Dutch whaling industry off

---

[3] Southern New Jersey.

[4] Several references will be made to latitude coordinates of Lewes in a number of cited
historic references in this text. Lewes and its environs lies between 38 degrees 45
minutes and 38 degrees 50 minutes latitude.

[5] Delaware Bay and River. This citation from de Laet may be found in J. Franklin
Jameson, *Narratives of New Netherland 1609 – 1664* (New York: Charles
Scribner's Sons, 1909), 37-38. See also Weslager, 1961, 32-33 and the earliest
description of Delaware Bay written in the English language by Robert Juet as
cited on p. 33.

Spitsbergen, owned a soap factory in Haarlem, and had been one of the largest pearl dealers in Amsterdam.[6]

Another notable group, known as the Hans Claesz (or Claessen) Company also prepared plans to establish a trading stronghold which developed strong rivalries, particularly with the Van Tweenhuysen Company. Much competition existed among these merchant groups, who petitioned the States-General for grants of exclusive trade rights in New Netherland. Moreover, the competitive nature of these early mercantile associations to explore and reap an economic harvest in the New World would spill over and beyond national boundaries. The European drive to colonize would involve growing tensions among the Dutch, English, and Spanish

Among the early Dutch explorers in the employment of these merchant groups who visited American waters after Hudson were Hendrick Christaensen (Corstiaenssen), Adrien Block, and Cornelius Jacobsen Mey (May). Based on their reports sent back to Holland, an exclusive right to trade was finally passed in the States-General on October 11, 1614, and granted to the "United Company of Merchants who have discovered and found New Netherland, situated in America between New France and Virginia, the sea coasts whereof lie in the latitude of forty to forty-five degrees."[7]

As one scholar has pointed out, the New Netherland Company became a monopoly formed by the principals of the four separate companies that had been involved in the trade to New Netherland—the Van Tweenhuysen Company, the Hansclaesz Company, the Witsen

---

[6] Simon Hart, *The Prehistory of the New Netherland Company: Amsterdam Notorial Records of the First Dutch Voyages to the Hudson* (Amsterdam: City of Amsterdam Press, 1959), 25-39. Van Tweenhuysen became director of the Northern Company that was the first company to trade in the Hudson River between 1613-1614.

[7] *N.Y. Colonial Documents* 1: 10. By the terms of the pact the New Netherland Company was to have the right to make four voyages to the exclusion of all competitors for a three year period beginning January 1, 1615. This is the first recorded use of the term "New Netherland."

Company, and the Hoorn Company.[8] Meanwhile as the navigators continued to explore the northern areas around Cape Cod and Long Island, Captain Mey turned his attention to exploring the Atlantic Coast to the south. In 1614 he had sailed into Delaware Bay and anchored his vessel between two capes—one which today bears his name (Cape May, New Jersey) and the other called Cape Cornelis (now Cape Henlopen).[9]

After these expeditions had returned to Holland, a further, more detailed examination of the coast was commissioned to Captain Hendricksen, who proceeded in his yacht *Onrust* (Restless) "which he had left on the coast for further use, to the Delaware, to ascertain the nature of that country; and to open a trade with the natives there."[10] On August 19, 1616 he submitted a brief report to the States-General, claiming to have "discovered and found a certain country, bay and three rivers situate in the latitude from 38 to 40 degrees."[11] Hendricksen attached to the report a "figurative map" showing the Delaware River system as he observed it.[12] Although brief in content, Hendricksen's report awakened an increased trading interest in this new uncharted area of New Netherland since he "did there trade with the inhabitants; said trade consisting of Sables, Furs, Robes, and other Skins." "Moreover," continued Hendricksen, "he hath found the said country full of trees, to wit: oaks, hickory and pines; which trees were, in some places, covered with Vines. He hath seen, in the said country, Bucks and does, turkeys and partridges. He hath found the climate of the said

---

[8] Thomas J. Condon, *New York Beginnings: The Commercial Origins of New Netherland* (New York: New York University Press, 1968), 23.

[9] Originally Cape Henlopen was the name applied to Fenwick Island. See E.B. O'Callaghan, *History of New Netherland Or New York Under the Dutch* (New York, 1855), 1: 73 and Scharf, 1888, 2: 1201.

[10] Condon, *New York Beginnings,* 74.

[11] *N.Y. Colonial Documents* I, 13.

[12] The "figurative map" is reproduced in Ibid., facing p. 11. See also Weslager, 1961, Chapter IX, 215-232 that discusses "Dutch Maps and Geographical Names," prepared by Professor Dunlap.

country very temperate, judging it to be as temperate as that of this country, Holland."[13]

During its three-year existence, the New Netherland Company made overt attempts to maintain its exclusive trading rights received in 1614. Following Hendricksen's explorations and report, the Company petitioned the States-General in 1616 for a special grant of trading rights in this "newly discovered" area for a period of three years. This, of course, included the geographical area drained by the Delaware River. However, during the period between 1614 and 1616, there developed a general discontent among some of the merchant groups who were opposed to a grant of exclusive trade rights to selected merchants. The opposition, which primarily included those merchants who were not members of the New Netherland Company, called for no more special favors to this Company. Under such pressure, the States-General procrastinated, and repeated petitions by the New Netherland Company to have their grant endorsed were consistently postponed. The result was that the monopoly came to an end, and by 1618 the trade was thrown open to all.[14]

The New Netherland Company continued its trading operations in the years after the expiration of its charter in order to protect the geographical area of its established trade. After 1617 the Company was sometimes referred to by its chartered name, but at other times, it was known as the Van Tweenhuysen Company.[15] The major difficulty facing this "second" Van Tweenhuysen Company was simply competition.

After 1618, a number of companies interested in the New Netherland trade petitioned the States-General for trading rights in New Netherland. This did not please the Van Tweenhuysen group, but since their grant had expired, there was nothing that they could do to prevent others from trading in New Netherland.

---

[13] Ibid., 14.

[14] See *N.Y. Colonial Documents* 1: 13-15. Cf., Condon, *New York Beginnings*, 26-27.

[15] Ibid., 27.

The principal competitor of the Van Tweenhuysen Company was the company belonging to Hendrick Belkens and Adriaen Jans Engel who had previously been "owners and partners in the New Netherland Company."[16] As the problem of competition became a matter of great concern to the Van Tweenhuysen Company, threats and intimidations began to be hurled at their rivals. While this may have succeeded in discouraging some groups, it did not work with the Eelkens Company who threatened legal actions if their right to free trade to New Netherland was obstructed.[17] Various ploys were used by these groups which kept maneuvering in order to protect their interests. One such method was the building of trading posts, which had been a common practice of earlier Dutch traders in establishing a de facto monopoly of trade in a particular area.[18] In the face of rising difficulties in controlling the New Netherland trade, as well as the increased activities in New Netherland itself, it was inevitable that a Dutch West India Company would be formed patterned after the East India Company. The chief purpose of the new company would be to first open avenues for trade, and, secondly, promote the establishment of colonies in New Netherland. Thus, on June 3, 1621, a charter to the newly formed Dutch West India Company was granted by the States-General with the "power to make contracts, leagues, and alliances with the princes and natives...to build any fortresses and strongholds there;...moreover, they may promote the settlement of fertile and uninhabited districts, and do all that the service of this country and the profit and increase of trade shall require."[19]

The first resolution passed by the States-General after the establishment of the West India Company to specifically trade in the Delaware Bay and River was granted on September 28, 1621. The

---

[16] See O'Callaghan, *History of New Netherland*, 81-82.

[17] Hart, *The Prehistory of the New Netherland Company*, 54, n. 3, and 69. See also Condon, *New York Beginnings*, 28-29.

[18] *N.Y. Colonial Documents* 1: 94 and Condon, 30.

[19] *VRB*, 91.

petitioners included Claes Jacobse Harincarspel, Petrus Plancius (a theologian and geographer), Lambrecht Van Tweenhuysen, and Hans Claessen and Company. The resolution granted

> ...that the aforesaid petitioners, for the purpose aforesaid [i.e., trading] mayt accordingly send to the above mentioned countries, coasts, and rivers, by them discovered, lying between Virginia and New France, in the latitude of forty to forty-five degrees, called New Netherland, also to the adjoining countries and a great river lying between latitude thirty-eight and forty degrees, two ships laden with all sorts of permitted merchandise; the one to the aforesaid New Netherland and the other to the aforesaid New River, lying in latitude between eight and thirty and forty degrees, and to the small rivers thereon depending, to trade away and dispose of their old stock which they have there, and afterwards to bring into this country, their goods, cargoes, clerks and seamen, on condition that they must be home with their ships and goods before the first of July, 1622.[20]

The "New River" referred to (also called in the resolution "a Great River") was obviously the Delaware River, which later was to be called by the Dutch the "South River."

It is clear that this consortium was the first authorized group by the West India Company to trade on the lower Delaware River. Although the author can find no additional documentation that refers specifically to the activities of this company immediately following September 28, 1621, it is curious to note that on June 18, 1622 Harincarspel petitioned the States-General "that the time allowed them, the petitioner, to bring over their returns from New Netherland

---

[20] *N.Y. Colonial Documents* 1: 27.

to this country, may be extended six months."[21] The resolution, how-ever, was postponed.

The activity of traders and explorers on the Delaware River, as well as other waterways on the East Coast of the New World, increased considerably as opportunities became apparent. Holland and England and France, particularly, were represented by various groups and adven-turers. In 1621 the following was recorded at a Court held for Virginia: "A third m(r) Dirmers Discouerris from Cape Charles to Cape Codd Delawarr River, and Hudsons River beings butt 20 or 30 leagues from our plantacon and within our lymit in W(ch) Rivers were found dive(rs) ships of Amsterdam and Horne who yearly had there a great and rich trade for Furs,...."[22]

Additionally, the Virginia historian, William Stith, and later the Delaware historian, Francis Vincent, wrote that "we have no account of their visit to Delaware, but information from several hands had reached the Virginia Company that the French and Dutch carried on a very profitable trade with the Indians on Delaware and Hudson Rivers."[23]

Swanendael Is Founded

On March 28, 1628, the executive committee of the Dutch West India Company issued a directive known as the "Charter of Freedoms and Exemptions" which provided for grants or patroonships for

---

[21] Ibid., 28.

[22] Susan Myra Kingsburg, *The Records of the Virginia Company of London* (Washington, D.C., 1906), 1: 505. Thomas Dirmers was associated with Captain John Smith, the founder of Jamestown, Virginia.

[23] William Stith, *History of the First Discovery and Settlement of Virginia* (1747), 198 and Francis Vincent, *A History of the State of Delaware* (Philadelphia, 1870), 108.

[24] It is important to note that the "term 'patroon' was not known to Dutch politi-cal nomenclature of the period, nor had it any association with the economic or administrative aspect of any by-gone feudalism. It was merely the equivalent of the English word 'patron' and was obviously used in the charter to distinguish those who would finance the specified number of colonists from those, for whom provision was also made...." S.G. Nissenson, *The Patroon's System* (New York: Columbia University Press, 1937), 26.

those persons or companies who wished to establish colonies in New Netherland.[24]

The events surrounding the early Dutch attempts to plant a colony on the west side of Delaware Bay in what is today the State of Delaware began prior to 1630. The dominant figure in planning that first settlement in New Netherland by patrons was Samuel Godyn, the president of the Amsterdam Chamber. He was not only well informed about the happenings in New Netherland, but had taken an active part in developing early guidelines and instructions for the formulation of Dutch interests in the New World. It had been reported to Godyn by Peter Minuit in New Netherland that whales were plentiful in Delaware Bay. The use of whale oil for both fuel lamps and as a lubricant made this a most desirable commodity in Holland. Thus an interest developed in the Delaware Bay area as a source for obtaining whale oil.

One of the provisions of the new "Charter of Freedoms and Exemptions" was that those who wished to participate in colonization could send "three or four persons to inspect the situation of the country."[25] As a result, Godyn, Kiliaen Van Rensselaer, and Samuel Blommaert notified the West India Company on January 13, 1629, that they were sending two men, Gillis Houset (Hossitt) and Jacob Jansz Kuyper, "with the intention, in case they made a favorable report to their honors, of planting a colony there."[26] The extent of the patroon's instructions to Hossitt and Jacob Jansz has so far not been documented, however, they must have been given the authority to acquire land if they found conditions satisfactory. In June, 1629, Hossitt purchased from the Indians lands for the founding of the Swanendael (literally translated as the Valley of the Swans) Colony.[27] This marked the first

---

[25] *VRB*, 137.

[26] Ibid., 154. See also Weslager, 1961, 257.

[27] A copy of the document which specifically mentions "Swanendale" or "Swansdale" for the first time may be found in Weslager, 1961, 258-259. On July 11, 1630 the deed was recorded by the Dutch at Manhattan, *N.Y. Colonial Documents* 12: 16-17. Cf., Leon de Valinger, Jr. "Indian Land Sales in Delaware," *Bulletin, ASD* 3 (February 1940), 29. See also Weslager, 1961, 266-267.

Indian land sale in the State of Delaware, and was negotiated with the "Ciconicins," the Algonkian-speaking Indians of the Lewes area.

Accompanying the contract of sale executed between Hossett and the native chiefs is the following reference to a missing map which at one time may have been part of this original Dutch document. "A caard [map] of ye South river in New Netherland made upon a newer View of itt done in ye yeare of our Lord Anno 1629 by order of Samil Godi gn by his Commiss. Gillis Housett in divers places amended and corrected by Hendrick Gerratsen. Upon ye 28th April."[28] This map, which also shows the position of various Indian tribes on both the New Jersey and Delaware shores, is the earliest demarcation of the territory purchased for the Swanendael Colony, and shows a considerably large area, originally intended for the settlement including most of the State of Delaware.

Meanwhile in Holland, Godyn notified the Amsterdam Chamber on June 19, 1629 "that he intended to plant a colony in New Netherland, ...he agrees to occupy in the capacity of patron the bay of the South River."[29] On February 1, 1630, four patrons – Godyn, Blommaert, Van Rensselaer, and Coenraets Burgh – entered into a joint account for their planned settlements.[30] Weslager has written, "We are not told the reason for this merger, but several advantages seem obvious; for example, they could have one capitalization for the whole venture, so that in the event of failure of one colony the principal patroon retained an interest in the other colonies to balance his losses; there were shipping advantages in sending vessels to distribute supplies or reinforcements to several points; one colony could assist a sister colony in time of need."[31]

---

[28] Dunlap and Weslager, "Toponymy of the Delaware Valley as revealed by an Early Seventeenth-century Dutch Map, "*Bulletin,* The Archaeological Society of New Jersey Nos. 15-16 (November 1958).

(1958): 2. Cf., Weslager, 1961, 220 and 258 and Dunlap, 1956, 54.

[29] VRB, 155 and Weslager, 1961, 260.

[30] Ibid.,164-165 and Weslager, 1961, 262.

[31] Weslager, 1961, 89.

At any rate, each patroon laid claim to several territories as put forth in an agreement dated October 1, 1630.[32] Principally, Blommaert was to locate his colony on the Connecticut River, Van Rensselaer on the Hudson, and Godyn and Burgh on the South River. Godyn, however, made arrangements to admit other partners, and by the time the settlement was made, there were ten subscribers. Captain David Pietersen de Vries, "a bold and skillful seaman," was one of these patroons.[33]

Godyn and his associates engaged the services of Captain Peter Heyes to master their ship, the *Walvis* (Whale), and Gillis Hossitt, who had returned from New Netherland in 1630, was employed as the agent in charge of the colony. de Vries explained that the main purpose in establishing the Swanendael settlement was "to carry on the whale fishery in that region, and to plant a colony for the cultivation of all sorts of grain, for which the country is very well suited, and of tobacco."[34]

The *Walvis* left Holland on December 12, 1630, with eighty persons, a cargo of lime, bricks, tiles, horses, cows and other provisions and necessities. After first discharging some passengers in the West Indies, the ship proceeded to Delaware Bay (known at the time as Godyn's Bay) where they landed in the spring of 1631 on the stream known as Blommaert's Kill. (Blommaert's Kill was probably named by Hossitt during his earlier voyage to New Netherland; it later was named Hoerenkil, Hoornkill, Whorekill, and finally Lewes Creek.)[35]

---

[32] VRB, 161-175 and Weslager, 1961, 263-265.

[33] In the literature two style variations are used: De Vries and de Vries. The latter will be preferred throughout this text.

[34] From de Vries', *Korte Historiael Ende Journaels Aenteyckeninge,* 1630-1633, 1643 (1655) as found in *Narratives,* Meyers, 8.

[35] Confusion as to the etymology of the name "Hoerenkil" has been described in Dunlap, 1956, 34-37, and by C.A. Weslager, "An Early American Name Puzzle," *Names* 2 (December 1954): 255-262. See also Dunlap, 1956 for a discussion of references to Godyn's Bay (Godins Bay, at 30) and Blommaert's Kill (Bloemaerts Kil, at 17 and 31).

Immediately after their arrival in the New World preparations were made to clear and plow the land for cultivation, prepare for the whaling season, and, most importantly, construct housing and fortifications. What these early colonists built was essentially a community house surrounded by "palisadoes." Instead of a continuous line of posts stuck into the ground, the "palisadoes" (palisades) or posts were placed every so many feet apart. The vertical posts were connected by a series of planks laid horizontally. The house was constructed of Dutch bezand Ijsselbrick (yellow brick) brought over by the colonists. The word "bezand" used in this connection indicated a step in the manufacturing process. While the molds were in motion, they were sprinkled with yellow sand to prevent the bricks from sticking together.[36]

Even though the settlement was called Swanendael, the small building surrounded with palisades has erroneously been called "Fort Oplandt" by several historians. Scharf, for example, in referring to the Dutch settlement of 1631, specifically gave it this name.[37] However, Professor Dunlap maintains that there does not seem to be support for this assertion in either de Vries or other sources of the period. It is therefore possible that the name Fort Oplandt came into use as a result of a mistranslation.[38]

No records of the names or occupations of the original settlers has, at the time of this writing, been found. Certainly it would appear an obvious assumption that among these settlers were bricklayers, carpenters, farmers, and, of course, harpooners, who could catch whales and refine their blubber.

---

[36] See O.H. Peets, "How Was the Stockade Built?" *Archeolog* 4 (November 1952): unpaged and a brief discussion of Dutch bricks by H. Geiger Omwake in *Archeolog* XV (1963): 40.

[37] Scharf, 1888, 1: 32.

[38] Dunlap, p. 29. The following clause appears in de Vries' *Korte Historiael ende Journaels Aenteyckeninge*, edited by H.T. Colenbrander ('s-Gravenhage,1911), 148 "...die buyten het Fort waren op Landt oxm haer wercke te doen." The words "Fort ...op Landt" are used here not as a name but as a description: "who were outside the fort working the land." See *Narratives*, Myers, 9.

In September, 1631, Hossitt was left with the settlement while Heyes in the Walvis departed for Amsterdam. When he arrived back home his report to the patroons was not entirely optimistic, since he only brought back "a sample of oil from a dead whale found on the shore."[39] Heyes reported, however, that he had arrived in Godyn's Bay too late for the whaling season which was from December to March. Although the patroons were disappointed and were not anxious to invest more money in the venture, Godyn convinced them that they would have to expect a short term loss for a long term gain. Finally, it was decided to outfit another ship and a small yacht to sail for Swanendael in time for the whaling season, carrying new settlers and fresh supplies. Captain de Vries was to lead this second expedition which included Hendrick de Forest, who was to relieve Hossitt in accordance with the "Charter of Freedoms and Exemptions" requiring the patroon(s) to replace the agent of his colony every two years. de Vries was prepared to sail early in 1632 when news was received that Swanendael had been destroyed by the Indians.[40] Finally on May 24th, de Vries sailed from the Texel (the island at the mouth of the Zuyder Zee in Holland) in the *Walvis*. With fifty men, accompanied by the yacht *Teencoorntgen* (Little Squirrel), they approached Delaware Bay on December 5, 1632, and apprehensively anticipated the first glimpse of their destroyed Swanendael. It is only fitting that de Vries himself tell the story of their arrival, what they saw, and of the events which, indeed, make a fascinating story in the history of New Netherland. de Vries in his journal wrote the following:

> The 5th the wind southwest, we weighed anchor, and sailed into the South Bay, and in the afternoon lay, with our yacht, in four fathoms water, and saw immediately a whale near the ship. Thought this

---

[39] *Narratives,* Myers, 8.

[40] Ibid., 9.

would be royal work – the whales so numerous – and the land so fine for cultivation.

The 6th we went with the boat into the river, [the Hoerenkill], well armed, in order to see if we could speak with any Indians, but coming by our house, [the Swanendael settlement], which was destroyed, found it well beset with palisades in place of breastworks, but it was almost burnt up. Found lying here and there the skulls and bones of our people whom they had killed, and the heads of the horses and cows which they had brought with them, but perceived no Indians and, without having accomplished anything, returned on board, and let the gunner fire a shot in order to see if we could find any trace of them the next day.

The 7th in the morning, we thought we saw some smoke near our destroyed house; we landed opposite the house, on the other side of the river, where there is a beach with some dunes. Coming to the beach, looked across the river towards the house where we had been the day before, and where we thought in the morning we had seen signs of smoke, but saw nothing. I had a cousin of mine with me from Rotterdam, named Heyndrick de Liefde, and as a flock of gulls was flying over our heads, I told him to shoot at it, as he had a fowling piece with him and he shot one on the wing and brought it down. With it came a shout from two or three Indians, who were lying in the brush on the other side of the river by the destroyed house. We called to them to come over to us. They answered that we must come into the river with our boat. We promised to do so in the morning, as the water was then low, and that we would then talk with them, and we went back to the ship. Going aboard, we resolved to sail in the river with the yacht, as otherwise in an open boat we might be in danger of their arrows.

The 8th of December, we sailed into the river before our destroyed house, well on our guard. The Indians came to the edge of the shore, near the yacht, but dared not come in. At length one ventured to come aboard the yacht, whom we presented with a cloth dress, and told him we desired to make peace. Then immediately more came running aboard, expecting to obtain a dress also, whom we presented with some trinkets, and told the one to whom we had given the cloth garment, that we had given it to him because he had the most confidence in us – that he was the first one who came in the yacht, and should they come the next day with their chief called Sakimas, we would then make a firm peace, which they call rancontyn marenit. An Indian remained on board of the yacht at night, whom we asked why they had slain our people, and how it happened. He then showed us the place where our people had set up a column, to which was fastened a piece of tin, whereon the arms of Holland were painted. One of their chiefs took this off for the purpose of making tobacco pipes, not knowing that he was doing amiss. Those in command at the house made such an ado about it, that the Indians, not knowing how it was, went away and slew the chief who had done it, and brought a token of the dead to the house to those in command, who told them that they wished they had not done it, that they should have brought him to them, as they wished to have forbidden him to do the like again. They then went away, and the friends of the murdered chief incited their friends – as they are a people like the Italians, who are very revengeful – to set about the work of vengeance. Observing our people out of the house, each one at his work, that there was not more than one inside, who was lying sick, and a large mastiff, who was chained – had he been loose they would not have dared to approach the house – and the man who had command, standing near the house, three of the bravest Indians, who were to do the deed, bringing a lot of beaver-skins with them to exchange, asked to enter the house. The man in charge went in with them to make the barter; which being done, he went down from the loft where the stores lay, and in descending the stairs, one of the Indians seized an axe and cleft the head of our agent who was in charge so that he fell down dead. They also relieved the sick man of life; and shot into the dog, who was chained fast, and whom they most feared, twenty-five arrows before they could dispatch him. They then proceeded towards the rest of the men, who were at their work, and going among them with pretensions of friendship, struck them down. Thus was our young colony destroyed, causing us serious loss.[41]

---

[41] Ibid., 15-16. See also Weslager, 1961, 96-97. de Vries first published his journal at Alkmoar, Holland (1655) which describes the six voyages to the New World under the partial title, *Korte Historiael, Ende Journaels Aenteyckeninge.* Portions of the original work relating to New Netherland were first translated into English by Dr. G. Troost and appeared in *Collections of the New York Historical Society,* 2nd ser. (New York, 1841), 1:245-273. Another English translation of sections of the journal relating to America by H.C. Murphy was published in an 1857 edition of the same *Collections,* 2nd ser. 1: 2-129. Excerpts from this later edition were taken and revised from the original Dutch text by A.J.F. Van Laer, New York State Archivist and appeared in *Narratives,* Myers, 3-29.

Survivors of the Swanendael Massacre

On July 18, 1962, Lena Thwing from Albany, New York came to Lewes to take part in the celebration of Historic Lewes Day. Mrs. Thwing told the sponsors of the event that "she had proof that there were survivors of the Zwaanendael [sic] massacre of 1632," and that "she is a descendent of one of the two survivors."[42] This bit of news excited historically conscious people in Lewes especially those who were of the belief that no one had lived through the incident.

One historian, C.A. Weslager, was perhaps most concerned about finding out whether or not this assertion was correct. After all his extensive work, *Dutch Explorers, Traders and Settlers in the Delaware Valley 1609-1664,* had just been published, and after examining source material, he had not found any factual evidence to support this claim.[43] Weslager immediately wrote to Mrs. Raymond R. Atkins in Lewes saying: "If Mrs. Thwing has documented information not known to us, I would certainly like to have the facts. Do you know on what document she based her judgment?" After a series of correspondence and detailed research, Weslager's findings were finally published three years after he began his inquiry. What follows has been, for the most part, synthesized from his article which appeared in the quarterly magazine of the Holland Society of New York, *de Halve Maen* in 1965.[44]

The story of survivors of the Swanendael incident is based on the Wiltsee family tradition as published by Jerome Wiltsee under the title *A Genealogical and Psychological Memoir of Philippe Maton Wiltsee and His Descendents* printed in Atchison, Kansas, by G.W. Myers in 1908. The family tradition begins in America, according to Wiltsee, when Philippe Maton along with his wife, two children, and two servants

---

[42] *Wilmington Morning News,* July 19, 1962. See also David S. Hugg, "How Many Survived the 1631 Lewes Massacre?" *Delaware Today* (June-July, 1963): 14-15.

[43] Weslager, 1961, 96-97 and 285.

[44] See C.A. Weslager, "Who Survived the Indian Massacre at Swanendael?" *de Halve Maen* 40 (October 1965): 9-10.

traveled from Holland to Fort Orange (Albany, New York) in 1623, where they assisted in the building of the fort. During the winter of 1631-1632, Maton and his two sons, Pierre and Hendrich, along with one of the servants went from Waal-bogt to Swanendael. The reason for their journey was to look into the prospects of settling there. Shortly after their arrival in Swanendael, Maton became ill and his children and servant awaited his recovery hoping to return to Waal-bogt. When the Indians raided the settlement in the spring of 1632, Maton, who was confined to his bed inside the house, and Hossitt were killed; the other settlers, working in the fields, also were killed. The two boys, hearing the cries of the victims and seeing the slaughter of the men, ran and hid in the brush. When found by the Indians, they were taken back to the village as prisoners and provided for. The young boys then came into the care of Mohawk Indians, who were returning to their village near Fort Orange after a southern expedition. Pierre and Hendrick continued their jaunt to Esopus (Kingston, New York), were then captured by the Mohican Indians who took them up the St. Lawrence River and were finally turned over to Jesuit priests in Canada.

Weslager carefully assails this story after examining documented evidence which challenges the credibility of the Wiltsee family tradition.[45] His main thrust was aimed at evaluating contemporary documentation of the Swanendael incident, particularly by de Vries, which contradicts the Wiltsee story. de Vries' account, as we have seen above, is based on both his own observations and the explanation of the killing as relayed by one of the Indians. It was characteristic of the man and his style to gather all facts about events worthy of recording, and discuss these items in a straightforward manner. Thus, with his information collected, de Vries categorically states that there were no survivors. Two of de Vries' subsequent translators, outstanding scholars in their own right, have praised the journal. Henry C.

---

[45] Weslager also examines the claim that the two boys changed their surname from Maton to Wiltsee in order to escape their Indian captors, which will not be discussed here.

Murphy has said that de Vries narratives "are entitled to the highest credit, for not only do they bear internal evidence of truth but they have been corroborated in many instances by other evidence, and by the records which we have."[46] The historian, A.C. Myers has stated, the journal "both internally and externally has well stood the tests of worthiness."[47]

Additional contemporary testimony was written by Kiliaen van Rensselaer, another patroon of Swanendael, in a memorial presented to the Assembly of Nineteen of the West India Company on November 25, 1633, in which he relayed, "With this aforesaid ship de Walvis, they [the Patroons] also in 1631 took possession of the bay of the South River in New Netherland, occupying the place of their colony with 28 persons engaged in whaling and farming, and made suitable fortifications, so that in July of the same year their cows calved and their lands were seeded and covered with a fine crop, until finally by error of their commis [Hossitt] all the people and the animals were lamentably killed."[48]

We do know the original contingent of men at Swanendael was twenty-eight men. Since thirty-two were listed as killed, four others must have joined the original settlement.[49] This may have been Maton, his two sons and servant, but to date there is no proof that they were in Swanendael.

A third and final piece of documentation refuting the contention that there were survivors of Swanendael can be found among the Cadwalader Collection of the Historical Society of Pennsylvania, which includes several depositions relating to the Dutch settlement on the

---

[46] Henry C. Murphy, *Collections of the New York Historical Society* (1857), 10.

[47] *Narratives*, Myers, 5.

[48] *VRB.*, 241.

[49] de Vries states this in his journal: "Before sailing out of the Texel we understood that our little fort [Swanendael] had been destroyed by the Indians, the people killed – two and thirty men – who were outside the fort working the land." *Narratives*, Myers, 9.

"Hoerenkil."[50] In March 1684-1685 the testimony of Aron Dirkson Horn was taken as follows: "this depont. heard and was informed by persons then arriving here [New York] from Dellowarre River, that the sd. River was settled by the Dutch West India Company, who had sent a parcel of men there in order to whale fishing; and this deponant saith further that some short time after, to his best remembrance it was about one yeare, or one yeare and a halfe after, news came here at New Yorke from Dellowarre; that all the sd people in Dellowarre where cut of by the Indians."[51]

Included in the letter book of the Van Rensselaer Bowier Manuscripts appeared the phrase, "you may engage Theunis Willemsen, who was left over in Swanendael." Van Laer in his translation made the following note: "this phrase may mean either that Theunis Willems was engaged in excess of the men required in Swanendael or that he survived the massacre." However, Van Laer goes on to say "from the account of the destruction of Swanendael in de Vries', *Korte Historiael,* it would seem that all the colonists were killed."[52]

In light of the foregoing discussion, it is clear from the several documented historical accounts available that there were no survivors of Swanendael. The Wiltsee family tradition has not been substantiated through recorded history and it, as well as any variations on the story, must be discounted, unless of course proven otherwise by uncovered historical documentation.

---

[50] These depositions were originally from the Penn Archives and were used in the later boundary dispute between William Penn and Lord Calvert.

[51] *Pa. Magazine* 80 (April 1956): 235.

[52] VRB, 223. Cf., Amandus Johnson, *The Swedish Settlements on the Delaware* (New York, 1911), 1: 171 who interprets the phrase to mean that Williemsen was a colonist at Swanendael who escaped. Johnson therefore maintains that there were 33 settlers which is at variance with de Vries' account. Still another version about a presumed survivor named Willemsen, again offered unsupported by documented evidence, may be found in Charles McKew Parr, *The Voyages of David DeVries* (New York: Thomas Y. Crowell Company, 1969), 122.

The Mystery of the de Vries (?) Sketch

In 1911 a facsimile of two charts, one of the South Bay and the other showing the coastline from Virginia to New England, were published as a supplement to the Linschoten-Vereeniging edition of de Vries' *Korte Historiael* and edited by H.T. Colenbrander.[53] The former was entitled *De Zuid – Boai in Niew Nederland* (The South Bay in New Netherland) and was reproduced from the original in possession of the States Archives in Holland.[54]

The question of who drew this map has never been answered, but a theory has developed that this was part of a series of maps or charts actually drawn by de Vries. When I.N.P. Stokes was meticulously gathering source material for his important work, *The Iconography of Manhattan Island,* he came across these sketch maps "both executed in the same style, and apparently by the same hand, one of which represents the vicinity of Cape Cod, and the other Delaware Bay, with an indication of the colony founded by de Vries and named 'Swanendael.'"[55] After carefully examining this find, Stokes concluded, "one of these sketches is numbered on the back '14', and I hazard the guess that it and its mate at one time belonged to a set which owed its origin to the initiative of de Vries, and was undertaken as a step in the foundation of a better knowledge of these coasts, and was intended to supplement and improve the delineation given by Block."[56] The acumen of de Vries' seamanship and his awareness of navigational details during his explorations is found throughout his journal.[57] To suppose

---

[53] Cf., P.A. Leupe, *Inventaris der Verzameling Kaarten berustende in het Ryks Archief* ('s Gravenhage, 1867), I. Nos. 517 and 518.

[54] See Colenbrander (1911), facing 154 and Weslager, 1961, facing 60, and 217 and 219.

[55] Stokes, *The Iconography of Manhattan Island* 2: 116-117.

[56] Ibid., 117.

[57] See for example Henry C. Murphy, *Collections of the New York Historical Society*, 39, 45, 85 and 121-122.

that he would either make new charts or at least up-date existing ones, whether by himself or through the help of a crew member skilled in cartography, is a reasonable assertion. Nonetheless, there is no entry in the journal that this was done, and until we learn otherwise, we cannot be certain who, in fact executed the map.

In researching the origin of this map, the Dutch Archives had the following to say: "We may presume that the map has belonged to the archives of the [Dutch] First West-India Company (1621-1674). The paper on which the map is drawn looks like two folio of a volume. In the 19th century all maps were taken out of the archives they belong to, in order to form a separate map collection. Unfortunately, however, it is not possible to find out the original place of the map in the whole of the archives...So after all it is not clear who drew the map."[58]

Let us turn now to a more detailed examination of the de Vries (?) sketch, since it was destined to play a significant role in later locating the settlement site of Swanendael. The only identifying mark — the number "17" — appears in the lower left hand corner. Obviously, this is the second sketch map Stokes had seen in the Dutch Archives. Delaware Bay is called "Godyns" and the River is given as "Willems," the two Capes — May and Henlopen — are also shown; "Blomaerts kil" was later to become the Horenkill and still later Lewes Creek.[59] It would seem clear that the sketch was drawn to show the location of Swanendael. The fort of the settlement is shown with a distinct north and south bastion surrounding a house. To the south of the stockade is a woods, no doubt from which the settlers secured the timbers for the palisade. Beyond the woods another European-type house is shown near four Indian abodes. There is no scale for measurement indicated on the sketch, and the palisade and the European dwelling are grossly exaggerated in size. Ostensibly, whoever did the drawing was primar-

---

[58] Personal communication to the author from J. Fox, Rijksarchivaris, the Hague, June 29, 1970.

[59] A discussion of the various place names that appear on the map may be found in Dunlap, 1956, passim, and in Weslager, 1961, 215-232.

ily concerned with depicting Swanendael as it related to its immediate geographical setting.

The de Vries (?) sketch, as I have decided to call this rather informative drawing, has been used by recent archaeologists and historians in two interesting ways: first, to examine the hypothesis that there was a Dutch trading post located here prior to the 1631 settlement; and second that the sketch, if accurately drawn, would thereby provide the location in uncovering the remains of Swanendael. Let us explore the reliability of the trading post hypothesis and, afterwards, cover the second aspect.

In referring to Lewes, the Delaware historian, J. Thomas Scharf, has stated that "The occupancy of this section by the whites dates from 1622. In that year some Dutch traders came and carried on a good business with the neighboring tribes of Indians."[60] This statement gave credence to the popular notion that there was a Dutch trading post erected on the west side of Delaware Bay before Swanendael.

When the Indian site found on the Russell Farm was being investigated in 1951, the archaeological report was concluded with the following: "…this encampment was recent (probably within the historic period), temporary or seasonal and of short duration. The suggestion is made that this camp may have sprung up because of a nearby trading post…."[61] The area of the Russell farm in colonial times had been owned by William Rowland whose home had once stood –as indicated by a survey in 1773 – roughly 200 yards northeast of the Russell site. A cursory examination of the vicinity of Rowland's colonial home (which became known as the Old House Site) was also made and the objects found there submitted to the Smithsonian Institution for analysis. C.M. Watkins, Associate Curator of the Division of Ethnology, concluded that "the horizons on this material extend from about 1630

---

[60] Scharf, 1888, 2: 1221. There is no reference of a source or document for this date.

[61] David Marine, "Report on the Russell Site," *Archeolog* 9 (May 1967): 6. Cf., H. Geiger Omwake and T.D. Stewart, eds., "The Townsend Site Near Lewes, Delaware," *Archeolog* 15 (1963): 2.

to about 1775 in their extremes... as a house site, it was probably in existence for some time, but had not remained long after 1750, if we judge from this material alone."[62]

The relics found at the Old House Site do not unravel the date of the structure nor the earliest occupation by Europeans. Yet O.H. Peets observed that,

> Under a section of the brick footing of the old house was found a rubble of charcoal, wood ashes, broken brick, and pieces of mortar – the latter less hard and seemingly older than that which covered the footing. This we took to be nearly conclusive proof that an earlier house had been burned at this place and brought to mind Mr. Leon de Valinger's [Delaware State Archivist] talk to us of the winter before on the sworn depositions of early settlers who, in 1683, had supplied William Penn with an account of the destruction of their houses and barns by a band of forty horsemen sent for this purpose from Maryland by Charles Calvert, son of Lord Baltimore.[63]

Peets went on to say "we know beyond question that the old house was on the land of Hermanus Wiltbank, one of the deponents, and we have found objects there of as early a date as the time of his living but as yet we have no proof that the house was his and the older house could well have been burned without the accompaniment of a troop of horsemen with drawn swords."[64]

---

[62] O.H. Peets, ed. "Examination and Report," *Archeolog* 3 (November 1951): 2.

[63] Ibid., 3. See Leon de Valinger, Jr. "The Burning of the Whorekill, 1673," *Pa. Magazine* 74 (October 1950): 473-487.

[64] Ibid., Relating to placing a date on the Old House Site State Archaeologist, Ronald A. Thomas, relayed to the author that "the evidence is suggestive, but inconclusive. Further excavations would certainly clear it up." Personal communication September 30, 1969.

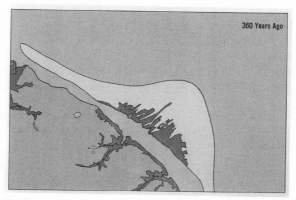

Lewes Harbor, 360 years ago. Courtesy, Kraft, J. C. 1988. "Geology." In The Delaware Estuary: Rediscovering a Forgotten Resource, edited by T. L. Bryant and J. R. Pennock, Newark, DE: University of Delaware Sea Grant College Program.

As has already been discussed in this chapter, European explorers and traders were quite active in Delaware Bay, yet thus far no evidence has been found, nor any historical documentation been uncovered, that a trading post was built before 1631. But the intriguing question still remains — why does the de Vries (?) sketch distinctly show two European type dwellings? One might conjecture that the settlement of 1631 actually consisted of the Swanendael fort plus a trading post. Therefore, let us explore the question as to whether or not the house drawn south of the fort was in fact part of the original settlement or was merely constructed later.

In his journal de Vries accounts for only one house which was destroyed, and there is no mention of any structure inland. Therefore, we must conclude that this second house was not constructed by the original settlers. We find from further reading de Vries' journal that he and his men viewed the remains of Swanendael on December 8, 1632, but that they did not set sail to continue their journey up the South (Delaware) River until January 1, 1633. On December 9th, the following entry appears: "We began to make preparations to send our sloops to sea, and to set up a kettle for whale-oil, and to erect a lodging hut out of boards."[65] Apparently at this time, de Vries entertained the notion that he and his patroon partners would re-establish a settlement and whale fishery where the abortive Swanendael settlement had been. This, however, would not happen. The three weeks or so from the time de Vries landed at Swanendael until he departed was plenty of time to construct this "lodging hut." One might venture to suppose that the house drawn south of the stockade—which is in the same vicinity as the "Old House Site"—was where de Vries and his men built their "lodging hut." However, the sketch shows a dwelling that appears to be larger than a board hut, and it is too far inland to serve as a refinery for whale oil.

From the above archaeological and historical information, we may conclude that there is no evidence to substantiate the viewpoint that a Dutch trading post was constructed at Swanendael prior to 1631 and that de Vries and his men did not build such a large structure inland in 1632. We will have to await the day when the definitive historical documentation is discovered—if, in fact it exists, as to who actually drew the de Vries (?) sketch, before the confusion will be straightened out.

The First Discovery of the Remains of Swanendael 1952, 1954, and 1964

Two hundred and seventy-eight years after the destruction of Swanendael, the first attempt was made to designate the spot where the Dutch had first landed on Delaware soil. The historical investigations that were published in 1909 by Rev. C.H.B. Turner, and others, resulted in the State of Delaware's placing a granite monument in memory of de Vries on the bank of Lewes Creek (the Lewes and Rehoboth Canal) on a hill about twenty feet above sea level.[66] Turner

---

[65] *Narratives,* Myers, 18.

[66] Today both the site and the Zwaanendael Museum are administered by the Division of Archives and Cultural Affairs of the Delaware Department of State.

concluded that this was the first suitable site for the fort, since it was located two miles southeast of the mouth of the Creek.

It has been generally believed that the seventeenth century Blommaerts Kill (Lewes Creek) had its beginning at or near the mouth of the Broadkill. Thus, the theory continues, when Hossitt in 1630 entered Godyn's Bay and sailed into the Blommaerts Kill, he had to travel down the waterway in a generally southeasterly direction until he reached the first high ground. This is based on topographical maps of the nineteenth and twentieth centuries which show only one "natural opening" between the Creek and the Bay at Veasey's Inlet. This, of course, was later closed when the Roosevelt Inlet was opened in 1937. A closer look at the de Vries (?) sketch, however, would refute this belief since Hossitt and later de Vries himself would have sailed directly into Blommaerts Kill from the Bay with the Swanendael site practically in front of them. The apparent discrepancy lies in the pattern of coastal geologic change that has occurred in and around Cape Henlopen over the last several hundred years. Professor John C. Kraft, Chairman of the Department of Geology at the University of Delaware, had completed detailed inquiries into this phenomenon. Kraft's findings, are based on geologic and historical interpretive analysis, and do, in large measure and for the first time, provided new and interpretive information about these coastal movements.

Kraft's thesis is that maps such as the de Vries (?) sketch may be very precise relative to the quality of the data presented by Dutch historians, or, for that matter, Dutch writers of the early and middle seventeenth century. Moreover, he takes the point of view that "one should believe the historical record and attempt to accommodate interpretations to fit it, rather than to disbelieve portions of the historical record that do not appear to match presently existing land forms."[67]

---

[67] John C. Kraft, *A Guide to the Geology of Delaware's Coastal Environment* (Newark: University of Delaware, 1971), 194. Cf., Kraft's "Sedimentary Facies Patterns and Geologic History of Holocene Marine Transgression," *Geological Society of America Bulletin* 82 (August 1971): esp. 2150-2152.

Kraft's analysis of accompanying series of six sketches that emphasize his thesis as applied to the changing coastal patterns of Cape Henlopen were succinctly written:

> A most interesting point to be noticed in the maps is the projection of the Lewes beach, probably by a littoral drift system in which flood tides, well supplied by sediment, flowed around the blunted Cape in a continuing sequence from 1631 to 1882. By 1882, the mouth of Lewes Creek and the Broadkill River had advanced from the Dutch Fort to Primehook, north of Broadkill Beach. A break-though south of Broadkill Beach opened the inlet that was finally sealed off with the construction of an artificial entrance at Roosevelt Inlet in Lewes. It is interesting to note that a littoral drift caused by the flood tide, flowing northwesterly and loaded with sediment from the Atlantic Beaches, can be projected to have paralleled the Lewes Beach coast until approximately 1882 when the advancing Cape Henlopen came abreast of the inner breakwater and effectively prevented the flood-tide currents from molding the coast. From that time on, flood currents increasingly flowed directly around the breakwater and into Delaware Bay. Studies of this type may significantly advance our understanding of coastal change in areas of man's intrusion.[68]

Although no archaeological investigation was made by Rev. Turner in 1909, yellow Dutch "tile brick" (bezand ijsselbrick) was found while digging in the foundation for the monument, as well as on the surface of the ground in the general vicinity.

---

[68] Ibid.

Early in the 1950s the Sussex Society for Archaeology and History had made some general investigations across from the monument on Pilottown Road in an old cemetery with the hope of finding the marks of an ancient road connecting this point with the Old House site and the dike or causeway across Canary Creek (see Chapter 1). At the same time, the possibility of locating the Swanendael palisades was discussed.

The de Vries (?) sketch indicated two bastions or gates – one north, one south – and it was assumed that if the northern bastion is taken to be the high point where the monument stood, then the brick house or fort would have to be somewhere on the old cemetery site.[69] This cemetery was called "the ancient burying ground" in a suit brought by the people of Lewes in 1687 against Jonathan Bailey, who attempted to close off the area as his private property. The ground occupied by the cemetery is at the beginning of a gentle slope toward the junction of Canary Creek and the canal, and it was surmised that this was the logical place for a fortification. How it came to be used as a cemetery cannot be explained, wrote O.H. Peets, "but the remains of the two persons killed in the house would almost certainly have been buried here by men of de Vries' party of whale hunters. They may also have collected bones of other victims lying in the fields nearby."[70] A cursory examination of the area by members of the Society challenged the belief that this was a private burial place of the Bailey family, since indications were found of several unmarked interments. In 1951, the land of the old cemetery came into the possession of St.

---

[69] O.H. Peets, "DeVries and the Old Cemetery in Pilot Town," *Archeolog* 4 (February 1952): 4. See the discussion and design of several Dutch built forts of the seventeenth century in John W. Reps, *The Making of Urban America: A History of City Planning in the United States* (Princeton: Princeton University Press, 1965), 147-154.

[70] O.H. Peets, ed., ""How Was the Stockade Built?" *Archeolog* 4 (November 1952), unpaged.

Peter's Episcopal Church of Lewes. Coincidentally, the church needed the land for a cemetery.

The Society met and decided that now was the time to make at least a preliminary excavation of the area in hopes of finding the Swanendael settlement. On January 21, 1952, the de Vries Site Committee was created and Chesleigh A. Bonine, Professor Emeritus, and former head of the Department of Geology at the Pennsylvania State University, was placed in charge of the project.[71] Since time was of the essence, the Committee decided to concentrate on trying to find the location of the stockade and the foundation of the brick house. After the cemetery had been surveyed, a bulldozer was used to begin the careful process of uncovering the layers of topsoil and subsoil.[72]

Their consistent and untiring efforts paid off. Nearly 200 separate post holes and molds were found along two sides of the cemetery plot at depths below the surface varying from seventeen to twenty-four inches. The postmolds were rectangular in outline and from twelve to twenty inches in diameter. They were closely spaced along the postmold line, and in some places almost touched.[73]

---

[71] The discussion that follows concerning the excavations at the Swanendael site is largely taken from several reports prepared by Bonine as cited in subsequent footnotes.

[72] Chesleigh A. Bonine, "Archaeological Investiagtion of the Dutch 'Swanendael' Settlement Under DeVries, 1631-1632," *Archeolog* 8 (December 1956): unpaged.

[73] According to Bonine "The words 'postmold' and 'posthole' are used by archaeologists more or less interchangeably. Strictly speaking, posthole is the cavity dug in which to put a post or timber and postmold is the filling of that cavity by the wooden post, plus a back fill of mixed subsoil and topsoil to fill the hole. The Dutch postmolds herein described consist of mixed topsoil, subsoil and decayed wood which makes them stand out as dark areas on the lighter colored subsoil surface. They are generally square or rectangular in outline in contrast to those of a farmer's fence which are round or oval and smaller in area. The square or rectangular Dutch postmolds reflect the type of digging tool used, either a square-edged shovel or hoe." Ibid.

The postmold line forming the northwest side of the cemetery plot was followed for 165 feet to Pilottown Road. Bonine noticed that across the road near the monument – a distance of 49 feet – three rectangular postmolds in contact with each other were found at a depth of about one foot. Here the line changed from a northeast to a northwest direction, which Bonine concluded was possibly the beginning of the north bastion. Unfortunately, this new direction could not be followed since the curbing of Pilottown Road interrupted the line of the postmolds.

After mapping all of the discovered postmolds, many of them were dug out to search for artifacts. Nothing to indicate the early Dutch settlement was found except a hand wrought iron spike and yellow brick.[74]

The old cemetery contained six marked graves when the work started, with the oldest dated at 1731 and the latest 1797. In addition four unmarked interments were encountered, but no artifacts were found in any of these graves, except a handmade shroud pin on one skull.

When a small house built in 1800, standing on the northeast corner of the plot was demolished in January, 1953, the soil beneath it was carefully examined. No evidence of the early Dutch occupation was found.

With their excavations completed, Bonine was sure that they had established the location of Swanendael as well as its relationship to other surrounding features. He concluded, "By placing a tracing of the [de Vries (?)] sketch, i.e., the stockade, European house outside to the south, and Indian habitations [these] fall approximately in line with

---

[74] Bonine points out that several experts were consulted during the field investigation including Dr. Frederick Matson, Archaeologist at the Pennsylvania State University, Dr. T.D. Stewart, the Smithsonian Institution, Mr. John Witthoft, The Pennsylvania Museum, and Dr. J.C. Harrington, The National Park Service.

the cemetery plot, the Old House Site and the Russell Indian Site. This can hardly be a coincidence."[75]

Permission to extend the work done in 1952, to the grass plot adjacent to the de Vries Monument, across Pilottown Road, was given by the Lewes Memorial Commission in 1954. The object of this continued search was to find the characteristic Dutch postmolds of the palisade and, possibly, some of the postmold pattern of the north bastion of the palisade, since most of the north bastion and the northeast boundary of the palisade had been obliterated by the construction of the Monument and Pilottown Road.

On October 21, 1954, Bonine, accompanied by Warren Callaway and David Marine, dug a trench from the curb of Pilottown Road northeastward near the edge of the canal. At a point two feet in from the curb, at a depth of fifteen inches, three rectangular postmolds of the Dutch type, (No. 244), were found exposed on the surface of the yellow subsoil. These were practically joined together and the long axis pointed in a northwest direction running into the curving curb near the Monument. No postmolds were found in the continuation of the trench toward the canal bank.

Since these postmolds were on the projected line of the northeast postmolds of the 1952 excavation, but nevertheless made a distinct right angled turn to the northwest, it was concluded that this point marked the west end of the portal of the north bastion of the palisade.[76]

The south bastion of the palisade was discovered in the final stages of the excavation made a decade later. Bonine's full account of the work is repeated below.

> Ten years passed before permission was obtained and search for the south bastion was resumed. In October,

---

[75] Chesleigh A. Bonine, "Archaeological Investigation of the Dutch 'Swanendael' Settlement Under DeVries, 1631-1632."

[76] Chesleigh A. Bonine, "The South Bastion of the DeVries Palisade of 1631," *Archeolog* 16 (1964): 15.

1963, the Lewes Historical Society had decided to apply to the National Park Service for certification as a National Historic Site or Area, and asked the Sussex Society for Archaeology and History to continue its investigation of the de Vries palisade in an effort to locate the south bastion.

Excavation was started where the digging along the southeast line had stopped in 1952 at the boundary line of St. Peter's Cemetery and the Bassett Brittingham lot lying to the southeast. A large scraper attached to a tractor was used to remove the dark topsoil which varied in thickness from fourteen to twenty inches, with an average of eighteen inches. Some digging by hand was necessary at the beginning point, however. Dark postmolds, number 181 to 190, were quickly discovered on the surface of the lighter colored subsoil. Then a large dark rectangular area, No. 191, was uncovered. This had a small oval dark area cutting slightly into the rectangle on the north corner. The small oval area was quite obviously a later intrusion dug into the rectangle. It was dug out and produced a bottle with pins in it! There was, also, a square postmold measuring about nine inches, in contact with the rectangle near the northeast corner. Later digging showed that this postmold was on the north postmold line of the bastion, which includes Nos. 191, 221, 196, 192, and 197. Rectangle 191 has been tentatively considered to be a latrine, underneath an overhead platform where sentries were posted and probably a cannon mounted. This rectangle was not dug out because it was desirable to preserve the entire postmold pattern of the bastion intact for future possible restoration.

The other postmold lines of the bastion were uncovered and plotted on cross section paper, using a scale of five feet equals one inch. The order of discovery of the various postmolds is indicated by serial numbers. It was necessary to scrape topsoil away from the area of postmolds, as they were discovered, so as not to mutilate them by tractor markings. This necessitated continually moving the tractor and scraper and accounts for the lack of continuity in the numbering of the postmolds.

When the northeast postmold line of the palisade was uncovered from Nos. 223 to 203 it became evident that the intrusion mentioned above had destroyed a postmold which, with No. 190, marked the portal or entrance to the fortified area. This portal measured about five feet, and a ladder was evidently placed here in order to reach the platform of the bastion. The northeast line of the palisade from the bastion portal to the corner north of Pilottown Road was not investigated beyond postmold 203 because an old photograph of the area involved showed a large farm house and several other buildings, now removed, had been built here. This previously occupied area undoubtedly had resulted in many intrusions interrupting or destroying the postmolds.

A heavy concentration of large postmolds along the south arc-like line of the bastion, Nos. 205-213, and also the large interior postmolds No. 194, 220, 215-218 and exterior postmolds Nos. 219, 221, 196 and 223, indicate supporting timbers for the bastion platform.

A farmer's fence line of a later time was found with

more recently installed red cedar posts. It extended from near postmold No. 181 cutting diagonally across the excavated area to near postmold No. 219. Two of these oval farmer's postmolds were found together near the Dutch rectangular postmold No. 181. In No. 181 a very badly decayed cedar post, part of the original palisade, was found while the cedar posts in the two farmer's postmolds were not so badly decomposed, and one was evidently used to replace the other post. Many small fragments of charcoal were found in the yellowish subsoil along the postmold of the south bastion, indicating that the timbers here had been severely burned by the Indians at the time of the 1631 massacre.

Practically no artifacts were found except what appears to be the handle of a metal spoon, badly decomposed, found about at the contact of the topsoil and subsoil near postmolds 212 and 213; also, a hand-made wrought iron spike, about five inches long, found on the subsoil surface but slightly embedded in the composite postmold No. 193. These may be of Dutch origin.

The dark postmold areas represent only the places where the deeper-set and larger timbers were placed; smaller and shallower-set timbers have long since disappeared in the topsoil where bacterial decay and chemical leaching by ground water has continued for three hundred and thirty-three years.

The postmold pattern found in the 1964 investigation clearly indicated the south bastion of the palisade as drawn by de Vries. No longer can there be any doubt about the location of this early colonial fort.

The previous work done in 1952 and 1954 along the two lines of the palisade and on the south bastion this year have furnished sufficient data so that it is now possible to reconstruct, in considerable detail, the dimensions and shape of the de Vries palisade.[77]

Swanendael: The Aftermath

Although much disturbed by the calamity that had taken place at Swanendael, de Vries did not contemplate any retaliation against the Indians.[78] He and his men, after burying the bones of the murdered colonists, remained in the area a short time and then set sail up the Delaware River, arriving on January 5, 1633, at Fort Nassau.

Back in Holland, the West India Company was engaged in internal disputes, and the anti-patroon faction in the company had received word that de Vries had traded for furs with the Indians. This group suspected that the patroons were attempting to take the fur trade away from the company. When de Vries returned home in July, 1633, he was so disappointed over this bickering, as well as disheartened over the failure of the Swanendael venture, that he severed his relationship with Godyn and the other partners. In 1636, Killiaen Van Rensselaer wrote to Johannes de Laet about the difficulty the patroons of Swanendael had. "...I fear that if we expand [our company] too much we may become the counterpart of Swanendael, as the large number [of patroons] causes confusion and, one pulling this way and another that may hinder one another and are in one another's way, so that I should conclude the fewer in number the better....When we got so many participants in Swanendael, then come our confusion."[79] Godyn and the remaining patroons gave up further attempts to colonize Swanendael; they also abandoned Burgh's land on the east side of

---

[77] Ibid., 15-18, the discovery of the South bastion was undertaken by Bonine, Warren Callaway, Paul Porter and Marion Tull.

[78] *Narratives,* Myers, 18.

[79] *VRB,* 334-335.

the Delaware Bay. In 1635, after continued disappointments, and after the land rights had lapsed according to the provisions of the "Charter of Freedoms and Exemptions," the patroons transferred the two tracts, Swanendael and Burgh's land, to the West India Company.[80] No further efforts were made to reopen a whale fishery or to begin another colony, although Dutch traders did visit the area from time to time. By 1656, the Company, sold Fort Casimir (New Castle, Delaware) as well as all the lands between the Christina River and Bombay Hook to the City of Amsterdam.

In 1657, two boatloads of Englishmen were shipwrecked near the creek called the Hoerenkill (today the Lewes & Rehoboth Canal), captured by the Indians, and later ransomed by the Dutch.[81] In the following year, the Dutch decided that some sort of action must be taken in order to fortify their territory on the South River and specifically at the Hoerenkill. Therefore, William Beekman, Alexander d'Hinoyossa and twenty soldiers were supplied with trade goods in order to reestablish contact with the Indians as well as to purchase additional land. After negotiations, the Indians deeded to the Dutch on June 7, 1659, all the land lying between Cape Henlopen and Bombay Hook extending westward (inland) about thirty miles.[82]

After the purchase, Peter Stuyvesant the Governor of New Netherland ordered that the Hoerenkill be prepared to ward off intruders and would-be attackers, especially from Maryland. Thus in 1659 a fort or garrison was determined to be of necessity.[83] Moreover, as the

---

[80] The transfer contract appears in O'Callaghan, *History of New Netherland* 1: 479-480 and in Weslager, 1961, 278-280.

[81] *N.Y. Colonial Documents* 12: 201.

[82] Weslager, "The Indians of Lewes, Delaware and an Unpublished Indian Deed Dated June 7, 1659," *Bulletin, ASD* 4 (January 1949): 6-14. In 1663 the City of Amsterdam purchased all of the South (Delaware) River including the Hoerenkill and adjacent lands.

[83] *N.Y. Colonial Documents* 12: 273 and Turner, 1909, 12. The fort tract was referred to in several early land grants on Pilottown Road as found in David Marine's study of the Duke of York patents in Appendix 2. Cf., Weslager, 1961, 293, n. 5.

*Monument commemorating
the failed colony at Swanendael
under the patronage of David
DeVries, located at westerly end
of Pilottown Road.
Courtesy of the Archives of The Lewes
Historical Society.*

settlers had continued to trade with the Indians up to 1659, they had made no attempt to protect their claim – another reason for the fort which would conveniently "legalize" the settled territory. Dutch-built forts or garrisons of the day were recorded under several variations such as "blockhouses," and "company's fort," apparently all for the same purpose – to offer a measure of security to the local population. We do not have any detailed records about the fort constructed at the Hoerenkill. However, on March 9, 1670, William Torn (Tom?) and Peter Alricks wrote to Governor Lovelace that they intended,

> ...to build a blockhouse 40 foote square wth 4 att every end for fflancks in the middle of the Towne the fort not being fitt to be repaired and if repaired of noe defence lying at the extreme end of the town and noe garrison therefore we beg that wee may [have liberty] to pull itt downe and make use of the tiles bricks

and other materials for the use of or new intended fortification wch if wee have noe occassion for, as wee fear wee shall, will be convenient for a courthouse notwithstanding.[84]

Thus the story of the founding and fateful end of the Swanendael colony comes to an end. But, its end was the beginning of a new era of colonization that would usher in the control of the lower Delaware by the English. By 1682 a youthful William Penn would arrive in the New World at New Castle, to take control of the land mass that comprises the State of Delaware. The very founding of Swanendael by the Dutch would play a pivotal role in the boundary alignment of the colonies of Delaware and Pennsylvania, as we shall soon see.

---

[84] Ibid., 493.

Chapter 3

Plockhoy and a *New Society*

A fascinating story in the colonial history of Delaware is the attempt of Pieter Cornelis Plockhoy, a seventeenth century Dutch reformer, to begin a colony in New Netherland in 1663. Of special interest is not the fact that a settlement was made—and within a year completely destroyed—but, the ideal behind the colony. Plockhoy had hoped his efforts would "grow and develop into the ideal commonwealth of love and equality." It was in the words of one nineteenth century historian, "among the most extraordinary of the early memorials of American colonization." [1]

Until not too many years ago, the political thought of this somewhat obscure reformer had never fully been discussed. [2] The association of Plockhoy's role to that of his contemporaries is of significance from

---

[1] J. Romeyn Brodhead, *History of the State of New York* (New York, 1874), 698.

[2] The most complete work is Leland Harder and Marvin Harder, *Plockhoy from Zurik-zee*, (Newton: Mennonite Historical Series, 1952). The early historical findings of Leland Harder were first published as "Plockhoy and His Settlement at Zwaanendael," *Delaware History* 3 (March 1949): 138-154. There is also an account in Turner, 1909, 285-288, and one to be found in Bertus Harry Wabeke, *Dutch Emigration to North America 1624-1860* (New York: The Netherlands Information Bureau, 1944).

two points: first, his philosophy was directly related to, and somewhat influential with, the intellectual and reform movements of the seventeenth century; and second, Plockhoy conceived a plan of government which was unique for its time. It was this plan of government that was attempted on the shores of the Delaware at Lewes.

Plockhoy and the Collegiants

Pieter Cornelis Plockhoy (1620-1700) was a Dutch Mennonite who actively participated in Church affairs during the critical period (1650-1664) when the entire Mennonite movement in the Netherlands was embroiled in internal conflict. The conflict involved a group of clergy and lay persons with whom Plockhoy was associated, known as the Collegiants. This group challenged the existing belief that the Christian life should be regulated by rules of conduct and prescribed confessions of faith. The Collegiants or Progressives, as they were also called, minimized the importance of creeds or strict applications of disciplinary rules, and emphasized in their place a spiritual life to be guided by an enlightened conscience. [3] In essence, the Collegiants were not an organized religious body, but were members of various religious denominations who met together to discuss the common faith. They were anti-Calvinist, advocated the separation of church and state and accepted no creed. [4]

It was Plockhoy's feeling that man does not have to accept a common interpretation of the Scriptures. On the contrary, a difference of opinion was to be expected, and for that reason, a combined state-church that would demand one interpretation and one creed, should be abolished. It was essential, however, that men attempt to resolve their differences of opinion, not through coercion, but by a free exchange of ideas, "that the weakness or ignorance of some may be remedied by the knowledge of others." [5] Thus if differences could be resolved in this

---

[3] See Harder and Harder, *Plockhoy from Zurik-zee*, 12.

[4] Ibid., 14.

[5] Ibid., 27.

way, tolerance of the divergent opinion would follow. "We must allow that liberty of speaking to others which we desire ourselves, without tying anyone to our opinion…without stumbling at any differences which do not hinder love and piety." [6] The most significant premise of Plockhoy's philosophy was tolerance—"It did not imply an acquiescence to ignorance nor a surrender to force. It was meant to insure peaceful relations between men in their pursuit of knowledge and truth" [7]

Little is known about Plockhoy's personal life outside of his reform activities and published pamphlets. However, it is known that he arrived in England in 1658 during the Interregnum under Oliver Cromwell. The Puritan Revolution (1642-1649) had raised England's hopes that the absolute power of the king could be replaced by a rule of justice and liberty. Unfortunately, under Cromwell, a dictator who ruled arbitrarily under the aegis of a benevolent despot, these hopes never came to pass.

Several attempts were made, particularly by the radical groups known as the Levellers and Diggers, to effect reform and political democracy within the new regime all to little immediate avail.[8] Nonetheless, Plockhoy went to England with the avowed goal "to see Christendom established as a universal state in the form reminiscent of the Collegia in Holland."[9] Plockhoy's initial strategy was to petition the English Parliament and, through the magistrates, have his

---

[6] Ibid.

[7] Ibid.

[8] See George H. Sabine, *A History of Political Theory* (New York: Holt, Rinehart, and Winston, 1962), 477-495. The ultimate influence of the Levellers and Diggers in England paved the way for much political reform that was to effectively materialize during the next two centuries. Although this development will not be discussed here it should be kept in mind by the reader that similarly what the Collegiants and Plockhoy ascribed to was at the time radical religious, social and even political thought. Cf., W. Schenk, *The Concern for Social Justice in the Puritan Revolution* (New York: Longman's, Green & Co., 1948), passim.

[9] Harder and Harder, *Plockhoy from Zurik-zee*, 24.

plan presented to Cromwell himself, but the latter's unexpected death in 1658 made this impossible. Additional attempts to see Cromwell's son and successor also failed. As a result, the undaunted Dutchman turned to having his letters, which were previously sent to Cromwell and the Parliament, published in order to "awaken the publick spirits in England." The first work was entitled *The Way to the Peace and Settlement of These Nations*, and was printed early in 1659.

A second edition of the letters concerning Plockhoy's initial plan for an ideal commonwealth was published in the same year under the shortened title, *A Way Propounded, To Make The Poor In These And Other Nations Happy.*

It was through this second pamphlet that Plockhoy's philosophy had become concerned with social problems and injustice in the world. He decided to give up working through the government and begin laboring directly with the poorer classes in society. Generally, his aim was to bring together all of the socially downtrodden people into communion with himself and with each other in order to improve their lives in a cooperative manner. They would live separated from the rest of society, but remain economically a part of it.

Plockhoy Plans His Colony

Repeatedly failing in his overtures to English authorities, Plockhoy returned to Holland in 1661, and petitioned the Burgomasters of the City of Amsterdam to establish a colony in New Netherland. From the beginning of his negotiations with the Burgomasters, Plockhoy had brought together a group of twenty-four families who wished to participate in his community experiment. After several overtures to the Dutch officials, the group finally petitioned for a tract of land on the South River along with a request for two hundred guilders in loan to each family.

On June 6, 1662, a contractual agreement between Plockhoy's group and the Burgomasters was completed. It stated "that he, Pieter Cornelisz Plockhoy, undertakes to present to us, as soon as possible, the names of twenty-five persons [families], who will agree to depart by the first ship or ships to the aforesaid colony of this city, to reside there and to work at farming, fishing, handicrafts, etc., and to be as diligent as possible not only to live comfortably themselves, but also that provision may thereby be made for others to come."[10] The contract went on to grant each member as much land as he could use at the "Horekill," the right to enact their own laws with the right of appeal to the "higher magistrates," exemption from taxes for twenty years, and a loan of money to each family.[11]

It took Plockhoy almost a year to get underway, with two factors mainly responsible for the delay. In the first place, the group was constructing an adequate framework of government, a privilege that had been granted them by the settlement contract, and second, Plockhoy wanted to have at least one hundred settlers before embarking.

Administration and Government for the Colony

Plockhoy's ideas for the administration and government of his colony had previously been submitted to the Burgomasters, ostensibly through an attorney or notary, who served as Plockhoy's agent during his negotiations with the city. His ideas had been outlined in the form of seven letters sent to the authorities between November 22, 1661 and May 25, 1662.[12] The fourth letter dated January 10, 1662, was the most significant since it contained one hundred seventeen "Articles of Government and Association." Selected articles from this fourth letter outline Plockhoy's theory of government.

---

[10] This petition appears in *N.Y. Colonial Documents* 2: 176-177.

[11] Harder and Harder, *Plockhoy from Zurik-zee*, 51.

[12] The seven letters became Plockhoy's third (although anonymous) publication and were promulgated in Amsterdam (1662) as part of *Kort Verhael van Nieuw Nederlants* (Brief Account of New Netherlands). Additional excerpts from the *Kort Verhael* which provide interesting descriptions of New Netherland, may be found in Weslager, 1961, 292-293.

Generally, he held that equality was to be the first and fore-
most basis of the "commonwealth" (colony). Popular government was
to be assured with a separation of powers, generally divided into the
executive, judicial and legislative functions. Moreover, new laws were
to be enacted by a majority vote of the people, which would then be
approved by a single executive also elected by the people. The following are the key excerpts as written by Plockhoy in his fourth letter that
describe the principles upon which he planned to incorporate into his
colony on the Delaware. [13]

> The principal basis or foundation for this society
> will be an equality for which purpose every man over
> 24 years of age who wishes to enter the society must
> seriously and earnestly promise that he will never
> strive for any special power, nor will allow anyone else
> to make the least efforts in that direction, but resists
> this with all possible means. Because all the rules will
> be instituted by a majority of two-thirds of the entire
> society, he will have to abide by them according to his
> best ability, as a good Christian.
>
> The common council meeting shall be held at the same
> time and place after the end of the above mentioned
> religious service.
>
> In order to conduct this meeting in good and proper
> form it is expedient now to set forth the organization
> of the government of the society.
>
> All laws and ordinances necessary for the benefit of
> this Christian civilian society will be enacted by at

---

[13] Excerpts from the fourth letter (Letter "D") of the Seven Letters or Articles of
Association ("Requesten, Vertoogen, and Deductien") published as part of *Kort
Verhael van Nieuw Nederants* (1662) by Plockhoy may be found in Harder and
Harder, *Plockhoy from Zurik-zee*, 189-205.

least a two-thirds majority, the votes being cast on ballots.

The same may be changed, increased, decreased or repealed by a two-thirds majority concurrence obtained in a written vote.

Such proposals to change, increase, decrease, or repeal existing laws will be made only by the public officers of that time, being the presiding members; and after some time of discussion with all who at one time have been public officers in the general assembly.

No law shall be proposed, let alone enacted, in the general assembly, with hurried thoughtlessness, which would be injurious to the state, city, and company, or might be considered so.

For which end as the highest goal of this society all will have to strive. This society could not operate with complete observance of the laws, advises and minor private procedures of the society, state, city or company.

Public Officials

Concerning the elections of the principal public servants the aggregate colonists, minimum 100 men, the unmarried men being not under 24 years and not being servant to anybody or having debts to the community in the form of a loan contracted for the beginning of the trip, will meet at the place determined by the highest supervisors.

Everyone of the voting colonists, according to his best knowledge, will nominate or choose as head of the colony the one whom he considers the most prominent in means, intelligence, and knowledge. The voting will be done on ballots rolled up.

The votes will be collected in the presence of all, and the ten names that have the most votes will be presented to the Burgomasters of the city of Amsterdam to select five of them to serve one year.

If it happens as is possible that the last of the list have an equal number of votes, a die will be cast to fulfill the ten.

And likewise those who are too near in blood-relationship will be decided upon by casting a die.

When the number of colonists increases by twenty men, a public servant shall be elected in order to increase the number of public servants.

The retiring officers will be eligible again after one year.

The oldest in years or the one who has been in office the longest should be most eligible for the office of presiding public servant.

The nomination may be sent over to the Magistrates a year beforehand. The selection could be made and the letter sealed until the last day of office. In such a way the officials would be chosen in time.

In addition to the public servants elected thus there shall be a nomination for one or two public servants chosen from the Mennonites, or those who will not defend themselves with arms. These will be elected in the above described manner, as assistant and supervising principal servants.

The public presiding servant shall be open to criticism on all his actions concerning the public interest as well as to lawsuits up to one year and six weeks after the expiration of his terms of service.

Common Rights

In order to stimulate and encourage those who lack of initiative, and in order to obtain a secure stock of provisions and a large area of common well-prepared lands, to be later divided by lottery, the best procedure according to our judgment would be to work together during the first five years in groups of ten men, each under supervision of a skilled foreman, working six hours daily on an assigned section of land, resolved to prepare the section during as many days which might be found fit to work.

The remaining time shall be left to each individual for his private affairs, comfort and welfare.

For which purpose each colonist might be given a separate piece of land situated nearby for private vineyards, gardens and play grounds, as much as space will permit, in order to provide for everyone's personal interests, desires and best pleasure.

Cattle would also during the first five years be the most profitable if bought, bred, and kept in common.

The common land, cattle, etc., could in no way be surety for anybody's private debts or arrears.

If after one, two, three or four years, new colonists should be added to society, they might (in order to obtain an equal status with those who were already there with regard to the land already under cultivation, and the common stock, as cattle, etc.) make an agreement with the society for requital perhaps by providing the oldest members with some relief from the common labor, or in another way to be arranged in each case.

In case of death of any colonist during the first five common-working years, his share in the common stock would be used to give relief (as in Article 58) to his dependents, unless they are able to provide for themselves without recourse to the community.

But if there is no heir in the society or among the colonists this would revert back to the community.

After the first five years have expired and as a result of the common labor of several hours daily a reasonable amount of cultivated land, grain and cattle have been secured, the time will have arrived for the best continuation of the common-wealth and for everyone in particular, for division of the landed property, cattle, etc., by lottery. For this goal every colonist and housefather should want to do his best on his own initiative, for this will be the most effective way to stimulate everyone's personal diligence and ambition for a higher standard of living.

Conflicts and Disputes

In regard to all personal conflicts and opinion differences (which might comprise injuries) it is believed that for the peace and welfare of the individual and the community nothing better could be proposed than:

That all those incorporated by oath, word of honor, or promise of loyalty in this society of Christian citizens shall understand that this oath also indicates that they submit to the laws of the community regarding private, large as well as small quarrels and disputes.

In this regard disputes should be submitted to the principal public servants for satisfactory solution, be they quarrelling or wrangling between husband and wife, parent and child, neighbors, teachers, women, servants, maids, etc.

If after a satisfactory settlement the individual persists in provoking a quarrel with reproaching or scolding words with the one to whom he had once been reconciled, or proves too stubborn for reconciliation, he should be fined an amount, two-thirds of which should be paid to the community, and one-third to the Sir Sheriff of New Amstel, who upon the recommendation of the before mentioned public servants might collect the fine.

After that, the obstinate, dissipated and unruly colonist (first under penalty of disenfranchisement, and after that expulsion from the society) will be required for a last time to adjust himself.

Protection of All

Our young and fragile society will have to be watched particularly carefully, so that the weaker members will always be protected as much as possible from oppression by the stronger ones, even to assist them so that they will not be deprived of the opportunity to obtain a better standing.

In 1662 Plockhoy published, a companion to his "Letters" and called, *Kort en Klaer Ontwerp...* (Brief and Concise plan). This became the actual Colonization Prospectus to enlist emigrants for his settlement at Lewes. It was here that he indicated that the colony in the New World could not rely on trade with the "outside world." Thus agriculture was to become the predominant interest to ensure self-sufficiency. "Land and livestock were to be owned in common for a period of time only, after which they were to be divided among the members, thereby providing a greater personal initiative to work hard at the beginning. [14]

It was also in this publication that an innovation forbidding slavery in the society was made: "since we do not want servile slavery in our society, everybody will have to work hard in order that we may show good progress."[15] Although this was consistent with Plockhoy's philosophy of equality, it nonetheless challenged the lucrative slave trading of the Dutch. It has even been said that "Plockhoy's was the first voice raised in America against slavery." [16]

The Fate of Plockhoy

In May, 1663, Plockhoy and his group set sail in the ship St. Jacob, bound for the New World with much enthusiasm and a new set of principles by which they would govern their lives. The St. Jacob arrived at New Amstel (New Castle) in July after having left "41 souls with their baggage and farm utensils at the Horekill."[17] At last the colony was started, but was doomed to be short-lived. In the fall of 1664, troops under the command of Sir Robert Carr sacked the young colony during the hostilities that accompanied New Netherlands' transfer to English rule.

Plockhoy's followers probably spread throughout the countryside, although there is no record of their fate. Plockhoy, however, remained

---

[14] Harder and Harder, *Plockhoy from Zurik-zee*, 61.

[15] *Kort en Klaer Ontwerp*, cited in Ibid, 182.

[16] *Year Book of the Holland Society of New York* (1914) p. 228. See also Turner, 1909, 286.

[17] *N.Y. Colonial Documents* 12: 436.

in the Lewes area for twenty-nine years after the destruction of his colony. There is a record that during the session of the court held January 9, 10, and 11, 1682, he received a grant for a "Towne Lott." He purchased a second lot soon after, and on December 8, 1693, sold his real estate to Cornelus Wiltbank.[18] By 1694 he moved to Germantown, Pennsylvania, where he later died totally destitute.

If this new experiment had had the opportunity to survive it most assuredly would have left a greater imprint on American colonial history. It was, without question, a unique concept for its time—the first attempt to establish a socialist utopia on American soil. Yet what will probably be remembered is that Plockhoy's misfortune was simply another Dutch failure to colonize Swanendael. It was, according to C.A. Weslager, "The final Dutch attempt to organize a colony on the Delaware."[19]

---

[18] *Sussex County Deed Record* A. no. 1, 107 and 145 and Turner, 1909, 87.
[19] Weslager, 1961, 102.

Chapter 4

The Boundary Controversy

The Dutch settlement, Swanendael, was destined to be the pivotal factor in how the future boundary alignment would be decided that demarked the limits of the States of Delaware and Pennsylvania. This story is a fascinating account of how colonial powers influenced the geographical bounds of the thirteen original colonies and ultimately the United States of America.

The Duke of York's Proprietary Grant

On March 12, 1664, King Charles II granted to his brother James Stuart, Duke of York (Later Kings James II) a patent conveying proprietary rights to lands in America from the St. Croix River in Maine to the east side of Delaware Bay and River. This encompassed almost all of New Netherland except that territory along the western shore of the Delaware River, which was still under Dutch control and included the territory of the settlement of Swanendael. It was this patent to the Duke of York that became England's first move toward eventually securing her economic and political position in America.[1]

---

[1] C.A. Weslager, *The English on the Delaware: 1610-1682* (New Brunswick: Rutgers University Press, 1967), 176-177.

The Dutch settlements on the Delaware posed a precarious situation for the English. They forced Charles II to decide whether to recognize the rights of the Dutch in New Netherland or to risk war with Holland. The latter course seemed more advantageous even though a tenuous peace had existed between the two powers since 1654. However, it was agreed in the Privy Council that the king should grant the territory occupied by the Dutch to the Duke of York, who would then seize the lands, somewhat underhandedly, and with a minimum of bloodshed. It was felt that the Dutch government could then declare war against England if they were so inclined. Yet this would be a weighty decision indeed, with the New World bases, in effect, under English control.

It was obvious that the Dutch were to be vulnerable to the English from several viewpoints. First the Dutch lacked not only military, but civil strength in the New World, despite the trading activity of the Dutch West India Company; and secondly, the population distribution was certainly not in their favor. New Netherland consisted of a population of approximately 10,000 while the English could claim roughly 50,000 people in New England, 35,000 in Virginia and 15,000 in Maryland.[2]

The Duke of York sent to New Netherland three armed ships carrying three companies of troops under the command of Colonel Richard Nicolls on May 15, 1664. The Conquest of New Netherland did not provide any great difficulty for the English. New Amstel surrendered in October 1664, and the name changed to New Castle. Fort Amsterdam, guarding the city of the same name, surrendered in September, 1665. The name of the fort was changed to James and the town to New York in honor of the Duke.

By August 1667, the war between the Dutch and English came to an end with the signing of the Treaty of Breda. For the next five years the political assimilation of New Netherland to English rule was to take place slowly but firmly.

---

[2] Ibid., 180.

The Claims of Lord Baltimore and the Duke of York

In 1671 a chain of events began which was to directly involve the precarious situation at the Hoerenkil. In that year, Charles Calvert, Lord Baltimore, decided to settle colonists on what he referred to as the "seaboard side" of his province, which comprised all the territory on Delaware Bay south of New Castle. His claim was based on his proprietary grant from Charles I dated June 20, 1632, which had included the land below the 40th parallel (approximately at Philadelphia) on the Delaware "hitherto uncultivated and occupied by savages." The grant made to Lord Baltimore was considerably earlier than the one given to the Duke of York. [3]

Lord Baltimore intended to challenge the Duke of York's claimed territory at the sparsely settled and poorly defended Hoerenkil in order to assert his right to ownership. He then proceeded to accomplish his purpose by creating in 1669 the now defunct County of Durham to include the area from the Hoerenkil as far north as the 40th parallel. The surveyor general of the province, Jerome White, was ordered to survey this territory and lay out at the Hoerenkil on the "seaboard side" two proprietary manors for Lord Baltimore each to contain at least 6,000 acres. [4]

Between 1671 and 1673, the settlers at the Hoerenkil had the misfortune of enduring three raids sent by Lord Baltimore to affect his control over the territory. The first occurred in June 1671 when Captain Thomas Jones rode with a party of horsemen and plundered the colony. A dispatch was sent to Governor Francis Lovelace in New York by Captain John Carr to inform him of the episode. Although Lovelace issued a protest as well as orders to bring Jones to justice, it

---

[3] Cecilius (Cecil) Calvert, the second Lord Baltimore became the first proprietary of the province of Maryland, named for the wife of King Charles in 1632.

[4] "Proceedings of the Council of Maryland 1667-1687/8," *Archives of Maryland* 5 (1887), 56-57. Cf., *N.Y. Colonial Documents* 12: 496-497.

ostensibly did no good. Jones went back to the Hoerenkill a second time in September and again plundered the settlement.

Perhaps the most terrifying raid of all occurred in December 1673 when another party was sent to the Hoerenkil, this time under the leadership of Captain Thomas Howell. What ensued has been referred to colloquially as the "Burning of the Whorekill." [5] The circumstances of this tragedy, as well as the two that immediately preceded it, were described in five contemporary depositions. Helmanus Wiltbank, one of the prominent citizens at the Whorekill, gave this account dated May 5, 1683:

> In the year of our Lord 1671 in the month of June Capt. Thomas Jones did come up in this place called Whorekill with 7 or 8 horsemen with force of arms, and came to the house of Helmanus Wiltbank and tyed him and rid to the rest of his neighbors and tyed them and kept a guard over them, and plundered the housing and carried the goods away and left us.
>
> In the month of September following came up the said Capt. Jones with a troop of horse with forces of armies and made forcible entry in this place, and called a court of their own men, and made us come to their court and demanded the oath of allegiance wherein we were not willing, whereupon the court did commit us to prison and kept us until the next day without meat or drink, and threatened to carry us for Maryland and confiscate our estate, so that we

---

[5] The name, *Hoerenkil* was the Dutch reference to the creek that is today part of the Lewes and Rehoboth Canal. Over time there have appeared in historical records a number of Dutch variations including *Hoerekil* and *Haert Kill*. Swedish writers used the form *Horn Kill* or *Hornkill*. During the seventeenth century the unfavorable English equivalent was *Whorekill* that was later dropped when the name *Lewes* became the standard place name reference to the town. The confusing etymology of the name has been cited in Chapter 2, footnote 35.

were forced to take the oath of allegiance to be true to my Lord Baltimore, and so we remained until the next year. 1672 in the month of August the Dutch recovering New York did send boat and men for to surrender this place, whereupon our Commissioner Francis Jenkins did take [to] them papers that were sent by the Dutch Governor and went to my Lord into Maryland and promised to bring speedy answer again which...[torn document] again for surrendering, if not w[e] should nothing except but fire and sword: So that the inhabitants for fear did surrender being the Commissioner was fled away, and my Lord in all this time never sent word nor answer nor protection.

In the month of December next following Capt. Howell did come with a troop of souldirs and demanded this place and we replyed we had been my Lord's tenants before, we will not or can defend the place. Capt Howell answered we are come now to defend you, and if it cost the province of Maryland a million in tobacco we will protect you and marched in the place, and did eat and drinke with us eighteen days, and then set our housing upon fire Christmas eave. What was not spended they burned and marched away and left us in [an] unbearable condition, so that all ye inhabitants (except a few) were forced to leave the place for want of provisions and them that were left in [the] place could not goe because their wives were bigg with child, and some men were famished at ye murder creek in this Bay.[6]

---

[6] This deposition as well as four others, plus a narrative of the incident, were first published in an article by Leon de Valinger, Jr., "The Burning of the Whorekill, 1673," *Pa. Magazine* 74 (October 1950): 473-487.

The nature of international politics being what it is brought the English and Dutch into another confrontation in 1672. And in the summer of 1673, word was received in New York that a Dutch squadron was on its way to the Atlantic Coast. During the short period of the Dutch reoccupation from August 8, 1673, with the seizure of New Castle from the English, and continuing to February 19, 1674, the Hoerenkil was once again under Dutch authority.

After the Duke of York had again regained his territory on the Delaware—the short war ended with the Treaty of Westminster—there was to be, not withstanding, a revival of the controversy between himself and Lord Baltimore pertaining to who owned the Hoerenkil as well as the entire Delaware.

Since no boundary lines were named, and the land area of today's Delaware became known as "an appendage of New York" and remained in possession of the Duke of York until he made deeds to William Penn in 1682, the description of Lord Baltimore's grant to Maryland, bounded on the east by the ocean, Delaware Bay and River, covered these same "lower counties." [7]

Typical of the controversy that was evolving can be found in a conference held between Lord Baltimore and William Penn on December 13, 1682, concerning the bounds of their respective territories. Excerpts from that meeting were recorded as follows.

> <u>Wm. Pen</u>. The King its true did command the laying out the line between us but if for a more ready way of accomodacon to us both he hath thought fitt to make other proposals I cannot tell why they may not be taken into consideracon but I shall concede and wave that letter wholly makeing this further offer. The Capes for several years have bin reputed to lye in the latitude of thirty seaven or between thirty seaven and

---

[7] See Walter A. Powell, "Fight of a Century Between the Penns and the Calverts Over the 'Three Lower Counties on Delaware'" TMs (typewritten manuscript, 1932), 8.

five minutes or thereabouts and hath bin soe generally taken and approved on by all persons for some considerable space of years and by which calculation all ships and Vessels have proceeded on their Voyages before such time as either interest or prejudice could sway them on the one side or the other soe then if the Lord Baltemore please to take his comencement from the Capes which has been generally and of soe long continuance reputedly to lye in thirty seaven degrees and five minutes and from thence measure by line two degrees fifty five minutes will just reach to the fortieth degree.

Lord B. My Pattent gives me the fortieth degree of northern latitude for my northern bounds and there is noe way certaine to find that as by an observacon to be taken by a sextant of six of seaven foote radies and such an Instrument you have belonging to Colonel Lewis Morris of New York besides your commencement by your Pattent is given at the fortieth degree of northern latitude.

Wm. Pen. Then I shall only say we will wave and wholly lay aside the King's letter at this time if the Lord Baltemore will begin at thirty seaven and a halfe insted of thirty eight he will indeed have more than was designed for him I therefore offer as a medium between us the more easily to accommodate this matter let the Lord Baltemore first begin at the antient [ancient] and generally reputed and knowne place of thirty seaven degrees and five minutes and thence with a direct line to forty what falls then within his bounds much good may it doe him I am contented and doubt not but he is soe worthy and soe much a Gentleman as not to endeavor to deprive me of anything shall appeare to be within by Grant. This I say I offer onely to lett the Baltemore know that altho' I am sensible the King's letter is grounded upon strong presumption and sound circumstance yet I am willing to wave that and accommodate the business between us a more equal way as I conceive viz. to commence at the common, generall and soe long reputed know place before either the Lord Baltemore or myselfe could challenge any interest in these parts of the world.

Lord B. It is other discourse that I expected to have heard from you at this time and well hoped I should have bin soe far favored by you as to have received some small advice from you before you had soe far proceeded upon that part of the Countrey which has bin always reputed and knowne to be justly claimed by me but to wave that I desire to be informed by you whither you have purchased the Dukes pretentions to Delaware.

Wm. Pen. Upon tearmes of the moiety of halfe the revenues thereof to be revenues thereof to be reserved for himselfe I hold it of his gift but this leads to other discourse I would willingly proceed first to the ascertaineing the bounds between us.

Lord B. The certaine bounds betwixt us must be the fortieth degree of northern latitude as I have already shewn you by my grant.

Wm. Pen. And to find out that I propose in my judgement the most equall way that I can be which is to begin at the Capes a place soe generally and soe

long knowne and reputed to lye within the latitude
of thirty seaven and five minutes by any observacon
yet taken and soe from thence to measure two degrees
fifty five minutes which will just make the fortieth
degree. [8]

In October, 1753, Lewis Evans, the noted eighteenth century car-
tographer, wrote a letter to the Maryland Governor, Horatio Sharpe,
in which he presented an argument specifically designed to support the
Baltimore claim. He described the location of Cape Henlopen this way.
"In August, 1682, the Duke granted the Delaware Counties to Mr.
Penn, to extend southward to Cape Henlopen. In December following an Act of Assembly of Pennsylvania expresly calls the present Cape
Hinlopen by the same Name. In March, following, the King grants the
lower Counties to the Duke [of York] under the Same Description.
The Cape Henlopen of the Dutch, and the Articles of Agreement, is
at four or five miles South of the present cape, so called; but neither is,
nor was ever at Fenwicks Island." [9]

When Evans' 1752 revision of the 1749 map of *Pennsylvania, New
Jersey, New York, and the three Delaware Counties* appeared, he referred
to Fenwick Island also as "The Old Cape Henlopen." However, on
his map of 1755 (of the *Middle British Colonies*), as described in an
accompanying "analysis," Evans repudiates this identity, admitting that
he was mistaken, as the following account provides.

A map I published of PENSILVANIA, NEW
JERSEY, NEW YORK and DELAWARE, in 1749,
is reduced to a smaller Scale in this, and forms those

---

[8] "Proceedings of the Council of Maryland," 384-385.

[9] Lawrence Henry Gipson, *Lewis Evans,* (Philadelphia: The Historical Society of
Pennsylvania, 1939), 47. See several depositions related to the boundary dispute
also concerning the confusion of the naming of Cape Henlopen in *Pennsylvania
Archives,* 2nd ser., 7: 348 and 355-356. Also see "The Calvert Papers" no.
2 (Selections from Correspondence), *The Maryland Historical Society: Fund
Publications* (1894), 136-138.

four Colonies. [10] So the three Lower Counties of New Castle, Kent and Sussex, upon Delaware, were called, before they were annexed to Pensilvania, when this name was given in Contradistinction to the three upper Counties of Chester, Philadelphia and Bucks. As it exceeds in Length and Barbarity all the savage Names in my Title put together, I have restored the Colony its old Name of Delaware.

The Errors are rectified, the principle of which were, Albany placed too far North, Shamokin too far West, and all the Route thence to Oswego five Miles altogether too much North; besides several Imperfections, in Places where later Observations and Discoveries have given us Knowledge of. In the first impression of my former Map I committed some mistakes in the Names of Places, near the entrance of Delaware Bay, on the West Side, and in my Attempt to rectify them, in the Second Edition, did but add to the confusion. I have since had an Opportunity of making a thorough Enquiry into this Affair, and conclude, that the Names that the Places thereabouts are now called by, and are the same as laid down in my General Map, are the only Names they ever had, and still retain amongst those acquainted with them; as Lewes, Whorekill Road, Cape Hinlopn [Henlopen], False Cape, and Fenwick's Island: Excepting that Mr. William Penn called Cape Hinlopen by the Name of Cape James, and Whorekill Lewes, on his first Arrival in 1682; the former is scarce known at this Day, and

---

[10] At this juncture in the manuscript the following two sentences were marked by an asterisk by Evans and actually appear at the end of his statement. The author has placed them here to restore a continuity to Evans' argument.

the name Lewes is confined to the Town, while the Creek still retains the Name of the Whorekill.

All must admit that the present Names are rightly laid down; but what is related in regard to the antient names must be understood only as my opinion. There are others who think, on no less Opportunity of forming a Judgment, that Cape Hinlopen was formerly called Cape Cornelius; and that Fenwick's Island was the False Cape, or Cape Hinlopn, of the Dutch, and others, till the arrival of the English in those parts under Mr. Penn. [11]

The Settlement of the Boundary Dispute

In the famous controversy as to whether the charter granted by Charles I to Lord Baltimore, or the charter granted by Charles II to the Duke of York and then William Penn, gave title to the territory which now constitutes the State of Delaware, the fact of the early settlement by the Dutch at Swanendael would become the crucial variable in its ultimate settlement.

The dispute over the Delaware territory was advanced for years, first between Lord Baltimore and the Duke of York, then Baltimore and William Penn, and finally by the legal heirs of both Baltimore and Penn. Inevitably, such a controversy was bound to be decided in a court of law. On the grounds that Lord Baltimore's charter gave no rights over previous settlements, the English Court of Chancery held that the shores of the Delaware as far south as Cape Henlopen were not included in the grant made to him in 1632, the year after the Swanendael settlement, and the decision was ultimately decided in favor of Penn. [12]

---

[11] Ibid., 147-148. See Dunlap, 1956, 31-34 for an in-depth discussion over the Henlopen place name confusion.

[12] See F.J. Kensman and George Gray, "Landing of the deVries Colony at Lewes,

The court case was argued before Lord Chancellor Hardwich of England in 1750.[13] Counsel representing both the Penn and Baltimore claims argued diligently. In fact, the jurisdiction of his Honor to try such a case "of a disputed claim to real estate and a princely province in the remote region of America" became one of the chief points of the defense. Lord Hardwich answered this charge when he read his final opinion:

I directed this case to stand over for judgment, not so much from any doubt of what was the justice of the case, as by reason of the nature of it, its great consequence and importance, and the great labor and ability of the argument on both sides; it being for the determination of the right and boundaries of two great provincial governments and three counties; of a nature worthy of the judicature of a Roman Senate rather than a single judge, and my consolation is, that if I should err in my judgment, there is a judicature equal in dignity to a Roman Senate that will correct it.[14]

Thus, the legal opinion in favor of Penn's claim effectuated the establishment of the boundaries of Delaware and Maryland, and finally ended the heated dispute that had persisted for so many years. The fact that there were Dutch settlers at Swanendael before 1632 became the final justification for the Court's decision.[15]

In 1909, a monument was erected on Pilottown Road not only in honor of de Vries and the Swanendael settlement, but as a symbol of

---

Delaware," *Papers HSD* LIV(1909): 4. Cf., Alfred N. Chandler, *Land Title Origins* (New York: Robert Schalkenback Foundation, 1945), 262-272.

[13] A comprehensive account of the boundary controversy, as well as the ultimate litigation, a crucial aspect concerning early Colonial history, may be found in Dudley Lunt, *The Bounds of Delaware* (Wilmington: Star Publishing Company, 1947). See also Nicholas B. Wainwright, "The Missing Evidence: Penn v. Baltimore," *Pa. Magazine* 80 (April 1956): 227-235.

[14] See John W. Houston, "Address on the History of Boundaries of the State of Delaware," *Papers, HSD* 2 (1879): 93-94.

[15] See C.A. Weslager, *The English on the Delaware*, 221-230.

Lewes' priority in Delaware history. It was dedicated by Baron Louden, the Dutch minister to the United States and has the following inscription.

ERECTED
BY THE
STATE OF DELAWARE
TO COMMEMORATE THE SETTLEMENT
ON THIS SPOT, OF THE FIRST
DUTCH COLONY, UNDER DEVRIES,
A.D. 1631
– HERE WAS THE CRADLING OF A STATE –
"THAT DELAWARE EXISTS AS A SEPARATE
COMMONWEALTH IS DUE TO THIS COLONY."
—BANCROFT

The Duke of York Patents: The Early Land Grants

For over two hundred years, Pilottown has been the name of a string of homes that border the southwest bank of the Lewes & Rehoboth Canal where many of the early Bay and River pilots lived. In the seventeenth century, the upper reaches of Pilottown Road had been the location of the first European settlement on Delaware soil by the Dutch. After the Duke of York had acquired title to the territory, he in turn conveyed or granted titles of land ownership of these lands in Delaware from 1657 to 1680.

These early English land grants are known and were published in 1903 as *Original Land Titles in Delaware: The Duke of York Record 1646-1679*. They have been the subject of an in-depth study by Dr. David Marine, and his findings, which first appeared in 1955, are reproduced in their entirety in Appendix 1. The *Duke of York Record* is a fragmentary and incomplete document of land titles and patents originally compiled from the records in New York under the direction of Thomas McKean by the authority of a law enacted by the colonial legislature of Delaware in 1770. Marine has found eight such patents which account for all the frontage on Pilottown Road northwest of Ship Carpenter Street, and provides good source material of the early land transactions in Delaware's oldest settlement. [16]

As the seventeenth century came to a close the little town of Lewes was now firmly under English control — and influence. The contentious boundary dispute between Lord Baltimore and the Duke of York had been settled, and land within the small, but now thriving community was being transferred to new owners and settlers. The next major event in the history of Delaware's oldest settlement would happen with the outbreak of the Revolutionary War.

---

[16] Cf., a compilation of source material, primarily from Fernow's Vol. 12 of *N.Y. Colonial Documents* that was done many years ago by Jeremiah Sweeney, "Early Delaware Land Grants, Plantations & Families" (Farnhurst, Del.: 1958) and exits in manuscript form.

Chapter 5

Independence, Treasure and War

The seeds of revolution in the American Colonies were intellectually planted when the earliest settlers arrived on these shores. These people possessed a spirit of adventure and a rugged sense of individualism. They came with a dedicated hope for a better life and a better future—that would not be undermined by a Royal prerogative. It was not until after the middle of the eighteenth century that a growing wave of opposition in the colonies toward the "mother land" began to develop. However, there was no universal American opposition toward Great Britain as many would have believed.

Lewistown in the Revolutionary War

Originally of English stock, much of the population of lower Delaware and the contiguous counties of Maryland were kept, by their location, out of touch with the general growth of resistance to British oppression. This greatly encouraged the Tory inclination to support England in her course of action. In 1777 the General Assembly of the young Delaware state ordered the death penalty for active Tories, and in the following month, Congress expressed alarm at "the spirit of Toryism" in Sussex County and the nearby Maryland Counties. [1]

Caesar Rodney as both militia commander and chief executive of Delaware, directed the struggle against *loyalism* with such success that Thomas McKean wrote that "the inhabitants of Delaware are said to be on the verge of total Revolution to *Whiggism*." [2]

During the American Revolution, several Lewestowners took an active role in the struggle for freedom. Shephard Kollock, the distinguished officer and journalist, fought at Trenton and other campaigns. Colonel David Hall raised a regiment in 1776 that became known as the celebrated "Delaware Line" which fought throughout the war. In the Battle of Germantown (October 4, 1777), Hall was wounded and did not rejoin his regiment. However, in October 1781, he petitioned the General Assembly stating that he had recovered his health but had been "unable to repair to his regiment being destitute of cash and of every other necessary for a Campaign." [3] In the spring of 1779 he was appointed a member of the court martial to try Benedict Arnold. However, the trial was not scheduled to begin until the following winter, and by that time Hall had gone on furlough and did not participate in the proceedings.[4]

One of the noteworthy revolutionary activists who, even today, has not received his just reward for efforts in the struggle for independence, was Henry Fisher. He was born in Lewes in 1735, the son of a physician of the same name who had come to America from Waterford Ireland, around 1725. It had been Dr. Fisher's intention to have his son educated in his own profession, but young Henry had developed a longing to become a pilot—and devote himself to a life on the sea.

---

[1] See Harold B. Hancock, *The Delaware Loyalists* (Wilmington: Historical Society of Delaware, 1940), 1-37.

[2] John A. Munroe, *Federalist Delaware* (New Brunswick: Rutgers University Press, 1954), 87-88.

[3] Christopher L. Ward, *The Delaware Continentals, 1776-1783* (Wilmington: Historical Society of Delaware, 1941), 524-526.

[4] See W. Emerson Wilson, *Forgotten Heroes of Delaware* (Cambridge, Md.: Deltos Publishing Company, 1969), 39-40.

By 1775, Fisher was firmly against the policies of the British colonial government. This attitude coupled with his reputation and integrity as an outstanding seaman and pilot prompted the first Committee on Safety of Philadelphia to engage him to remain in Lewes and supervise the defenses at the entrance to Delaware Bay. Fisher took command over the Bay and River Pilots, and at the same time was commissioned a major in the Delaware militia. It was in this position that he virtually became the eyes and ears of the American cause stationed at strategically located Lewestown. He and his men kept a constant vigil in the waters off Cape Henlopen and were prepared to notify the Committee of Safety and the Continental Congress of any new or unusual British naval movements.

The Delaware River just below Philadelphia was obstructed after September 9, 1775, with a "chevaux-de-frise," a series of spikes placed in the river in such a way as to be a formidable obstacle to vessels. Only a narrow channel was left open, the secret of which lay with two trusting pilots. All of the buoys and other markings in the river and bay were removed, and the pilots were ordered not to assist any ship unless on a specific mission in the cause of the Americans.

The birth of the American nation had not yet occurred in the spring of 1776; and the metamorphosis of a population from loyalty to the mother country several thousand miles away to a new political and social contract of government was slowly coming about. It was indeed a radical cause for its time; it was a cause inspired by a new philosophy of popular sovereignty; and it was a cause that challenged the established institutions of its day, demanding a new society of justice and freedom. It was the beginning of a revolution that had the promise to become *Novus Ordo Seclorum*—a new order for the centuries.

In March 1776 the threat of war was fast approaching the shores of the Delaware. Unaware to Henry Fisher and his pilots, the British war ship, *Roebuck,* consisting of forty-four guns, manned by 250 men, along with her tender, *Maria,* was making her way from Cape Henry, Virginia, to Delaware Bay. The *Roebuck* was commanded by Sir

Andrew Snape Hammond whose log books would give details of the British exploits to deter American resistance. [5]

Hammond's mission was primarily to guard the entrance of Delaware Bay and "to prevent any Supplies getting to the Rebels," and "to annoy them by all means."[6] On Monday, March 25, 1776, the *Roebuck* anchored within sight of the Cape Henlopen lighthouse. By seven o'clock that evening, Henry Fisher sent a note to the Committee of Safety informing them that a sloop-of-war with a small tender had been stationed in the bay.[7]

The next morning, a pilot boat came out from Lewestown. Captain Hammond wrote about the incident in his log this way: "I immediately dispatched all boats arm'd after her in hopes of getting some pilots for the river." [8] The pilot boat was captured along with two other vessels that were coming south down the river. Fisher later wrote of the incident that, after being captured, the three ships were striped, scuttled and set adrift.[9] During the next five days the *Roebuck* carried out its mission of harassing and chasing pilot boats and other ships

---

[5] Excerpts from Captain Hammond's ship's log have been published in William Bell Clark, ed., *Naval Documents of the American Revolution* 5 vols. (Washington, D.C.: U.S. Government Printing Office, 1960-1969), esp. Vols. 3 and 4. The complete logs of Captain Hammond as well as his acting Lieutenant, John Phillips, covering the period March 22 to May 19, 1776, have been transcribed for the author by Michael L. Richards, Research Associate at the Hall of Records and are available for the first time. A copy of the logs as transcribed by Richards has been deposited at the Lewes Historical Society. See Harold B. Hancock, "A Calendar of English Microfilms Relating to Delaware and Delawareans," TMs (typewritten manuscript, no date) on file in the Morris Library, University of Delaware. Hancock was in England during 1958-1959 on sabbatical from Otterbein College when he did this research.

[6] Clark, *Naval Documents of the American Revolution,* 3: 235.

[7] Ibid., 4: 510.

[8] Ibid., 529.

[9] Public Archives Commission, *Delaware Archives* 5 Vols. (Wilmington, 1919), 3: 1362-1363.

that were sailing in the bay. The following entry in Hammond's log for Thursday, March 28th, is indicative of the *Roebuck's* activities.

> In the morning Saw Several Sail in the Offing, the Tenders out examining all sails in Sight, exercised great Guns and Small Arms.

> Moderate and cloudy weather, in the afternoon found the Mizzen topsail Yard was Sprung, Ordered the Carpenter to make a new one; On the appearance of Several Small Vessels heaving in Sight from Sea, weighed and gave Chase, at 6 Spoke a Sloop in Ballast from New England taken by a Pilot boat, at 7 brought too and was joined by the *Maria* Tender, and at 8 made Sail after a Rebel Sloop of 10 Guns, which had chased the *Maria* at 10 lost sight of the chase, and made Sail towards the Lighthouse and Sent the *Maria* and Cutter after a Sloop which had anchored within the Hen and Chickens [shoals]. [10]

On April 10th Colonel John Haslet, the commander of the Delaware militia, wrote to President Hancock from Dover and enclosed the report of the commanding officer of the detachment of the Delaware battalion stationed at Lewes concerning the ensuing engagement with *Roebuck's* tender. The report stated:

> On Sunday, 7th April, an express came from the Light House Guard to Lewes, with intelligence that Capt. Field [Nehemiah Field was a Lewes pilot] who commanded a schooner sent by the council of that County to [St.]Eustatia for powder, had just arrived and demanded assistance to unload her. [11] I gave

---

[10] Clark, *Naval Documents of the American Revolution,* 4: 596.

[11] St. Eustatia was an important Dutch trading center in the Caribbean during the eighteenth century.

Colonel David Hall House (c. 1790), located at 107 Kings Highway.
Courtesy of the Archives of The Lewes Historical Society.

orders for the troops to march as soon as the boats
could be had to ferry them across the creek [Lewes
Creek], which the inhabitants procured with amazing
dispatch. We then marched with the utmost expedition
to reinforce our guard, which had taken post by the
schooner to assist in discharging her cargo – mostly
course linens. She then lay seven or eight miles to the
southward of our Cape. At the time of our arrival,
the tender making sail, bore down upon the schooner;
on observing this the men immediately ran her on
shore. Our troops were outdone by the tender, though
they marched at the rate of seven miles per hour. Just
before our arrival, the tender gave guard a broadside
with swivels and musketry, which they returned. On
our junction a constant fire was kept up for some
time, until we perceived the distance too great. We
then left off firing and unloaded the schooner, though

several hundred shots were fired at us to prevent it. Our people picked up many of their [cannon] balls rolling in the sand. The tender dispatched one of the barges to the ship [*Roebuck*] for assistance, who made sail immediately but was soon obliged to come anchor for fear of running on the Hens and Chickens [shoals on the Atlantic side of Cape Henlopen]. About the time the ship turned the Cape, the tender anchored within musket shot of the schooner and kept a continual fire with her swivels. We had by this time got the swivels in the schooner loaded with grape-shot, and a constant fire for two hours was kept up on both sides. We undoubtedly wounded their men, for we perceived some to fall and others to run to their assistance. They made several efforts to purchase their anchor, which were prevented by our fire, but at last they succeeded. Fortunately, however, one of our swivels cut their halyards and down came their mainsail, which compelled them to anchor once more. At last, the wind shifting, they had a boat to tow them off. We then turned our fire on the boat, where two men were seen to fall; the barge, returning from the ship, joined to tow them out, our men escaped unhurt. The militia officers at Lewes acted with a spirit which does honour to their country. [12]

Scharf in his history of Delaware comments that this skirmish was most effective "in removing from the minds of the patriots the exaggerated impression of the invincibility of the British ships and sailors, and they flocked to the shores of the bay in readiness for another encounter." [13]

---

[12] Scharf, 1888, 1: 226.

[13] Ibid.

The engagement at the mouth of Delaware Bay prompted Dr. James Tilton, who was in Lewes, to write the following to a friend in Philadelphia on April 17, 1776.

> Lewistown is at this time made up of officers and soldiers, and the people altogether seem determined to defend our little place. As for Tories, there are none among us. That infamous name is quite done away since danger came so near us. The *Roebuck* still remains in our road [in Delaware Bay] all alone, and has, I believe, lost her tender; a few days ago some say they saw a sloop take her to the southward of our Cape. We have been 50 and 100 men on guard at the Light-house, Arnold's and the Creek's mouth, and are determined to watch them closely. We would not let them, but desired them to go to New Foundland for that purpose. If they should attempt to fish on the beach, we are determined to show them Yankee play, as we did on Easter Sunday when we were unloading Capt. Field. I do assume that if you were here you would be pleased with the spirit of the people. [14]

As for the *Roebuck*, it remained in the vicinity of Cape Henlopen for several weeks and then sailed up the Delaware to confront the newly formed and underestimated American colonial navy. [15]

The fort (or battery) for the defense of Lewes was located on Pilottown Road at the site of the original

---

[14] Ibid., 1:226-227. Dr. Tilton entered the army as the surgeon in Colonel Haslet's regiment and later was appointed Surgeon General of the Army during the War of 1812.

[15] See William Bell Clark, "The Battle in the Delaware," *Year Book* (New Jersey Society of Pennsylvania, 1930), 52-73. A curious account of the activities of *Roebuck* is told in the deposition of a captured American seaman, William Barry, and may be found in *American Archives*, 4th Ser. (1846), Vol. VI: 809-811.

Swanendael settlement. There was also an arsenal consisting of a bombproof artillery storehouse at the corner of Shipcarpenter and Second Streets where the Hannah Beebe House now stands. Both the battery and the arsenal were used during the Revolution and later during the War of 1812. One historian has indicated that the latter "…was the first regularly established arsenal in the colonies taken from the Dutch, and was used as a source of supply for arms used in early Indian warfare as well as against marauding pirates from the lower seas." [16]

The Legend of the "Treasure" Ship, de*Braak*

There have been many shipwrecks near Cape Henlopen over the centuries, but there is one incident that occurred over two hundred years ago that captivated the interest of the people of Lewes—as well as treasure hunters—for many generations.

The legend that has grown around the de*Braak,* since it sank on May 25, 1798, was popularized by the theory that the ship was carrying anywhere from two to thirteen million dollars worth of gold (with some estimates as high as seventeen million dollars). The legend of the treasure is attributed to "Spanish prisoners" who had swum ashore to Lewestown after a violent squall sank the ship. They told of a fabulous treasure that had been aboard a Spanish ship that the de*Braak* had captured and looted. Another interpretation of the legend was that the de*Braak* had secret orders to harass the Spanish in the West Indies and had put into Jamaica to take on board a cargo of gold.

In 1967-1968 the first scholarly investigation of the de*Braak* was published in *The Smithsonian Journal of History* and delved into the story behind the legend. Based on British Admiralty records, it was found that "on examination of papers relating to de*Braak* shows that

---

[16] B.S. Albertson, Jr., *Picturesque and Historic Lewes, Delaware* (Milford, Del., 1929), 3.

regular inventories have been made, with no pertinent records posted as missing or stolen: and no obvious gaps, except for logs lost when the vessel sank." [17]

Originally, the d*eBraak* was a Dutch-built cutter, a one-masted vessel with fore-and-aft rig and had an eighty-four foot long deck. In 1795, the ship was captured by the British during the war between Great Britain and the Dutch Batavian Republic. In 1796, the de*Braak*, along with other Dutch vessels, was sent to the Plymouth Naval Yard to be checked for possible refitting. As a result, the de*Braak* was re-rigged as a brig and became a two-masted vessel. On June 13, 1797, the ship was ready for service in His Majesty's fleet, and Lieutenant James Drew, an experienced seaman, was made the commanding officer.

By February 8, 1798, the Royal Navy ordered the dispatch of the de*Braak*, along with the ship, *St. Albans*, commanded by Captain Francis Pender, to accompany convoys of trade in North American waters. The two vessels, along with their respective convoys, were to meet in Delaware Bay and then proceed to sail to Philadelphia, New York, Boston, and ultimately join Vice Admiral George Vandeput in Halifax. Toward the end of February the convoys approached Chesapeake Bay.

On April 1, Captain Pender signaled the de*Braak* to chase two strange sails which proved to be *H.M.S. Magnamine* and her prize, the French Privateer *Victory* from Boston. On April 2, 1798, with de*Braak* almost out of sight astern, Pender signaled her recall with a gun. For the next two days the weather was stormy. On April 4th only seven of the convoyed vessels were in sight—de*Braak* had parted company. [18]

From a statement made by the de*Braak's* quarter gunner, Samuel Mitchell, as well as correspondence from the British counsel at Philadelphia to the Foreign Office, it appeared that after leaving her convoy the de*Braak* captured a Spanish ship which was on passage from

---

[17] Howard I. Chapelle and M.E.S. Laws, "H.M.S. deBraak: 'The Stories of a Treasure Ship'" *The Smithsonian Journal of History* 5 (Winter 1967-1968): 57-60.

[18] Ibid., 62-63.

Rio de la Plata to Cadiz with a cargo consisting of two hundred tons of copper bars and cocoa. A special crew that included a master, one midshipman, and about eleven sailors, was placed on board the captured vessel while the *deBraak* took some of the Spanish crew. [19]

The *deBraak* entered Delaware Bay on May 25th and began to anchor a mile or so off Lewestown when "a sudden and very violent squall struck her, she heeled over, filled through the open hatches, and sank very rapidly." [20]

Three days later, the British Consul, Phineas Bond, came to Lewestown and dispatched a letter to Lord Granville, the Secretary of State for Foreign Affairs in London, reporting the loss of the *deBraak*. In the meantime, the Spanish prize ship was sent to Philadelphia. The Admiralty, having been informed of the tragedy of the *deBraak* on June 23rd by Vice Admiral Vandeput in Halifax, decided that since the *deBraak* lay in shallow water, an attempt should be made to salvage her. On September 15th, by Vandeput's orders, *H.M.S. Hind and Vixen*, a brig fitted for salvage work, arrived off Cape Henlopen to try to raise the hull. After several sweeps with special gear *Hind and Vixen* failed to move the wreck, apparently already well settled in the sandy bottom. Vandeput reported to the Admiralty on October 20th that in spite of excellent weather, the *deBraak* was not able to be raised even though the best means available had been used. The Admiralty agreed, and the British decided to abandon their efforts. [21]

The argument has been made that if the British knew there was a gold cargo on the *deBraak*, they would have persisted in the efforts to salvage her rather than the seemingly casual attempt that was made. Nevertheless, there have been serious attempts over the years by groups feeling certain that there was a fortune in gold aboard the *deBraak*. Subsequent attempts to recover the ship first began in 1880,

---

[19] Ibid., 63.

[20] Ibid., 63.

[21] Ibid., 64.

when a group of American entrepreneurs tried their salvaging skill – all to no avail. During 1932 and 1933 another try was made with no success. Another try was made during 1935 and 1936, when the Colstad Corporation of New England picked up the search. They also experienced failure. In 1952 another private group searching for the lost ship was halted while salvaging in the "restricted" area off Cape Henlopen. [22]

One of the chief reasons that made it difficult to pinpoint the location of the *deBraak* can be accounted for by the fact that over the years, the sea currents and winds have shifted Cape Henlopen. Undercurrents also may have lodged the vessel and moved it some distance from where it actually sank. With this in mind, and still clinging to the old legend, another try was made to find the *deBraak*. Beginning in 1965, the D. and D. Salvage Company from Pennsylvania, headed by Mario S. Busa and Dr. William T. Defeo, made its bid to find the treasure—again without success.

The story of the search for the *deBraak* and its fabled treasure came to a close by 1986. Beginning in 1984 and for the next two years the location of the *deBraak* was discovered and it was ultimately raised by a Reno, Nevada, commercial salvage firm, Sub-Sal, Inc., on August 11, 1986. No treasure was found in the deteriorating hull, but over 20,000 historic artifacts have been preserved by the State of Delaware. [23]

The War of 1812

In March 1813, the British has assembled a large naval force near Norfolk from which was detached a fleet including the frigates *Poitiers*

---

[22] See Virginia Cullen, *History of Lewes, Delaware* (Lewes: Colonel David Hall Chapter, Daughters of the American Revolution, 1956), 46-47. See also Gilbert Byron, "The Challenge of the 'debraak,'" *Delaware Today* 8 (August-September 1969): 7-9 and 24-25.

[23] A comprehensive account of the *deBraak*, its history and ultimate discovery may be found in Donald G. Schomette, *Hunt for H.M.S. De Braak: Legend and Legacy* (Durham: Carolina Academic Press, 1993).

and *Belvidere*, along with several smaller vessels. Their mission was to blockade the entrance to Delaware Bay. The fleet took its position within sight of Lewestown on March 13th placing the inhabitants in "a great state of alarm." The enemy was carefully kept under surveillance, especially by the bay and river pilots who, once again, changed their occupations during this time of hostilities.

Less than a week had gone by after the start of the blockade when the British found themselves in need of food and supplies. It was logical that a demand should be made on the coastal town of Lewes for such provisions, and so a letter was sent "to the first magistrate of Lewestown" from "His Britannic Majesty's ship *Poitiers*, in the mouth of the Delaware, March 16," and read as follows.

> As soon as you receive this, I must request you will send twenty live bullocks [ox or bulls], with a proportionate quantity of vegetables and hay, to the *Poitiers*, for the use of his Britannic Majesty's squadron, now at this anchorage, which shall be immediately paid for at the Philadelphia prices. If you refuse to comply with this request, I shall be under the necessity of destroying your town. [24]

This threat had the following ironic conclusion: "I have the honor to be, sir, your obedient servant, J. Beresford, Commodore Commanding the British squadron in the mouth of the Delaware." [25]

The letter was received by Colonel Samuel B. Davis, a native of Lewes, who was in command of the militia and soldiers that had been quickly assembled for a defense of the town. [26] Davis in turn transmit-

---

[24] William M. Marine, "The Bombardment of Lewes by the British," *Papers, HSD*, No. 33
(1901): 14-15.

[25] Ibid, 15.

[26] The Life of Colonel Davis, the "Defender of Lewes" is discussed by W. Emerson Wilson, *Forgotten Heroes of Delaware*, 77-78.

ted the demand to Governor Joseph Haslet in Dover, who at once left for Lewestown and arrived there on March 23rd. Haslet officially responded to Commodore Beresford saying:

> As governor of the State of Delaware, and as commander of its military force, I improve the earliest time afforded me, since my arrival at this place, of acknowledging the receipt of your letter of Lewes. The respect which generous and magnanimous nations, even when they are enemies, take pride in cherishing towards each other, enjoins it upon me as a duty I owe to the State over which I have the honor at this time to preside, to the government of which this State is a member, and to the civilized world, to inquire of you whether upon further and more mature reflection, you continue resolved to attempt the destruction of this town. I shall probably this evening receive your reply to the present communication, and your determination of executing or relinquishing the demand mentioned in your letter of the 16th inst. If that demand is still insisted upon, I have only to observe to you that a compliance would be an immediate stigma on the nation of which I am a citizen; a compliance therefore cannot be acceded to. [27]

As soon as Commodore Beresford received Haslet's initial reply, he immediately sent the following response.

> In reply to your letter received to-day, by a flag of truce, in answer to mine of the 16th inst., I have to observe, that the demand I have made upon Lewistown is, in my opinion, neither ungenerous nor wanting in that magnanimity which one nation ought to observe with

---

[27] Marine, "The Bombardment of Lewis by the British," 15-16.

another with which it is at war. It is in my power to destroy your town, and the request I have made upon it, as the price of its security, is neither distressing nor unusual. I must therefore persist, and whatever sufferings may fall upon the inhabitants of Lewes must be attributed to yourselves by not complying with a request so easily acquiesced in. [28]

With this letter, the correspondence was concluded. The enemy had wasted too much time and now it was felt they must take action. On April 16th, Beresford ordered an attack which was participated in by four launches of twenty-four and-eighteen-pounders, two sloops carrying thirty-two pounders and a mortar, a pilot boat having six-pounders, the schooner, *Paz*, mounting twelve-pounders, and finally the frigates *Belvidere* and *Poitiers* belonging to the formidable group of naval warships known as "seventy-fours." In all, two hundred and forty-one guns fired at the defiant town. Indeed, the concerns of a nation were focused upon this little spot on the Delaware. A dispatch which appeared in the Baltimore Patriot on April 7th read as follows:

> This morning a very steady smoke was seen in the direction of Lewistown, supposed to be occasioned by throwing rockets into that place....Our brave citizens being short of cannon-balls, the enemy was so accommodating as to fire eight hundred on shore, which on picking up and finding they suited the caliber of our cannon remarkably well, the loan was immediately returned with interest. [29]

On the shore, the people of Lewes were kept busying preparing a defense of their community. Schemes were attempted to get the British

---

[28] Ibid., 16-17.
[29] Ibid., 20.

"ashore and trap them, but they seemed to have anticipated our purpose, and kept close to their boats." [30]

The bombardment lasted twenty-two hours during which time there were no injuries incurred, although some property had been heavily damaged. Most of the shots fired by the attackers seemed either to fall short or pass over the town. Scharf has suggested that the reason why Lewestown escaped extensive damage from the attack was because "the trees on the marsh [of Lewes Beach] obstructed their view to such an extent that their aim was not effective." [31]

Colonel Davis had a command of about 1,000 men including both regular militia and volunteers. Because they only had one eighteen- and one nine-pounder for artillery, the militia fired but few shots, hoping to save their ammunition in case the British attempted a landing. Such a threat became certain on April 8th when the British sent several small vessels carrying their soldiers toward the shore. Davis quickly decided that the invasion could perhaps be thwarted if he succeeded in convincing the incoming British that there was an advancing American army descending on Lewestown. "He marched the militia and volunteers along the water front up to where, unseen by the enemy, they could enter a back street of the town, countermarch to the water front and along it, go and return." [32] The deception worked and the British signaled for the landing party to return to ship. Thus Davis had tricked the enemy by making them believe that there were substantial numbers of soldiers in Lewestown.

Many contemporary historians of the War of 1812 either fail to mention the attack on Lewestown, or treat it very lightly. Certainly it could not be considered a major engagement. However, the very fact that a British fleet was discouraged from continuing up the Delaware River might suggest that a major attack on Wilmington, the duPont

---

[30] Ibid., 21.

[31] Scharf, 1888, 1: 1236.

[32] Marine, "The Bombardment of Lewes by the British," 24.

Powder Mills, and even Philadelphia was averted. Colonel Davis' successful efforts to defend Lewestown, first by his refusal to send the British supplies and, second, by his foiling the invasion, had to be the key element in driving off the enemy. [33]

In 1869 one historian wrote about the attack this way.

> So spirited was the response of a battery on an eminence, worked by Colonel Davis' militia, that the most dangerous of the enemy's gun-boats was disabled, and its cannon silenced. On the afternoon of the 7th [April 1813] the British attempted to land for the purpose of seizing live stock in the neighborhood, but they were met at the verge of the water by the spirited militia, and driven back to their ships. For a month the squadron lingered, and then, dropping down to Newbold's Ponds, seven miles below Lewistown, boats filled with armed men were sent on shore to obtain a supply of water. Colonel Davis immediately detached Major George H. Hunter with a few men, who drove them back to their ships. Failing to obtain any supplies on the shore of the Delaware, the little blockading squadron sailed for Bermuda...." [34]

Shortly after the incident, Lewes native, Governor Daniel Rodney, made notice of the strategic importance of having sufficient defenses in Lewestown to protect the entrance of Delaware Bay. In a communication to the Secretary of War in Washington, Rodney wrote on June 25, 1814: "I am persuaded Sir, when you consider the situation of Lewes that all ships of war coming into the Bay must pass or anchor near it;

---

[33] See Daniel Rodney's description of the events during and after the British attack on Lewes in C.H.B. Turner, *Rodney's Dairy and Other Delaware Records* (Philadelphia, 1911), 1-18.

[34] Benson J. Lossing, *The Pictorial Field Book of the War of 1812* (New York, 1869), 669.

that there are two batteries here with 18, 12 & 6 pounders mounted on each, and a considerable quantity of powder, arms and other military stores belonging to the United States, you will deem it expedient to order some troops to this station." [35]

There were two forts in Lewestown, one on Pilottown Road and the other on Front Street, now the site of the 1812 Memorial Park, that were used during the engagement. The arsenal was located at Second and Shipcarpenter Streets. There was also an encampment consisting of some five hundred troops, along with most of Lewes' citizens at Block House Pond (behind the present day Beebe Medical Center). Until the closing of the war, the battery was garrisoned by troops and was finally discharged on March 15, 1815. In charge was commander William Marshall—a pilot who had been Lieutenant Commander under Davis during the Bombardment—who wrote in his diary of his last official duty: "this day discharged all the men: took the keys of the magazine; nailed up the guardhouse, and stopped the touch holes of the cannon." [36] Perhaps someday all of mankind will perform the same "duty."

---

[35] Public Archives Commission, *Governor's Register State of Delaware* (Dover,1926), 125-126.

[36] Marine, "The Bombardment of Lewes by the British," 37-38.

CHAPTER 6

The Town of Lewes and Its Community

There are many facets that add an important human and community dimension to the early history of Lewes. Individually and collectively they have had their impact on how this settlement on the Delaware grew and changed over time. These are more than simply tid-bits of history. They comprise events, activities, and the all-important factor of human engagement that makes a community.

The Early Court

There was a Court of Law in what is today Lewes as early as 1659, which was held "first in the fort, next in the residence of one of the trusties, and later in a suitable tavern room, until a courthouse was finally built at Lewes about 1735-1740." [1] In 1673, the *Whorekill Court,* as it was called in official records, was formally recognized to have jurisdiction over both Sussex and Kent Counties. This lasted until 1680, when separate courts were established for each county.

---

[1] Ignatius C. Grubb, "The Colonial and State Judiciary of Delaware," *Papers, HSD* 17 (1897): 12. The old Lewes courthouse stood at the corner of Second and Market Streets on the present cemetery of St. Peter's Church. The tavern mentioned is the Ryves Holt House.

When the new courthouse was constructed in Georgetown in 1792, the county seat for Sussex was transferred there from Lewes where it remains today. [2]

The First Town Planning

William Penn has been regarded as an important colonial advocate of town planning. Evidence of this is found in his plan for Philadelphia in 1682. Under the auspices linked with Penn's acquisition of Delaware, a new interest was inspired in Lewes (referred to as Lewestown in official records after 1690) with the specific hope of making it a merchant port. Therefore, the Court granted titles upon "conditions implying the building of good-sized houses on pain of fine and forfeiture, upon which basis various improvements were encouraged...." [3] It was desirable to have a well-planned town to serve as an impetus in attracting the kinds of craftsmen and merchants who would be the backbone of a prosperous community. There is no evidence that a physical plan was drawn (as in the case of Philadelphia), so directions for a well laid out community were made by verbal or written instructions. For example, on March 6, 1694, the following was issued:

> The Court gives Liberty for a Ditch to be Cut through the most Convenient place of the Town of Lewes into the Creek for the Convenecy of Draining the Savannah on the back part, next to the Second Street Lots, between the Lott of Nehemiah Field, (Behind the Second Street and fronting on Mulberry Street) and the four acre Lott of Captain Thomas Pemberton, adjoining upon Richard Holloway, be reserved for a Market Place, and the vacant peace of Land next

---

[2] See Dudley Lunt, *Tales of the Delaware Bench and Bar* (Newark: University of Delaware Press, 1963), as it pertains to the Whorekill Court at 19-31.

[3] Pennock Pusey, "History of Lewes, Delaware," *Papers, HSD* 38 (1903): 20-21.

Adjoining on the Southwest side of John Miers, his Lott, to the Block House pond, and between the Block House Field and that be used as a Common Burying Ground.[4]

Later on we see that the Court changed its mind, for the following was issued on September 6, 1696.

Whereas at a court held the sixth and seventh days of March 1694 a Certain peace of Land In the Town of Lewes, In the Mulberry Street, Lying and being between the 4 acres of Captain Thomas Pemberton, and the Lott of Nehemiah Field was ordered to be reserved for a Market place the Court upon a second Vue thereof Do find the same not to be convenient as was expected, and so order the same to be free, to be granted out unto Town Lots 60 foot in breadth and 200 foot in Length.[5]

Seventeenth Century Pirates

Because of Lewes' strategic position at the entrance to Delaware Bay, pirates on several notable occasions accosted the town primarily to obtain fresh provisions. The first recorded incident seems to have been in 1672, when a party of privateers made a landing on the bay coast and attacked Lewes. Evidently there was considerable damage done since "...an impost of four guilders in wampum on each anker of strong liquor was authorized for one year to repair the losses occasioned." [6] Again in 1698, the French pirate, Canoot, plundered a

---

[4] Turner, 1909, 40.

[5] Ibid., 40-41, see also 25.

[6] William M. Marvine, "Pirates and Privateers in the Delaware Bay and River," *Pa. Magazine* 32 (1908): 460.

Philadelphia sloop below Cape May, "and manning her landed fifty men at Lewes and looted the town." [7]

In 1700, the notorious Captain Kidd anchored his ship off Cape Henlopen for several days. "...Inhabitants of ye town of Lewes in Sussex County, had gone on board Captain Kidd, ye privateer, ...and corresponded wt him & received from him and his crew some muslins, calicoes, monies, and other goods which wer [from] East India & Prohibited goods...." [8] For their actions, the unassuming citizens were arrested for being accessories in promoting illegal trade. To protect themselves from future attacks, each citizen of the town was required to arm himself and wait for the firing of a gun and beating of drums which was the signal of an oncoming raid.

Cape Henlopen Lighthouse

In 1765, a lighthouse was built by the British Colonial Government on the Atlantic side of Cape Henlopen. It was the second oldest lighthouse on the Atlantic coast, constructed a few years after the one built at Cape Henry in Virginia. According to local tradition, there had been a crude whale oil light at the Cape since 1725 to warn incoming mariners of their approach to the Hen and Chickens Shoals and to guide their way into the shelter of Delaware Bay. During the days of the sailing ship, the bay was the only place of refuge within three hundred miles from New York to the Chesapeake. [9]

The Cape Henlopen Lighthouse was built on the highest point of land in the area at the time: 50 feet above sea level and 1,400 feet

---

[7] Ibid., 461.

[8] Turner, 1909, 42. The activities of the pirates in Delaware Bay have prompted several fictional accounts, notably: Howard Pyle's story of "Tom Christ and the Treasure Box" in *Stolen Treasure* (1907), about Captain Kidd burying his cache on Cape Henlopen; also Pyle's *Within the Capes* (1899); *Kings Pardon* (1937) by Gertrude Crownfield; Rupert S. Holland, *Pirates of the Delaware* (1925); and *Crooked Eye* (1930) by Katherine Virden.

[9] See John W. Beach, *The Cape Henlopen Lighthouse* (Henlopen Publishing Co.: Dover, 1970) that tells the full story of this ancient light.

inland. It was in the shape of an octagonal tower, eight stories high with walls of brick and granite seven feet thick. The local historian, Virginia Cullen, says that "the first mention of the lighthouse was in an advertisement in the 'New York Mercury' of January 4, 1762, regarding 'a scheme of a lottery for raising 3,000 pounds to be applied to erection of a lighthouse on Cape Henlopen.'" [10]

The important function of the lighthouse was interrupted on two notable occasions. During the Revolution, it was extinguished by American patriots although the British later burned the interior. It was restored in 1784, but during the War of 1812, suffered a similar fate.

In 1788, a Committee of Wardens visited the lighthouse and noticed how the sand dune on which it was built was slowly being intruded upon by the sea. They reported their discovery to none other than Benjamin Franklin, who was then President of the Pennsylvania Council. In their report to Franklin, the Wardens mentioned the changing surface of the land over the entire area, and stated that where there had been deep ponds a few years before, there were now substantial sand dunes. [11]

As a result of the Warden's report, an effort was made to retard the erosion by anchoring the dunes with "underwood" and through the planting of various shrubs. It was this erosion on the ocean side which concomitantly caused a sandspit to be built up on the northern bay side of the Cape, and it was this process of nature – accentuated by man-made breakwaters forming a harbor of refuge—which over a period of time caused the metamorphosis of Cape Henlopen from a smooth rounded peninsula to the jutting point we see today. [12] The protective measures did not work, and the dunes moved even faster,

---

[10] Virginia Cullen, *History of Lewes, Delaware* (Lewes: Colonel David Hall Chapter, Daughters of the American Revolution, 1956), 29-30.

[11] Edward Rowe Snow, *Famous Lighthouses of America* (New York: Dodd, Mead & Company, 1955), 146.

[12] See an interesting article on the subject by John R. Spears, "Sand-waves at Cape Henlopen and Hatteras," *Scribners Magazine* (October 1890): 508-512.

especially after the breakwater workers lit fires along the beach at night which destroyed the vegetation. This left the dunes unstable and subject to continual shifting. Dr. David B Tyler, the noted maritime historian, has written about the shifting sand dunes.

> In 1860 it was estimated that the sand moved at the rate of eleven feet a year. The northwest wind was the propelling force. When the wind was from the southeast it brought rain and the wet sand did not move but the resultant surf cut into the beach below the light. Jetties, buttresses and brushwood anchors were ineffective. [13]

Time will take its toll, and nature would rule and determine the inevitable fate of the Cape Henlopen Lighthouse. On April 13, 1926, the crew of the pilot boat *Philadelphia* witnessed the sea claiming the "old man of the Atlantic" which for a century and a half had aided many a sailor in distress.

Early Education Under the Dutch and English

Little is known about the early Dutch efforts to establish formal educational institutions at their Swanendael settlement. There were no public schools in the traditional sense, even though the pursuit of education was firmly encouraged. For example, in the "Charter of Freedoms, Privileges and Exemptions" granted by the States-General to the patroons of New Netherland between 1630 and 1635, it was clearly stated that, "the patroons shall also particularly exert themselves to find speedy means to maintain a Clergyman and Schoolmaster, in order that Divine Service and zeal for religion may be planted in the country...." [14]

---

[13] David B. Tyler, "The Cape Henlopen Lighthouse," *Estuarine Bulletin* 2 (University of Delaware, August 1956): 3.

[14] *N.Y. Colonial Documents* 1: 99.

Historian, James Wickersham, writing in the nineteenth century, points out that even though Holland was the first European nation to develop a system of public schools, "let no one expect to find well organized schools and skilled teachers, for this mere handful of people in a wilderness, three thousand miles from home and help, had to win the battle for existence before they could give much attention to the arts that cultivate and refine." [15]

When William Penn came to the New World to take control of his massive land grant in 1682, a positive effort was made to establish formal education through the following order in his frame of government: "that the Governor and provincial council shall erect and order all public schools, and encourage and reward the authors of useful sciences and laudable inventions."[16] Universal education was contemplated by Penn, which unfortunately was not to be carried out by the governmental authorities. According to Wickersham.

> The provincial authorities of Pennsylvania [we can assume the same held true for the "three lower counties"] did next to nothing to promote the course of general education during the long period from the beginning of the eighteenth century to the end of their rule in 1776. Charters were granted to a few educational institutions, some laws were passed securing to religious societies the right to hold property for school purposes, and in special cases enabling them to raise money by lottery to build schoolhouses; but this was all. Penn's broad policy respecting public education was virtually abandoned. Intellectual darkness would have reigned supreme throughout the

---

[15] James Pyle Wickersham, *A History of Education in Pennsylvania: Private and Public, Elementary and Higher* (Lancaster, Pa.: 1886), 2.

[16] Samuel Hazard, *Annals of Pennsylvania From the Discovery of the Delaware 1609-1682* (Philadelphia, 1850), 564.

province had not the various churches and the people themselves been more alive to the importance of the subject than the government. [17]

Keeping this general situation in mind we turn to Lewes where the earliest attempt at formal education can be attributed to William Penn's Quaker background of which education was of fundamental importance. Quakers are said to have held meetings in Lewes as early as 1692,[18] and the historian, Walter Powell, states that there was a Society of Friends living southwest of Lewes in an area still known as Quakertown in about 1697.[19]

Although there is no documental evidence to substantiate the claim that the noted Penn Charter School was located in Lewes, there is evidence to suggest that Lewes was an early colonial center for education. [20] The establishment of the Penn Charter School in Philadelphia had its impetus when William Penn sent a letter in 1689 to Thomas Lloyd, then President of Philadelphia Council and later Deputy Governor of the province, instructing him to set up a "public grammar school." The Friends Public School as it was known – and then the Penn Charter School – began in 1689, and was formally chartered in 1697.[21] This digression from the story of Lewes is necessary in light of remarks made by John F. Watson. "At this early period of time, so much had the little Lewistown at our southern Cape the pre-eminence in female tuition, that Thomas Lloyd, the deputy Governor, preferred to send his younger daughters from Philadelphia to that place to finish their education." [22]

A curious connection with Watson's statement can be made with a metallic seal one inch and a half in diameter that was unearthed many

---

[17] Wickersham, *A History of Education in Pennsylvania,* 78.

[18] See Scharf, 1888, 2: 1232.

[19] Walter A. Powell, *A History of Delaware* (Boston: The Christopher Publishing House, 1928), 397.

[20] See Virginia Cullen, *History of Lewes, Delaware,* 41-42.

[21] Wickersham, 41.

years ago in Quakertown. The seal had no date but was inscribed with the words "Trustees of Penn's Charter School in Lewes." What additional clues does the maze of history still possess? Can it be supposed that Penn's plans for organizing education in Lewes were formulated at the time he was considering establishing himself there? Shortly after his arrival on the Delaware in 1682, he issued an order to the Justices of the Peace at the Court of the Whorekill instructing them to lay out a manor of 10,000 acres for the Duke of York and one of equal size for himself, "to be between the Bounds of Cedar Creek and Mispillion Creek or in the most Convenient place Towards the north side of the County." [23]

Another interesting association took place in 1692 when the Rev. Samuel Davis, leader of the first Presbyterian Church in Lewes was visited by a Quaker, George Keith, who had been appointed in 1689 to take charge of the first Friend's Public School in Philadelphia.[24] What the purpose of their meeting was is not known. However, it would not seem inconceivable that the subject of education was a prime topic.

An additional insight into the early educational efforts in Lewes has been set down by historian, Thomas Scharf, who stated the following:

> In 1754, John Russell is spoken of as the schoolmaster of the town serving also as deputy recorder, but there is no account of a school house in that period. Two years later Thomas Penn ordered that the income from the Great Marsh should be devoted to the support of the school in Lewes, but it is probable that no building

---

[22] Watson's two volume work, *Annals of Philadelphia and Pennsylvania in the Olden Time Being a Collection of Memoirs, Anecdotes, and Incidents of the City and Its Inhabitants* went through a number of editions from 1850 to 1927. This citation is from the 1870 edition, 1: 287-288.

[23] See Turner, 1909, 84.

[24] See Scharf, 1888, 2: 1230, and Wickersham, *A History of Education in Pennsylvania*, 42.

for that especial purpose was erected until 1761. That
year a frame house was erected on Second Street, near
Shipcarpenter Street, in which the youth of the town
were instructed more than one hundred years. [25]

The Rev. Francis Hindman conducted a school in Lewes as early
as 1795, which emphasized instruction in the classics. This led to the
establishment of the Lewes Academy shortly thereafter, and a large
frame building was erected for educational purposes, at the intersection
of Savannah Road and Third Street. [26] The Lewes Academy effectively
provided the educational needs of the community until 1875 when the
Lewes Union School was created and controlled by a Board of Public
Education. Today public education in Lewes is conducted under the
administration of the Cape Henlopen School District, that was formed
from the school districts in Lewes, Rehoboth Beach and Milton in July
1969.

As early as 1738, the Presbytery of Lewes laid the foundation for
an educational institution that was later to become the University of
Delaware. In that year, the Presbytery, concerned about the lack of a
suitable school for the education of youths for the "sacred work of min-
istry," [27] sent the following "memorial" to the Synod in Philadelphia:

That this part of the world where God has ordered our
lot, labours under a grievous disadvantage for want of
the opportunities of universities and professors skilled
in the several branches of useful learning, and that

---

[25] Ibid.. Scharf.

[26] A general discussion of the early schools, as well as the instructors who served them,
may be found in accounts of "Lewes Schools" and "The Genesis of Education in
Lewes" from the notebook of Virginia L. Mustard, copies of which are deposited
in the Hall of Records. Walter A. Powell, *A History of Delaware,* 449, cites the following institutions in his list of schools established or incorporated in Delaware:
Grammar school at Lewes prior to 1750; school at Lewes, 1761; and Francis
Hindman's Classical School, Lewes, 1795.

[27] See Powell, 427.

many students from Europe are especially cramped in pursuing their studies, their parents removing to these colonies before they have [had] an opportunity of attending college, after having spent some years at the grammar school; and that many persons born in the country groan under the same pressure, whose circumstances are not able to support them to spend a course of years in the European or New England colleges. [28]

The "memorial" was received favorably by the Synod, which immediately ordered "two standing committees to act in the above affair for this year, one to the northward and the other to the south-ward of Philadelphia." [29]

By the following year, 1739, at a meeting of the Synod, "an overture for establishing a seminary of learning was unanimously approved. In 1744, a school was established under the care of the Synod where, "all persons who please may send their children and them instructed, gratis, in the languages, philosophy, and divinity." [30] The school opened in New London, Pennsylvania, with the scholarly Reverend Francis Alison, who had served as a member of the "Southern Committee," as principal. In 1752, the New London Academy, as it was called, was moved to Elkton, Maryland, where it was operated until 1767, and then moved again, this time to Newark, Delaware. In 1769, Thomas and Richard Penn granted the Newark Academy a charter, the immediate predecessor of Delaware College, which today is the University of Delaware. [31]

---

[28] Turner, 1909, 318.

[29] George H. Ryden, "The Relation of the Newark Academy of Delaware to the Presbyterian Church and to Higher Education in the American Colonies," *Delaware Notes* 9th ser. (University of Delaware, 1935): 10.

[30] Edward D. Neill, "Matthew Wilson, D.D. of Lewes, Delaware," *Pa. Magazine* 8 (1884): 46-47.

[31] See William D. Lewis, "University of Delaware: Ancestors, Friends, Neighbors,"

Improvements and Ship Building in a Coastal Town

Lewes was incorporated by an act of the Delaware General Assembly on February 2, 1818, and Samuel Paynter, James F. Baylis, Benjamin Prettyman, David Hazzard, and Peter F. Wright were appointed as "Commissioners" with their initial task to have all of the houses and streets throughout town surveyed. During the coming years, the little community was to grow, mainly due to the extension of the first railroad, the *Junction and Breakwater* completed in 1869. [32]

One of the most far reaching projects began in 1828 when the Federal government began constructing one of two breakwaters in Lewes harbor. The inner barrier of the Delaware Breakwater was begun that year, and was completed about 1834, for a total cost of approximately $1,160,000.In 1870, the United States government appropriated $225,000 for the construction of a 2,000 foot long "iron pier" extending from Cape Henlopen into the bay. It was never completed by the government, whose original intent was to utilize the pier when navigation on the Delaware became obstructed. [33]

The Harbor of Refuge was begun in 1892, and was completed in 1901. Scharf, writing in 1888 about the Delaware Breakwater, said that it was "the most important improvement of [its] kind in the United States.... It is a massive work of granite masonry, two thousand eight hundred feet long, exclusive of the Ice Breaker, above it, which is seventeen hundred feet long." [34] Today the Delaware Breakwater and Harbor of Refuge provide over one thousand acres of safe anchorage for vessels.

Delaware Notes 34 (University of Delaware, 1961): 14-17. See also, John A. Monroe, *The University of Delaware: A History* (Newark: University of Delaware, 1986), esp., 9-36.

[32] By 1883 this branch was to consolidate with other lines under the name of the *Delaware, Maryland, and Virginia* Railroad. See Scharf, 1888, 2: 1226. See also William H. McCauley, "Junction and Breakwater Railroad Primarily a Sussex County Project," *Archeolog* 2 (July 1959).

[33] Scharf, 1888, 2: 1226-1227.

[34] Ibid., 1225.

In 1880, the Federal government established a signal station at the end of the Breakwater, which later became the Maritime Exchange serving the area until 1942. [35]

> During the early days of the bayside community, the Lewes Creek (today the Lewes and Rehoboth Canal) afforded a good channel for the navigation of sloops and schooners, and since there was an abundance of good timber on the creek's inland shores, ship building became an important enterprise. [36] As early as 1683, John Browne "petitioned the Court [in Lewes] for A towne Lott Convenient to build a Sloope or Shallop." [37] Shipcarpenter Street recognizes those Lewes residents who were employed in this livelihood. According to Boyd's *Delaware State Directory*, there were two shipyards in Lewes in 1859. [38] John and Peter Maull, two well-known boat builders, operated a yard at "Pilottown," finishing their last boat in 1866. [39]

The Pilots of the Bay and River Delaware

One cannot write about the early history of Lewes and overlook one of the most integral aspects of this coastal town—the bay and river pilots. This stalwart profession has been referred to as the "…act of

---

[35] For a discussion about the Maritime Exchange in Lewes as well as the early Life-Saving Station, see Frank H. Taylor, *The Handbook of the Lower Delaware River* (Philadelphia,1895), 59-72.

[36] A brief discussion of the changes experienced along this waterway may be found in William J. Cohen and George Nocito, "The Changing Lewes and Rehoboth Canal," *Delaware Conservationist* 21 (Summer 1977), 22-23.

[37] Turner, 1909, 109.

[38] At 258 in the *Directory* published in 1859-1860.

[39] A full account of ship building activities, including many historic photographs, may be found in James E. Marvil, *Sailing Rams: A History of Sailing Ships Built in and Near Sussex County, Delaware* 2nd ed. (Lewes: The Sussex Press, 1974).

conducting a vessel in channels and harbors and along coasts, where landmarks and aids to navigation are available for fixing; where the depth of water and dangers to navigation require a constant watch and frequent changes of course.

Piloting required the greatest experience and nicest judgment of any form of navigation." [40]

The early Indian inhabitants were the first pilots. They showed the Europeans how to avoid the dangerous shoals and how to maneuver their large vessels in the Delaware River and Bay. John Griffith, one immigrating Quaker, wrote in 1765: "On the [ninth day] of the sixth month we made Cape Henlopen and a pilot came on board and [he] proved to be an Indian." [41]

Lewestown seemed to be the logical home for many of the first colonial pilots, who began a tradition of service which exists even today. In addition to their navigational duties, the pilots had become involved in both the Revolution and the War of 1812 when British ships blockaded Delaware Bay and frequently attacked American merchant and naval ships. The pilots became instrumental in making it difficult for the enemy to navigate in the bay by removing buoys and extinguishing the light at Cape Henlopen.

Stories of unusual heroism have been associated with the pilots who have, over the years saved many vessels that have been caught in stormy seas. Probably the most notable disaster occurred in 1889 when winds of gale force piled up more than forty vessels on Lewes Beach and carried out to sea the pilot boat, *Enoch Turley*. The two masted schooner was lost with its crew of four men and six pilots who had stayed out looking for ships to guide into port. It has been recounted by Captain Thomas J. Virden.

Many a courageous man with less fixity of purpose

---

[40] James E. Marvil, *Pilots of the Bay and River Delaware*, (Laurel: The Sussex Press, 1965), 15.

[41] Ibid., 125.

would have sought shelter of the pilot house when the storm broke, but it was the duty of the pilot to face the storm and keep his ship headed for her destination and out of danger. He did and paid the supreme price because of his devotion to duty. [42]

The Pilots' Association for the Bay and River Delaware was formed in 1896 when the owners of eight pilot schooners joined together. Groups of about eight pilots each owned and operated their boats previous to 1896, and while operating independently, demonstrated sharp rivalry in finding ships to guide. Thus when the association was created the pilots began to cooperate to their mutual benefit. After completing an apprenticeship of four years, a new pilot was granted a license to become a member of the Pilots Association. In the first year of the Association, there were ninety-two pilots and twelve apprentices, who guided a total of seventy-nine vessels in and out of Delaware Bay during the first month alone. [43]

African and Indian Descendents

As has been true of so much of America's recorded history, the emphasis has traditionally been on European discovery and achievement. The explorations and settlements under the auspices of, for example, the Dutch, Swedish, French, Spanish, and English have become woven into the story of the evolution of a unique American culture. To a large extent the very notion of an *American culture* suggests that it is composed of a number of variables that represent the full scope of both the human mind and body, and a blending of other cultures.

The non-Europeans did have an important place in the history of Delaware's oldest settlement, and as elsewhere, is often overlooked. We have studied and documented, as best as possible through archeological

---

[42] Ibid., 292-293.
[43] Ibid., 49.

and historical investigations, the Indian inhabitants (as was detailed in Chapter 1). They were the first to live here; to cultivate the fields, build their huts, and search the bay and river for food.

In addition to the Indian inhabitants, the other significant non-European group that lived in Lewes and its environs, and, over time, prospered here, were those of African decent—brought to these shores as slaves by the Europeans in the seventeenth and eighteenth centuries. What is perhaps most significant is that despite the original social status of African slaves, as time changed so did status. With the Constitutional prohibition against slavery enacted as Article 13 in 1865, black Americans would, in many places such as Lewes, fashion and carve out their own version of "community." Originally, it was a tight-knit community, propelled by the desire to survive and sustain. It was in its own way—not by choice, but by happenstance—a segregated community that would, in the twentieth century, slowly became integrated into the larger Lewes community.

There are several black families who have lived in Lewes for generations, descendents of some of the earliest residents. The first meeting house in Lewes town of the African Methodist Episcopal Church was begun by Richard Allen in the early part of the nineteenth century. Allen, born a slave in Dover had served in the Continental Army during the Revolution, later became the founder and first bishop of his independent denomination. This first church for blacks in Lewes was located on Pilottown Road next to an old cemetery that still exists today. The original building was unfortunately destroyed by fire, yet the current St. George's A.M.E. Church on Park Avenue, dedicated in 1930, serves as the modern version of Bishop Allen's first efforts.

Ship building was an important craft, and clearly an indispensable trade for many Lewes citizens, both European and non-European. The natural advantages of the easy access to the river and bay opened up much entrepreneurial potential, and boat building prospered. Scharf has pointed out that during the nineteenth century, two black ship carpenters, Peter Lewis and Cato Lewis, operated a small boat building business in Lewes, adding their skills to this ancient craft. [44]

Lewes, like many old settlements, has, over the centuries, nurtured tales and folklore which have passed from family to family and generation to generation. When Virginia Cullen wrote her *History of Lewes* (1956), she included many stories which have aroused the curiosity of many.[45] One of the most interesting and little known legends that has been recounted pertains to the coming of the *Moors* to the Delmarva Peninsula.

The Moors have been called by C.A. Weslager, a "forgotten folk." They are neither European, African, nor Indian—but a racial and ethnic composite of all three. [46] There are several stories that have been passed down through the years relating to the coming of these people to Delaware's shores. [47] There is one story that, sometime prior to the American Revolution, a group of Spanish Moors sailed to America to start a colony. After settling along the Atlantic Coast they intermarried with the indigenous Indian tribes and over time, developed a "race" of people called Moors. There is another legend which tells about Spanish or Moorish pirates who were shipwrecked near Indian River Inlet and rescued by Nanticoke Indians. Again, through intermarriage with the Indians, Delaware's unique Moors had their origin. [48]

The best known and most frequently cited account of the origin of the Moors was first given in 1855 at the court in Georgetown

---

[44] Scharf, 1888, 2: 1226.

[45] Cullen, 54-63.

[46] Historically the Moors were natives of Mauretania, a geographical area that includes Morocco and Algeria. Later they represented a mix of Berbers and Arabs, who in the eighth century conquered Spain.

[47] The Moors have generally contained themselves in two individual settlements one at Cheswold, near Dover, and the other on the north shore of Indian River in Sussex County. See C.A. Weslager, *Delaware's Forgotten Folk* (Philadelphia: University of Pennsylvania Press, 1943), 1-24.

[48] See Ibid., 25-29.

in the case of the *State of Delaware v. Levin Sockum.* The trial was an important test of the racial laws of that time which forbade the sale of ammunition and firearms to blacks. Sockum, an Indian descendent and owner of a general store, had been accused of such an act when he sold powder and shot to Isaiah Harmon, one of his "mixed-blood" customers. In order to establish whether or not Harmon was of African descent, the testimony of Lydia Clark, "one of Harmon's relatives, and in appearance a perfect Indian type," was entered into the proceedings.

The following account was written some years after the trial by Judge George P. Fisher who had been prosecuting attorney in the *Sockum* case. The account of the court proceedings first appeared in the *Milford Herald* on June 15, 1895, and was later published in C.A. Weslager's, *Delaware's Forgotten Folk* (1943).

> About fifteen or twenty years before the Revolutionary War, which she [Lydia Clark] said broke out when she was a little girl some five or six years old, there was a lady of Irish birth living on a farm in Indian River Hundred, a few miles distant from Lewes, which she owned and carried on herself. Nobody appeared to know anything of her history or her antecedents. Her name she gave us as Requa, and she was childless, but whether maid or widow, or a wife astray, she never disclosed to anyone. She was much above the average woman of that day in stature, beauty and intelligence. The tradition described her as having a magnificent complexion, large and dark blue eyes and luxuriant hair of the most beautiful shade, usually called light auburn. After she had been living in Angola Neck quite a number of years, a slaver was driven into Lewes Creek, then a tolerable fair harbor, and was there weather-bound for several days. It was lawful then, for those were colonial times, to import slaves

from Africa. Queen Elizabeth to gratify her friend and favorite, Sir John Hawkins, had so made it lawful more than a quarter of a century prior to this time.

Miss or Mrs. Requa, having heard of the presence of the slaver in the harbor, and having lost one of her men slaves, went to Lewes, and to replace him, purchased another from the slave ship. She selected a very tall, shapely and muscular young fellow of dark ginger-bread color, who claimed to be a prince or chief of one of the tribes of the Congo River which had been overpowered in a war with a neighboring tribe and nearly all slain or made prisoner and sold into perpetual slavery. This young man had been living with his mistress but a few months when they were duly married, and Lydia told the court and jury, they reared quite a large family of children who as they grew up were not permitted to associate and intermarry with their neighbors of pure Caucasian blood, nor were they disposed to seek associations or alliance with the Negro race; so that they were necessarily compelled to associate and intermarry with the remnant of the Nanticoke tribe of Indians who still lingered in their old habitations for many years after the great body of the tribe had been removed further towards the setting sun. This race of people were for the first two or three generations confined principally to the southeastern portion of Sussex County and more particularly in the neighborhood of Lewes, Millsboro, Georgetown and Milton, but during the last sixty or seventy years they have increased the area of their settlement very materially and now are to be found in almost every hundred in each county in the State, but mostly in Sussex and Kent. From the first origin to the present time, they have continued to segregate themselves from the American citizens of African descent, having their own churches and schools as much as practicable.[49]

Architecture

The stylistic changes and evolution of Delaware architecture generally followed political changes. After 1664 when the English took control from the Dutch and the Swedes, their ideas began to influence style. In the early period, skilled workman, especially in Sussex County, were extremely scarce. Nevertheless, after 1664 as the smaller communities grew, builders became an established group, and there developed, to some degree, a stabilizing in the methods of construction.

Although styles and periods of architecture overlap, changes in Delaware architecture generally lagged behind what was happening in larger and more populous colonial centers. However, the dates of the various styles can be approximated as follows:

Early American	From the early settlements to 1700
Georgian	1700-1800
Post Colonial	
(Post Revolutionary	
or Transitional)	1790-1830
Republic or Greek Revival	1800-1857
Pre-Civil War	1835-1865
Victorian	1865-1900
Twentieth Century	After 1900

In Manhattan on May 30, 1649, a contract was signed to build two houses, apparently on the Delaware. The specifications provide an insight into the early Dutch architecture of New Netherland:

2 houses each 32 feet long, 18 wide and 9 feet of a story; breastwork 3 feet; the wooden frame for a

---

[49] Ibid., 34-35.

double chimney, with the 5 outside and inside doors
3 window-frames
1 transom window-frame
1 circular window-frame
Three partitions, according to circumstances the
roof thereon to be covered with planks. Doors and
windows, as proper.

The contractor shall cut and trim the pine timber in
the woods, about 200 paces from the place, where the
house shall stand. The owner shall deliver the timber
at his own expense on the ground, where the houses
are to be erected. 2 planked closets cut off from the
square room 2 bedsteads. [50]

Probably the most distinguishing characteristic of early Sussex
County architecture is in the type of building material used, particularly since the style in this area was different from that found in either
Kent or New Castle Counties. Stone and clay for brick making were
not indigenous to Sussex County. What stone or brick was used in
the foundations of many homes of the early period was brought from
England. This was known as ballast stone and served a dual purpose
in stabilizing the weight of the ship as it traveled the unpredictable
seas, and then as the subsequent foundation material in building construction. One of Delaware's preeminent architects, George Fletcher
Bennett, described what happened in Lewes this way.

They didn't improvise, at least from my experience, or
try to invent anything. You will find a house in Sussex
County of the same general dimensions, such as roof
lines, as in New Castle County. But, the material is
different. The carpenters used what they found in

---

[50] "Papers Relating to the Provincial Affairs of Pennsylvania," *Pennsylvania Archives*
2nd ser. (1878): 469-470.

Lewes. They had no stone or brick to work with. The influx of English people were from the south of England where wood was the answer to everything. [51]

Many older homes in Lewes today exemplify the kind of construction found in Sussex County during the later seventeenth and eighteenth centuries. Generally, these homes were built of pine framing with cypress shingles for the roof and sides. Both the bald-cypress and juniper (a white cedar) were in great abundance in the area and used primarily as a sheathing over frame and timber construction. "Frames of hand-hewn Black gum timbers were covered with shingles from the Big Cypress Swamp. These shingles were very large; in contrast to the modern nineteen-inch shingles, they were often thirty inches long. They were not sawed, but riven out of the solid bolt by hand." [52]

Although it is obvious to think of the Great Cypress Swamp between Frankford and Selbyville as having been the main source of the cypress shingles for Lewes homes, there is documentary evidence that there was a closer source of supply, namely near the present Broadkill River. In a grant made to Bryand Rowles in 1681, specific reference was made to a "cypress swamp on the main branch of the said Broad Creeke" (also cited as the Great Creek). It is quite feasible, then, that the old Lewes homes built in this and later periods used cypress materials from the Broadkill Marsh. [53]

Even after clay (used to make brick) was found near Milford around the middle of the eighteenth century, the wooden materials continued to prevail in Sussex County. Eberlein and Hubbard in their notable study of historic homes of Delaware have explained how the early homes were constructed.

---

[51] George Fletcher Bennett, interview with the author May 23, 1969.

[52] Anthony Higgins, "The Swamp Where They Mined Cypress," *The Baltimore Sun*, April 1, 1932.

[53] *Duke of York*, 60-69. An early description of the "Dimensions and Bounds of Prime Hook near the Horekil," refers specifically to a "Cypress Swampe" adjacent to "Slaughters Creeke." See *N.Y. Colonial Documents* 12: 573.

These early one-room houses, built in the seventeenth and early eighteenth centuries, were of the one-story and attic type. They were typical in Virginia and Maryland, and recall medieval precedent, as well as they may, built as they were by artisans who had learned their trades under men imbued with what was left of the medieval spirit, a set of men whose ideas change slowly. [54]

Most of the early colonists came from England and they brought with them the English building traditions handed down by generations of "country" carpenters. The eighteenth century architecture, exemplified in many old Lewes buildings, was untouched by the classic ideals of the important city architects like Inigo Jones, John Webb, and later, Sir Christopher Wren, whose influences were to be paramount in larger colonial communities during the eighteenth century. Rather, the early buildings in Lewes provide an example of rural colonial America and how local craftsmen adapted their desire to provide adequate shelter using the building materials they had available. [55]

Architecture during the period 1775 to 1814 was influenced by such styles as late Georgian, post-Colonial (post-Revolutionary or Transitional), and, to a lesser degree, by the emerging Republic, Regency or Greek Revival styles. New design trends ushered in modifications to floor plans, elevations, and decorative details. Overall, the robust rigor of the Georgian spirit was somewhat slow in making its influence felt in Sussex County architecture, yet it did come into vogue.

A unique aspect of Delaware Georgian domestic architecture is what has been referred to as "Quaker Georgian." Beginning

---

[54] Harold Donald Eberlein and Cortlandt V.D. Hubbard, *Historic Houses and Buildings of Delaware* (Dover: Public Archives Commission, 1963), 5.

[55] The first comprehensive source for Delaware architecture may be found in George Fletcher Bennett, *Early Architecture of Delaware* (New York: Historical Press, Inc., 1932), passim.

about 1720, the Quaker penchant for austerity was increasing and, albeit there was an acceptance of the utility in architectural expression, Quakers were nonetheless "principled" against the contemporary Georgian graces and amenities. [56] The practical effort of such attitudes resulted in a rather functional exterior plainness.

After the War of 1812, the architectural tradition of Regency design (in some cases Greek Revival) and later the Victorian style became popular, and Lewes possesses some examples of these architectural forms. Even though the exuberant wave of romanticism that sparked these architectural traditions was slow to come to Sussex County, it nonetheless did have its influence. Many homes in Lewes today still exhibit the intricate design work of "ginger-bread" reminiscent of the Victorian period.

The history of Lewes is very much reflected in the homes and buildings lining the streets of this oldest Delaware settlement. More than any other individual, Dr. James E. Marvil, the founding president of the Lewes Historical Society, became the principal advocate for preserving Lewes' architectural past. His lasting legacy is representative of the many buildings he personally preserved and encouraged others to do the same. [57]

Over two hundred years of slowly changing architectural styles can be appreciated only by seeing first hand the houses where the townsfolk have lived for generations. It is a unique heritage that has survived—a living example of a vernacular, historic tradition. But it may well be that this tradition will be lost, and so must be protected from the impetuousness of that cultured predator – twenty-first century man.

---

[56] Ibid., 10.

[57] See James E. Marvil, ed. *A Pictorial History of Lewes, Delaware 1609-1985* (Lewes, Del.: Lewes Historical Society, 1985).

Chapter 7

The Story of the Public Commons

The community of Lewes is located at a truly distinctive geographical spot. Lying just inside the sandy arch of Cape Henlopen, this quaint coastal town has found its protector against the raging Atlantic storms. Cape Henlopen possesses unique and fascinating natural features; it includes two and three-fourth miles of Atlantic Ocean beach and one and one-fourth miles of Delaware Bay shore and beach. Shifting sand dunes affected by wind and tide have changed its contours over the years; salt water marshes, beach grasses, several species of orchids, pitch pines, insects of all denominations, gulls, sandpipers and rabbits are just a few of the characteristic features and natural inhabitants of this area. No other place in Delaware and few other parts of the Atlantic Coast provide similar natural beauty and serenity than "Henlopen's Jeweled Finger."

Historically, the Town of Lewes has claimed that certain lands on Cape Henlopen as well as the vast marshes northwest of the community are a public commons. This claim and its story comprise one of the most interesting and little known aspects of Delaware history. Indeed it is a unique study in the evolution of a moral allegation ultimately perfected under the sanction of law. The long chain of events which underlies this story began in the seventeenth century and was to continue for well over 200 years.

The Federal Government Acquires Cape Henlopen 1940 - 1941

With the approaching storm clouds of World War II, in the third decade of the twentieth century, it became apparent to the United States government that provisions for strong coastal defenses of our shores must be made. During the summer of 1940, the U.S. Army Corps of Engineers began, rather secretively, surveying government and state-owned land that had been acquired on Cape Henlopen over the years. By July 7, 1941, it was evident that plans were being carried out to establish a coastal defense installation on the cape when the War Department issued through the authority of the United States government condemnation proceedings on 1010.8 acres of land adjacent to other area previously ceded to them by the State of Delaware. At the same time, the Federal government issued a "Declaration of Talking" and acquired title to this land.

Soon hundreds of workmen were busily constructing, at the cost of millions of dollars, what was to be declared the "largest defense project on the Atlantic seaboard." [1] On August 8, 1941, the new fortification was named in honor of Lieutenant General Nelson Appleton Miles, who had been commanding general of the United States Army from 1895 to 1903. When the war came to an end, Fort Miles served as a separation center as well as a German prisoner-of-war camp. Activities at the once busy fort were slowly phased out, so that by 1964, the State of Delaware acquired from the Federal government 705 acres of "excess land" considered no longer necessary for coastal defense. This has become the nucleus of Cape Henlopen State Park.

Although the United States had obtained title to much of the cape through the power of condemnation in 1941, several parties pro-

---

[1] See William H. Connor and Leon de Valinger, Jr., *Delaware's Role in World War II*, 2 vols. (Dover: Public Archives Commission, 1955), 1: 56.

fessing various claims to this land sought compensation. In the following year, these parties filed briefs claiming an interest in the lands that had been condemned. As a result, the District Court for Delaware appointed Clarence A. Southerland, as a "Special Master" on May 1, 1943, "with power to summon witnesses, issue subpoenas, and take further testimony as might be required, and to make findings of fact and conclusions of law." [2] Southerland, a highly respected member of the Delaware Bar would prove to be well suited to the assignment. In 1951 he would be appointed the first chief Justice of the reorganized Delaware Supreme Court.

The District Court's instructions continued, "It thus appears that the matter before the Court and referred to the Special Master for decision is the ascertainment of the person or persons who, at the time of taking, owned or had any interest in the real estate so condemned by the United States, and the nature of the interest so held." [3]

The parties who asserted a claim to the condemned lands—and whose representatives came before the Special Master—included the State of Delaware, Sussex County, the "inhabitants of the Town of Lewes and County of Sussex," the Commissioners of Lewes (the governing body) and several other private individuals and corporations. In order to prove rightful ownership or title, the "parties claimant" relied on records and other factual data that were contained in a treatise with the succinct title, "Cape Henlopen," prepared by Houston Wilson, a Sussex County attorney who had a strong interest in history. "Cape Henlopen" was originally prepared at the request of the Delaware Society for the Preservation of Antiquities and the State Highway

---

[2] The compiled stenographic minutes that were published of the hearing subsequently held on July 6, 1943, are known as the "Draft Report of Special Master Clarence A. Southerland." It will be cited in this chapter as the Southerland Report. Quote on p. 2. The legal citation of the condemnation action is U.S. vs. 1010.8 Acres, 56 f. Suppl. 120 (Dist. Ct. Del. 1944). Technically, the court proceedings were not completed until November 24, 1948, when the final judgment was made.

[3] Ibid.

Department in 1940 to serve as a basis by which the Attorney General of the State of Delaware could advise them of their respective rights, claims, and interests over the lands of Cape Henlopen in the condemnation proceedings. [4]

Houston Wilson's report, was accepted by Judge Southerland "in evidence," during the proceedings, and because of its comprehensiveness became the significant research document that the Court would rely on in deciding the various claims. The report was referenced by Judge Southerland as simply, the "Wilson Report," and it will be cited as such throughout the remainder of this chapter. It consisted of ten parts and a voluminous number of exhibits and exists only in typewritten manuscript form. Much of the valuable information and findings that appeared in the report has not been available to the general reader and appears in print for the first time. [5]

When Wilson began his research, he found himself faced with a tremendous amount of relevant, entangled, and conflicting material. He had anticipated conflict, otherwise the report would not have been necessary. "The status of the title of these lands," he wrote, "possesses all the ingredients required to concoct a first rate nightmare for the legal mind which may be called upon to disentangle it." [6] Special Master Southerland was to be that "legal mind," and fortunately Wilson's foreboding would not materialize.

---

[4] In 1939 Houston Wilson was asked by the State Highway Department to research the department's jurisdiction over certain lands of Cape Henlopen, from which the Town of Lewes was selling sand. He accepted the assignment casually, yet he was keenly aware that such an investigation would be of major historical and legal significance.

[5] Although there is no date of reference on Wilson's "Cape Henlopen" treatise, it was initially received in evidence in the case on May 4, 1942. Therefore the present author will assign the date of 1942 to the Wilson Report. Very few copies of the Wilson Report are known to exist, however, there is one on file at the Hall of Records.

[6] Wilson Report, Part 1: 3.

In order for Wilson to deliver as logical a presentation as possible, he had to first, rather arbitrarily, make two general assumptions; first, that the title to the lands in question, initially acquired by William Penn, passed to his heirs, and later perfected by the State of Delaware, is valid and good; and second, that there is no known present claim to the lands in question preceding Penn's claim.[7]

The Origin of the Public Commons Claim Before 1682

When Houston Wilson began investigating the origin of the public commons claim, he began his inquiry with Penn's acquisition of his American property which took place on August 24, 1682. The subsequent court action in the 1940s – as we shall soon see – which established the legal basis of a public commons claim was predicated on specific actions after 1682. Acknowledging that the claim of Cape Henlopen and the Great and Beach marshes as a public commons is an "ancient one," Wilson wrote, that he had "...found it difficult to uncover the records if any, upon which this public commons claim is based." [8] However, he had "been successful in uncovering once again those records upon which that claim might be said to be based. Generally speaking, one might say that the early inhabitants of Delaware and Pennsylvania felt that they were entitled to all marsh lands as and for a common pasture by virtue of some unwritten law." [9]

Since Wilson was only concerned – for the purposes of his investigations – with the events beginning in 1682, the present author, in attempting to determine the origin of the public commons claim, has undertaken a search before that year.

In Chapter 4 it was recounted how the settlers at the Hoerenkil (the Dutch name for Lewes Creek, or River, that became known as the Whorekill after the English regained control of New Netherland

---

[7] Ibid., Part I: 2.

[8] Ibid., Part III: 48.

[9] Ibid., Part III: 48-49

in 1674), were thriving under most precarious conditions. The disputes between the Dutch and the English and the destructive raids and vandalism undertaken by forces sent by Lord Baltimore to claim the western side of Delaware Bay provided a constant state of upheaval for those who tried to make the Hoerenkil their home.

This unfortunate state of affairs would create one noteworthy dilemma. The granting of land titles became entrenched in confusion, creating many discrepancies in legitimizing land ownership. In 1674, Edmond Andros became the Governor of New Netherland, after the territory was recaptured from the Dutch in the same year. His primary responsibility was to act on commission of the Duke of York in exercising the Duke's newly expanded authority. The Duke of York's laws had previously been published on March 1, 1664, when the English originally captured New Netherland from the Dutch. The people were therefore reasonably familiar with these tenets, particularly as they affected the acquisition of land. However, as far as the people of the Hoerenkil were concerned, there still existed serious questions about valid titles.

On May 11, 1676, Captain Edmond Cantwell, Surveyor General for the Delaware and formerly the sheriff at New Castle, wrote to Governor Andros requesting that he approve an order, "...to Lay out ye bonds of ye Horekill for there are already people in Dispute where they Live and under whoos governmt; ye Indyans Declares how far ye Dutch has had ye said Bay southward of ye Horekill sum people are Doutfull it might Ly under Baltemore and will not take it up." [10] Cantwell continued in his letter that "when ye patents come from New Yorke I shall go to ye horekill and wth your honors order Ly out ye Line that ye people may know how far to take up land." [11] Hermanus Wiltbanck, a resident of the Hoerenkil, sent several letters to Andros in which he stated that Lord Baltimore intended to control the area

---

[10] *N.Y. Colonial Documents*, 12: 545-546.

[11] Ibid., 546.

once again, and that surveyors from Maryland were surveying "Severall thousand acres... Lyeing within the Limitts of these governmt." [12]

To definitively resolve how a public commons claim to certain lands had its beginning, we might rely on the above situation as a major ingredient. An early reference as to why lands were determined to be held in common is contained in a treatise by Daniel Denton, an Englishman, who traveled extensively in New Netherland. Denton wrote in 1670 concerning the process of procuring land:

> ...the usual way, is for a Company of people to joyn together, either enough to make a town, or a lesser number; these go with the consent of the Governor, and view a tract of Land, there being choice enough, and finding a place convenient for a town, they return to the Governor, who upon their desire admits them into a Colony, and gives them a Grant or Patent for the said Land, for themselves and Associates. These persons being thus qualified, settle the place, and take in what inhabitants to themselves they shall see cause to admit of till their Town be full; these Associates thus taken in have equal privileges of the Land suitable to every mans occasions, no man being debarr'd of such quantities as he hath occasion for, the rest they lie in common till they have occasion for a new division, never dividing their Pasture-land at all, which lies in common to the whole Town. [13]

On June 14, 1671, during the Council meeting held at New York, it was ordered that "about ye Whorekill...what is past granted

---

[12] Ibid., 571 and 576-577; see also 583

[13] Daniel Denton, "A Brief Description of New York" [1670], in William Gowan, *Bibliotheca Americana* (New York, 1845), 39. Denton also stated that one of the chief reasons why this area was so sparsely populated was because "The Dutch gave such bad titles to the lands," 38.

there, bee confirmed upon the conditions as the rest of ye Land with the Provisoe that each planter bee Obliged to settle upon the Land and each Person be enjoyed to settle a House in a Towne to bee appointed neare them." [14]

Although there was no specific mention of lands to be held in common by the Council, we find that less than a month later on July 1st, a confirmation for a parcel of land at the Whorekill was granted to Hermanus Frederick Wiltbanck, reputed to have been the first permanent settler in the Lewes area. The document describing Wiltbanck's land reads: "beginning at Aroskes Kill, and stretching South East and North West to Beaver Kill in breadth and in length as it runs into ye woods South West and North East till it comes behinde ye Creeke which is by ye common land of ye Whore Kill containing by estimacon about eight hundred acres." [15] Aroskes Kill may be present day Arnell or Arnold Creek, a tributary of Rehoboth Bay, Beaver Kill is Holland Glade located between Lewes and Rehoboth Beach and drains into the canal. With Beaver Kill established, the common land mentioned in this confirmation refers to Cape Henlopen. However, the perplexing aspect of this apparently isolated documentation concerning the public lands is that it evidently stands by itself as the earliest reference to lands to be held as a public commons in the vicinity of Cape Henlopen.

In reviewing the records of events at the Hoerenkil the author has found what he believes to be the first official recognition of a public commons claim to lands on the lower Delaware River. After the Duke of York's laws were "re-introduced," Governor Andros ordered in September 1676, that Courts of Law (specifically at New Castle and the Whorekill) be organized and procedures established for the selection of magistrates who would make known to the people and adjudicate the Duke's laws. It was decreed that any person desiring land

---

[14] *N.Y. Colonial Documents*, 12: 484. A list of persons "living at the Horekil, Del," made in 1671 indicated a population of "47 souls," 522.

[15] *Duke of York*, 147.

should make application to the appropriate court, which would then grant a certificate to survey the same. [16]

On June 26, 1680, the magistrates of the Whorekill Court – Luke Watson, John Rhoades, John Kippshaven, William Clark, and Otto Wolgost – sent a letter to Governor Andros concerning several matters including the "settling of land." To them must be credited the earliest official mention of protecting certain lands for public use. The letter included the request that the lands of the Cape as well as the marshes northwest of the town should "lye in common." They went on to say:

> There was sume Certain Land formerly laid out by Capt Cantwell for a Towne; which was to be divided into Lots of 60 foot in breadth and 200 foot in Length, and the Land woods that lye back was to be common: for food for cattle and firewood, it being in all about 130 Acres of Land; …Here is a greate marsh that lyes at the north west side of the Towne, which it should be at any time here after taken up by any perticolar person it would be a great Inconvenancey to those that doe or shall here after live here; as also the Cape, where there is good pin[e] Trees for building; the Land Lettel worth; both which wee desire may Lye in common for the use of the Towne…[17]

Four months later on October 14, 1680, William Clark sent to Governor Andros a "memorandum of public matters at the Horekil to be attended to," where he reiterated that "the marsh at the north west end of the towne and the Cap[e] to be Common to the Use of the Inhabitants." [18]

---

[16] Ibid., 561-563.
[17] Ibid., 654-655.
[18] Ibid., 659.

We know that in May, 1676, Cantwell had written to Andros concerning the surveying of the Whorekill (as discussed above), but it was not until 1680 that it was actually done. Although the author can not find any survey or confirmation of a survey that the "towne" was in fact laid out, it should not go unmentioned that beginning in November, 1677, the then magistrates at the Whorekill Court wrote to Andros informing him that Cornelis Verhoofe had surveyed the lands of Thomas Wellburne and William Anderson, but that a short time later, Cantwell had blotted out their names "and putt in his owne friends which appears to be done with his owne hands."[19] What the extent of the chicanery was we may not know for certain, but it might be reasonable to suppose that if Cantwell was inclined to tamper with one survey, he may have altered others to suit his own designs or for that matter not performed them at all!

Basic Title to Cape Henlopen: The Deed to William Penn in 1682

The first task before Special Master Southerland's District Court in 1943 was to examine the basic title to the lands and waters of the State of Delaware. This title derives from two deeds conveyed by James, Duke of York, to William Penn, each dated August 24, 1682. One of these deeds conveyed a tract of land lying with a circle of twelve miles from New Castle, and the other "all that tract of land upon Delaware River and Bay, beginning twelve miles south from the town of New Castle, otherwise called Delaware, and extending south to the Whorekills, otherwise called Cape Henlopen." [20] Both deeds contained a "covenant for further assurance," contained in letters of patent issued by King Charles II to the Duke of York on March 22, 1682, for the same lands conveyed in the deeds. Essentially, this had the effect of granting to the Duke powers of government and other proprietary and seigniorial rights, along with absolute ownership of the land.

---

[19] Ibid., 587. Cf., 602-603.

[20] Wilson Report, Part 1, 20-22 and Exhibit E.

On December 7, 1682, the Three Lower Counties of Delaware were annexed to Pennsylvania. In the same month, a Provincial Council and Assembly – the first step toward an organizational government – was set up. Following the establishment of this early government, Penn and his successors, as Proprietaries and Governors, and the Assembly and Council of the Province (along with the Assembly of the Three Lower Counties) exercised the power of authority over the Pennsylvania and Delaware territory until the American Revolution. [21]

After 1682 there were to be several challenges, both to the proprietary interest and governmental powers of Penn and his heirs. Penn had been a favorite of King James II (formerly the Duke of York), but when the latter was deposed by William and Mary in February 1689, Penn's relationship with the new monarch became strained. In 1692, he was removed from the government of Pennsylvania and the Delaware territory. However, by August 1694, he was restored once again to his previous position. Letters patent, subsequently issued by the crown, restored Penn to the administration of the government of the "said province and territories." In 1934 when the case of *New Jersey v. Delaware*, involving the boundary between the two states was argued before the Supreme Court, Justice Benjamin Cardozo offered the following opinion: "This patent [letters patent of August, 1694], it would seem, had settled for all time the validity of his [Penn's] exercise of governmental powers, however much it may have left in doubt his title to the land." [22]

After William Penn arrived at New Castle on October 27, 1682, he took action in the form of several directives to insure the proper utilization of his holdings. On November 7th, he issued a commission to the "justices at Whorekill" for the establishment of a "Court of judicature for the County of Whorekill alias New Deal, to act in the said employment and trust for the preservation of the peace and justice

---

[21] See Richard S. Rodney, "The End of the Penns' Claim to Delaware," *Pa. Magazine* 61 (April 1937): 182-203.

[22] *New Jersey v. Delaware*, 291, U.S. 370.

of the Province." [23] On December 25th Penn issued another commission superseding the one of November 7th. He ordered the name of the county changed from Whorekill to Sussex; and more importantly, he directed the court at the Whorekill (the court held at Lewes for the county) with the following:

> Receive peticons from the time that may be made by such persons as designe to take up land among you and that you grant them a warrant to the surveyor to admeasure the same, provided always that you exceed not three hundred acres of land to a master of a family, nor a one hundred acres to a single person, at one single penny per acre or value thereof in the produce of the county, which done, that the surveyor make his returne into court and that the court made thereon returne unto my secretary's office." [24]

This authority of the court at Lewes to grant land was exercised until 1700 when it became evident either through neglect, error, or inexperience that the question of land titles was causing a great deal of confusion. [25]

In order to rectify the confusion, "An Act for the Effectual Establishment and Confirmation of the Freeholders of this Province and Territories Their Heirs and Assigns, in Their Lands and Tenements" was issued. Excerpts from this Act as well as several important items of source material referred to throughout this Chapter are classified as Public Commons Documents in Appendix 2.

---

[23] Scharf, 1888, 1: 516.

[24] Ibid., 2: 1203.

[25] Wilson Report, Part 1, 33. The proceedings of the court held at Lewes from 1682 to 1700 may be found in Turner, 1909, 58-126.

The Public Commons Claim to Cape Henlopen 1682 - 1901

It should not be an unusual assumption to make that William Penn, by the very character of the man, perpetuated such a public commons claim that, as we have seen, in actuality had originated before his acquisition of Pennsylvania and the Three Lower Counties.

He was more than a staunch Quaker simply trusting the tenants of his faith; he was a man who felt very close to nature. His love for his new province, with all of its natural wonders, became deeply embedded in a philosophy of life – a philosophy which to some degree has left its imprint on Pennsylvania and the Three Lower Counties. Penn wrote, in August 1683, to the Free Society of Traders of Pennsylvania residing in London the following:

> The country itself in its Soyl, Air, Water, Seasons, and Produce, both Natural and Artificial is not to be despised. The Land containeth divers sorts of Earth, as Sand, Yellow and Black, Poor and Rich: Also gravel both Loomy and Dusty; and in some places a fast fat Earth, like to our best Vales in England, especially Inland Brooks and Rivers, God in his Wisdom having ordered it so, that the Advantages of the Country are divided, the Back-lands being generally three to one Richer than those that lie by Navigable Waters....The Air is sweet and clear, the Heavens serene... rarely overcast. [26]

Penn's excitement and concern over the bounties of his Colony were predicated on a deep personal view that extolled the relationship of man to his God, and how best man should not entreat on the works of his maker. "The Earth is the lord's," he wrote, "and his presence fills it, and his power upholds it, and it is a precious thing to enjoy and use

---

[26] *Narratives*, Myers, 225-226.

it in a sense and feeling of the same…. Have a care of cumber and the love and care of the world." [27]

Returning to Penn's role in establishing specific principles for settling the land in his colony, we find that in 1701 he prescribed a direct warrant declaring certain lands be held in common in the town of New Castle. The warrant required that a survey be made of 1,000 acres adjoining or near the town "to lie in common." [28]

Specifically as to Cape Henlopen, the first attempt to guarantee certain public rights to land in common was made by a grant of the court at Lewes and by commission of William Penn on January 9, 10, and 11, 1682, as the following attests. This would become known and referred to as the "Warner Grant," in the Wilson Report and in the hearing before Judge Southerland.

> Upon the petition of Edmond Warner the Court grant unto him the land of the Cape Commonly called Cape Inlopen Lying on the North East side of the Creek formerly called the Whorekill to make a Coney Warrin on and Liberty to Build a House and seat a Warriner upon the said land upon the condition that the Timber and feed of the said land and marshes thereunto Belonging be and forever hereafter Lye in Common for the use of the Inhabitants of the Town of Lewis and County of Sussex, as also free Liberty for any or all of the Inhabitants of the said County to fish get and take of there oysters & cockle shells and gather plums, cranbereys and Huckleberys on the said land as they shall think fitt always provided that no person

---

[27] William and Thomas Evans, eds. "Memoirs of the Life of William Penn," *The Friends Library* 12 Vols. (Philadelphia,1841), 5: 185.

[28] Cited in the Southerland Report, 34. See also *Trustees of New Castle Commons v. Megginson*, 1 Boyce 361, which presented the question whether common lands were exempt from taxation as the property of a corporation for charitable uses.

whatsoever shall not hunt or kill any Rabbits or hares on the said land without the Leave and consent of the said Edmond Warner his Executors Administrators or Assigns....[29]

During the 1943 hearing before Southerland he evaluated the construction and validity of the Warner Grant this way: "The wording of the grant is unusual, but it seems reasonably clear that it was intended to create two rights or privileges, viz., a right in Edmond Warner to establish a coney or rabbit warren and a right of common in the inhabitants of the Town of Lewes and county of Sussex." [30] Southerland continued that "the important consideration is the clear intention of the grant to create a right of common in the cape lands for the benefit of the classes of persons defined in the grant." [31]

The next incident that can be found to substantiate the public commons claim to Cape Henlopen arises out of the attempt of certain persons to take up a portion of these lands during 1796. However, prior to 1796 several acts were passed by the General Assembly of the State of Delaware relative to land sales and land titles.

In 1793, an act was passed for the opening and establishing of a land office in the State to conduct the sale of all vacant and uncultivated lands. In addition, any matters in dispute would be heard by a Board of Commissioners. [32] In the following year, a supplement was passed to this act which provided that all patents, warrants, and grants for land within the State made by the Duke of York, William Penn, and any subsequent proprietaries or authorized agents before January 1, 1760 (as well as all surveys made in pursuance of such patents, warrants, and grants) were deemed to be valid. This supplement also pro-

---

[29] Sussex County Deed Record, A-1, 14. Wilson Report, Exhibit. V. Cf., Deed Record A-1, 109 for a second transcription of the above which is a paraphrase of the entry on p. 14; see also Wilson Report, Part 3, 49-51 and Exhibit W.

[30] Southerland Report, 23.

[31] Ibid.

[32] 2 *Laws of Delaware* 1160 (1793). Wilson Report, Exhibit X.

vided that appeals from any ruling of the Board of Commissioners would be brought before the High Court of Errors and Appeals which would have the final determination in any case to be judged. [33]

After the act of 1793 and the supplement of 1794 were implemented, the Recorder of Deeds for Sussex County issued between June 15th and June 21st, 1796, four separate warrants for the surveying of land on Cape Henlopen. In order, these warrants were issued to the following: On June 15th a warrant to survey a parcel of vacant land and marsh (not exceeding 200 acres) on the northeast side of Lewes Creek near "a place called Long Neck in the marshes of the said creek," issued to Nicholas Ridgely, Theodore Wilson, Rhoads Shankland, Jr., and Thomas Marsh;[34] on the same day a similar warrant was issued to William Russell;[35] on June 16th, another, and similar warrant, was issued to William Perry, Peter and John Marsh;[36] and finally on June 21st the Recorder of Deeds issued a warrant to William Coleman for vacant marsh lands (again not to exceed 200 acres) on the northeast side of Lewes Creek, "not already granted, surveyed and appropriated." [37]

Inevitably the issuance of these warrants for the surveying of lands on Cape Henlopen was most disturbing to many persons who still believed in the public commons claim. It was one of Lewes' prominent citizens, Caleb Rodney, a future Governor of the State, who filed caveats (a restraining order) against those who had received these warrants. After some nebulous negotiations, the caveat against Russell was

---

[33] 2 *Laws of Delaware* 1174 (1794). Wilson Report, Exhibit Y. The High Court of Errors and Appeals was created by the State Constitution on June 12, 1792. See 1 *Laws of Delaware* 44 (1792) and Wilson Report, Exhibit Z. Several other acts supplementing the original act of 1793 were passed between 1796 and 1843 and need not be concerned with here.

[34] Sussex County Land Warrants, Certificates V, No. 20, 173. Wilson Report, Exhibit AG.

[35] Ibid. Wilson Report, Exhibit AH

[36] Ibid. Wilson Report, Exhibit AI

[37] Ibid. Wilson Report, Exhibit AJ.

finally heard as a test case before the Board of Commissioners. On July 19, 1797, after proceedings had been completed, the Commissioners did "order, judge and decree that agreeable to the laws of the State of Delaware it is considered that the said William Russell take nothing by his said warrant, and that the said William Russell shall not be permitted to hold the land contained in his said survey." [38]

This decision of the commissioners does not determine upon what basis the warrant and survey were voided. Wilson wrote that "it also appears that an appeal was taken and the record made out and sent up to the High Court of Errors and Appeals," which, "Pursuant to the Act of 1793, should have heard and determined the appeal at its sitting on the first Tuesday, in August, 1797."[39] A thorough search for the original records of the High Court of Errors and Appeals issued on that day has proved futile. Therefore, we must rely on a secondary source of evidence as to the issue determined by the Board of Land Commissioners in the case *Rodney v. Russell* in order to have an understanding of the basis for the decision reached by the High Court of Errors and Appeals. This secondary source is in the form of a petition (see Appendix 2) signed by sixty-nine citizens of Lewes to the General Assembly and dated January 6, 1817. The petition clearly states that both the Board of Commissioners and the High Court of Errors and Appeals held the original Warner Grant of 1682 to be valid, and consequently denied the right of any individual to take possession of any lands and marshes of Cape Henlopen.

What happened to the rights granted to Edmond Warner is difficult to say. There has not been found any deed, bill of sale, assignment of rights or any will executed by Warner. However, in the executive correspondence files at the Hall of Records, there are three letters addressed in the year 1901 to Governor John Hunn from James C. Beebe, a resident of Lewes. These letters seem to throw some additional

---

[38] Wilson Report, Part 3, 58. See a copy of the Caveat Docket concerning Russell in Appendix 2.

[39] Ibid.

light on Warner's interest in these lands, and appear in print for the first time in Appendix 2.

Beebe wrote that since Warner died intestate, the land covered by his grant in 1682 therefore reverts to the state: "The timber, feed, of said land and marshes thereunto belonging be and forever hereafter bye in common for the inhabitants of Lewes and Sussex &c. The beach is not feed or timber [or] marshes, therefore, it escheats to the state,... no one has an equitable right to sell or convey it." [40]

Special Master Southerland's analysis is particularly relevant:

> The Warner Grant appears to create rights which, by their very nature, call for supervision and control by the public authorities, in order that the benefits which the grant seeks to confer may be equitably enjoyed. If such control be lacking, the benefits will be lost, since unrestricted use will defeat the very purpose of the grant. Can it be supposed, for instance, that the first man to go upon the common lands may take all the timber and feed for himself? And if not, how much? And if it be answered – 'a reasonable quantity,' then how is that quantity to be ascertained, and how is the limitation enforced?
>
> The rights of common created by the Warner Grant are public or collective in their nature and not individual, and, if not enforceable only through governmental authority, are certainly a proper subject of governmental control as constituting a species of charitable use or trust for the benefit of an indefinite group or class. [41]

---

[40] "Executive Correspondence Files," Hall of Records. Wilson Report, Part 3, 63

From the foregoing it may be concluded that this is the legal basis upon which a public commons claim may be made to Cape Henlopen. [42]

The Public Commons Claim to the Great and Beach Marshes
1680 - 1739

Interwoven with the history of a public commons claim to Cape Henlopen is the claim that the marsh lands northwest of the town are also to be reserved for public use, as we have seen by the letter sent by the magistrates in 1680 to Governor Andros. The next reference to a public commons claim to the marshes came in October 1687, in a lawsuit entered in the court at the Whorekill:

> Jonathan Bailey was summoned to this Court... [for] violently by force of arms Wickedly Maliciously & feloniously oute of a sordid base Covetous desire, aboute the beginning of the last yeare 1686... Contemning & despising, thy Neighbors, fence Not onely the Kings Hyeway [Pilottown Road], to thy owne use, which said Hyeway hath bene Made Worne & Accustomed for Many years, Neither had thy Neighbours, any other roade or hye way to ye Commons Commonly called Marshes either ffetch Hay Looke after their Catle, or other ocations; but allsoe the onely Known Antient place of A burying ground for the Towne of Lewis....[43]

---

[41] Southerland Report, 33. Cf., *State v. Griffith*, 2 Del. Ch. 392, 409. Southerland points out that the term "Commons" or "common land" has often been applied to lands dedicated to public use (3 Tiffany, Real Property, Sec. 934) and the rights created by the Warner Grant are somewhat similar. Therefore "the right of public authority to regulate the use of such land is unquestioned." Southerland Report, 33-34.

[42] Wilson Report, Part. 3, 62.

[43] Turner, 1909, 119.

The court found that Bailey had infringed upon the rights of the public. It was then ordered that the "Hyeway" to the marshes be restored, and one acre of the ancient burying ground be set aside for the public. [44]

The earliest test of the proclaimed right of sanctioning the marshes as a public commons occurred in the early part of 1734 when reports were circulated in Lewes that Joshua Fisher had acquired a grant for "Lynks Island." [45] The townspeople became quite incensed over this intrusion and felt that this grant to Fisher would violate their nebulous, but claimed right to the marshes as a common. A letter substantiating the public common's right was therefore sent by Ryves Holt to the proprietaries on March 6, 1734. In the letter, Holt carefully explained the basis of the ancient public commons claim.

> Sir: Having lately presumed to write a few lines yre self and Hon'ble Bro're, annex'd to the Lewes Petition for Lynks Island and the great Marsh, I beg leave to give Y're Hon're, to whom I am more known, the following acc't of the ground thereof. As soon as a report was spread that Mr. Jos'ae Fisher had a grant for Lynks Island, the Towns People assembled together, and showed an almost gen'l Discontent, many of whom alleged that y're Honr's Father [William Penn] had given ye s'd places, as a common of pasture, to the inhabitants of this Town; vain was it (during the first haet) to call upon them to make out a title thereto, but at length some of our Seniors being questioned about the affair, and nothing appearing, save only, that some verbal promises had been made to give them

---

[44] Ibid., 120. Cf., Scharf, 1888, 2: 1223-1224.

[45] As part of the evolution of land forms, islands existed in the "town marsh" and Lynks Island is clearly defined on the Shankland survey of June 11, 1736. Subsequent man-made and natural changes eventually eliminated these "islands."

and successors, the s'd Island and Marsh, it was then resolved to Petition Y'r Hon'ble Family for a grant of the places afs'd; and having adventured to say to my fellow Townsmen, upon that occasion, that I was confident, that if your Hon'ble Proprietaries knew that we were desirious of taking up the said marsh, etc. they would not deny us, provided we made a proper application; I thought it would not be taken amis, to trouble y're Honour with the foregoing narration, the importinence whereof; if you'll please excuse, it will lay me under a great obligation of being at all times ready, to manifest the duty and affection that owe to that Hon'ble Family; under whose ancestors government, and upon whose land, I first drew breath, I am,

Honorable Sir,
Y'r most Humble
& obedient servant
R's Holt[46]

The letter was received favorably by the proprietaries, and after several months, they issued an order to the town representatives, Ryves Holt, Simon Kolloch, and Jacob Kolloch, to instruct William Shankland, the Deputy Surveyor, to survey and plot the two "Islands" lying to the Southwest of Lewes Creek. This Shankland proceeded to do, and on June 11, 1736 he filed his return in the Office of the Recorder of Deeds for Sussex County identifying "a certain parcel of marsh Situated in the County of Sussex formerly called and known by the name of the Town Marsh lying and being on the South side of the Broadkill [River] and on the Northwest side of Lewes Town Bounded with Cold Spring Creek on the West and on the South with Pagan

---

[46] The original is in the Hall of Records. Wilson Report, Exhibit AO.

A view of the Great Marsh from near the mouth of Canary Creek near the
westerly end of Pilottown Road.
Courtesy of the Archives of The Lewes Historical Society

[Canary] Creek and on the East with Delaware Bay and Lewes Creek now called by the name of Penns Bounty." [47]

Subsequent to this Survey, the proprietaries, over the signature of Thomas Penn, issued a warrant on June 23, 1739, to the Surveyor General, Benjamin Eastburn, authorizing and requiring him to accept the Shankland Survey of 1736. In addition, the warrant made clear that Eastburn should make his return to the Secretary's office in order for confirmation to Ryves Holt, Simon Kolloch, and Jacob Kolloch as the trustees of the marshes for the use of the Town of Lewes. There was to be a yearly quit rent on this land paid by the people of Lewes, which would go for the support of a school within the town. A complete copy of this warrant appears in Appendix 2.

---

[47] Sussex Surveys A-1776, 506. Wilson Report, Exhibit AP.

**Vested Control Over the Public Commons by the Town of Lewes
1773 – 1907**

We have examined the pertinent details concerning the public commons claim to Cape Henlopen and the Great and Beach marshes. Beginning in 1773 several indirect and direct measures in the form of legislative acts were started which ultimately established the vested control over the public lands in the Town of Lewes.

Cape Henlopen 1773 - 1857

The story of this curious chain of events begins on November 6, 1773, when the proprietary, John Penn, by and with the advice and consent of the General Assembly, appointed a commission with the delegated authority to build a bridge over Lewes Creek at the point near or where the early colonial fort had stood. [48] On March 29, 1775, a supplement to this authority was approved which authorized the appointed commission to cut a canal in the creek ten feet wide and two feet deep "until it passes through the place where a passage of ninety feet is left between two abutments of the bridge now erecting." [49] In addition, the commission was authorized, after the canal had been cut, to stop or fill up the existing channel or the Creek on the Cape side and to continue the causeway across the filled area. The causeway was completed by August 12, 1775. [50] Although the construction of the bridge across Lewes Creek made access to the Cape considerably better,

---

[48] 1 *Laws of Delaware* 530 (1773). Wilson Report, Exhibit AR.

[49] 1 *Laws of Delaware* 540 (1775). Wilson Report, Exhibit AS.

[50] Scharf, 1888, 2: 1223 and Wilson Report, Part 4, 73. Several supplements to the original Act of 1773 were passed as follows: On January 29, 1791, which provided that the bridge be kept in good repair (2.*Laws of Delaware* 1011 [1791] and Wilson Report, Exhibit AT); on January 28, 1794, David Hall and Caleb Rodney were named as commissioners in place of John Rodney and Henry Fisher (2 *Laws of Delaware* 1170 [1794] and Wilson Report, Exhibit AU); and on February 9, 1796, provisions were made for the charging and use of tolls to be collected (2 *Laws of Delaware* 1308 [1796] and Wilson Report, Exhibit AV).

a real disadvantage became evident from the point of view of preserving and conserving the green timber and feed of the Cape.

Before the bridge was built the Creek had afforded a degree of protection to the Cape commons, the addition of the bridge greatly improved access and aided those seeking to ravage and destroy the area. On January 24, 1779, the General Assembly met this threat by imposing certain fines to be levied against any persons who shall "fall, cut, cart or convey any green timber wood, on or from said Cape, for any private use whatsoever." [51]

However, there was one exception – which illustrated the importance of maintaining the Cape Henlopen Lighthouse – an act of the General Assembly that granted to the keeper of the lighthouse the privilege "…to cut and make use of as much timber on said Cape as will support him or them in firewood, fences, and repairs on said Cape for said lighthouse, and for no other purposes whatsoever." [52]

Another provision of the 1799 act recognized that keeping the Cape in its natural state would be advantageous. It was wisely stated in the preamble that "the timber, is a defense against the sea, and if once destroyed, the navigation of said creek may cease." [53] The Act having to do with trespassing upon and pillaging the Cape (as supplemented) was followed by still another act passed on February 15, 1814, the title of which sufficiently shows its purpose.

> An Act Authorizing the Court of General Quarter Sessions of the Peace and Goal Delivery, of the State of Delaware to Appoint Trustees to Take Charge of, and Secure, the Rents of the Lands and Marsh Commonly Called Cape Henlopen, for the Use of the County of Sussex. [54]

---

[51] 3 *Laws of Delaware* 67 (1799). Wilson Report, Exhibit AW. See also a later supplement (January 30, 1813) to raise the fine in 4 *Laws of Delaware* 607 (1813) and Wilson Report, Exhibits AX and AY.

[52] Ibid.

[53] Ibid.

Section 1 of this act authorized the Court to appoint Trustees, "to take possession of, and rent to the highest and best bidder, in lotts, the aforesaid lands and marsh for any time not exceeding three years; and the money arising therefrom to be paid over to the county treasurer for the use of the County of Sussex only." [55]

The effect of this move by the General Assembly imposed even greater restrictions on the use of the Cape than the townspeople of Lewes were willing to accept without protest. Consequently, a petition was drafted to oppose the action and sent to the legislative body in Dover (see Appendix 2). However, the petition did not convince the General Assembly to modify its previous course. By February 20, 1837, additional legislation was enacted, again as a supplement to the original act of 1799. This latest legislation included four important changes:

First, the Superior Court of Sussex County was authorized to appoint the trustees for the public lands. Second, one of the trustees had to come from the Town of Lewes. Third, one half of the proceeds received by the trustees was to be used for ditching and draining the lands and marshes of the Cape. Finally, the supplement was to remain in effect only for a period of ten years. [56]

On February 19, 1841, the General Assembly passed an act to improve the navigation of Lewes Creek by cutting a canal near Green Bank situated northwest of the junction of Canary and Lewes Creeks. Moreover, this was to be re-enacted February 3, 1849. According to the provision of the 1841 Act, certain trustees were appointed "in behalf of the State, of all the lands and marshes in Lewes and Rehoboth Hundred, on the northeast side of Lewes Creek, belonging to this State, called Cape Henlopen." [57]

---

[54] 5 *Laws of Delaware* 40 (1814). Wilson Report, Exhibit AZ.

[55] Ibid.

[56] 9 *Laws of Delaware* 167 (1837). Wilson Report, Exhibit BB.

[57] 9 *Laws of Delaware* 411 (1841). Wilson Report, Exhibit BF. A supplement to this act was approved on February 3, 1847, that was similar to the act of 1841, only changing the term of the trustees from four to eight years. See 10 *Laws of Delaware* 134 (1847). Wilson Report, Exhibit BG.

Attention should be directed to an important technicality as contained in the clause that appeared in Section 9 of both the Act of 1841 and the Act of 1849 that referred to the lands "belonging to this state." This would be changed on February 15, 1849, by a supplement that read, "belonging to the inhabitants of the Town of Lewes, in the County of Sussex." [58]

All of these legislative acts had to do with the appointing of trustees with power to sell the timber and rent the land and marshes of Cape Henlopen. Yet the lands and marshes were to remain unimproved. The only material profits to be derived were from the cutting of the timber or the pasturing and cutting of the marsh hay that grew on the Cape. It will be recalled that the original Warner Grant provided that "the timber and feed of the Cape should forever lie in common for the use of the inhabitants of the Town of Lewes and County of Sussex." This provision was emphasized by the Act of 1799; by 1849, however, a new twist came when the Legislature created the trustees to administer the lands of the Cape belonging to the State. The supplement of 1849 amended the words belonging to the State to read "belonging to the inhabitants of Lewes, in the County of Sussex."

From all of these legislative gymnastics it becomes difficult (confusing to say the least) to ascertain exactly to whom the designated public lands belonged. As to the statement contained in the last supplement, it may be said that the trustees charged with protecting the interest of the Town of Lewes in and to these lands must have realized that a subtle change in the context of the Warner Grant could be made simply by striking out the word "and" to read "in the." Therefore, instead of the timber and feed of the Cape lands remaining forever *in common for use of the people* of Lewes and Sussex County, they would lie forever *in common for the people* of Lewes, in the County of Sussex. This was indeed a clever change to make—one that would have far-reaching land use implications in the future. [59]

---

[58] 10 *Laws of Delaware* 309 (1849). Wilson Report, Exhibit BH.

[59] Wilson Report, Part 4, 80-81.

The Town of Lewes had originally been incorporated by the General Assembly on February 2, 1818. By an Act of March 2, 1857, shortly after the expiration of the eight-year term of the trustees over the lands of the Cape as fixed by the Act of 1847, the Charter of the town was altered in several respects. Of importance to this discussion is the transfer of the trustee power to the Commissioners of Lewes (the governing body). Section 6 of this act provided "that the said commissioner [the town commissioners] shall also have the general supervision and trusteeship of the public land on the north-east side of Lewes Creek, called 'the Cape,' with the power to 'lease the same or any part thereof, for terms not exceeding three years and to sell the timber and wood thereon, and to sue for and recover damages for any trespass that may be committed by any person on said Cape lands, timber or wood." [60]

All of the foregoing legislative acts, initiated ostensibly with the hope of perfecting the public commons claim to the Cape, did not make any reference to the Great and Beach Marshes. It is quite probable that some readers may already have given up all desire in trying to follow this legalistic trek through history, and do not wish to continue. For those who have had the interest or perseverance to stick it out, we shall now turn to the Great and Beach Marshes to find out their fate.

Great and Beach Marshes 1863 - 1907

The first Act of the General Assembly directly affecting the Lewes marshes was passed on March 24, 1863 empowering the Commissioner of the Great and Beach Marshes to build a bridge across Canary Creek and, in order to maintain it, "cut, take and use such timber as may be necessary from the Cape Henlopen Pinery." [61] A more specific legislative act was passed the following year, on February 11, 1864, which

---

[60] 11 *Laws of Delaware* 486 (1857). Wilson Report Exhibit BW.

[61] 12 *Laws of Delaware* 358 (1863). Wilson Report, Exhibit BJ. This act was another of the series entitled "To Improve the Navigation of Lewes Creek and Other Purposes."

appointed commissioners vested with full authority and control over the Great and Beach Marshes. They were authorized to sell and dispose of the hay and grass once a year at a public sale. The proceeds from this annual sale were to aid the "construction and repairs of bridges and necessary causeways on any public road which may be laid out from Lewistown, across Canary Creek, over the public marsh to Broadkiln Creek, and to such other public improvements about Lewistown as they may deem proper." [62]

It was discussed earlier that the original Proprietary Warrant provided that the yearly quit rent from the Great and Beach Marshes be used "for and towards the support of a public school to be kept within such town." Additionally, the act went on to provide that the Commissioners so appointed and their successors should be elected every four years by the "qualified legal voters" of the Town of Lewes. [63]

On August 10, 1864, the General Assembly passed an amendment to include the Cape and Cape Marshes within the original scope of the original act thereby transferring to the Commissioners of the Great and Beach Marshes jurisdiction over the lands of the Cape. [64]

On January 11, 1810, a petition was made to the General Assembly by the Town of Lewes seeking approval for a Charter of Incorporation. The petition was presented in Dover and was signed by fifty-eight inhabitants of the town (see Appendix 2). However, the petitioners either purposely or otherwise made one error in their presentation. They stated that the land and marsh of the Cape as well as the Great Marsh had been granted to the town as a commons and they therefore asked the Legislature for the authority to dispose of these lands and marshes. Obviously, it was not foreseen by the subscribers

---

[62] 12 *Laws of Delaware* 447 (1864). Wilson Report, Exhibit BI.

[63] Ibid.

[64] 12 *Laws of Delaware* 473 (1864). Wilson Report, Exhibit BK. The Act of 1863 along with the amendment of 1864 is found in 12 *Laws of Delaware* 475 (1864). Wilson Report, Exhibit BL.

that their request would receive strong rebuttal from other quarters. Immediately, forty-four citizens of Sussex County filed an answer.

> It is a notorious fact scarcely disputable that the Great Marsh and Cape was granted by a propriety warrant for the express use of the said town and county as a common pasturage. This grant invested the citizens with a complete and indefeasible title and cannot consistently with the constitution be divested or suffer any modification unless the consent of a majority of the inhabitants of the county is first obtained. [65]

This rebuttal provoked a "memorial" from the Lewes petitioners who countered with a further statement. They admitted that the Great and Beach Marshes were granted to the inhabitants of Lewes specifically for a school, yet they avoided making any reference to the question of the grant of the Cape as a commons, except to state that: "It has been represented to the people of the county adjacent to Lewes that it was the intention of the petitioners to debar them from the privilege of pasturing their cattle on the Cape, this together with the erroneous impression that the Great Marsh was granted for a common we believe is the entire cause of their having signed the remonstrance." [66]

As a result of this dispute the General Assembly did not incorporate the Town of Lewes until February 2, 1818. For some unknown reason – possibly because of the furor over the public lands – Lewes' initial charter of incorporation was hidden under the unassuming title, "An Act to Improve the Navigation of Lewes Creek, to Survey and Regulate the Streets of the Town of Lewes, and for Other Purposes." [67]

It should be pointed out that before Delaware became a state, the northeastern boundary of Lewes did not extend beyond the southwest

---

[65] Wilson Report, Exhibit BQ.

[66] Wilson Report, Exhibit BR.

[67] 5 *Laws of Delaware* 309 (1818).

bank of Lewes Creek.[68] However, in Section 9 of the 1818 act the northeastern boundary line of Lewes was defined as the northeastern bank of Lewes Creek or the southeastern portion of the Cape. [69]

In the Charter of Incorporation, no direct powers or authority were granted to the town Commissioners relative to the public commons claim over the Cape and the Great and Beach Marshes. Yet fifty-three years later on March 2, 1871, the General Assembly passed, this time without resorting to secrecy, "an Act to Incorporate the Town of Lewes," and, for the first time spelled out specific regulations by which the public lands were to be controlled – by the Town of Lewes. By this Act of 1871, the northeastern boundary of the town, for the first time, extended across the Creek and included a portion of the Cape. It is even more significant that through this latest legislative enactment the Commissioners were successful in having acquired vested control over "all the public and vacant lands lying within the corporate limits," as well as "full and exclusive authority and control over the Great and Beach Marshes, Cape and Cape Marshes, near Lewes." [70] The act also contained the provision that the commissioners were not to prohibit or restrain citizens of the town or the State of Delaware from fishing along Delaware Bay or from grazing their cattle on the "Cape or Beach or Cape Marshes." [71]

Several subsequent legislative acts would broaden the original powers granted to the Commissioners over the Great and Beach Marshes, established when the town was originally incorporated in 1818. In summary, these have included a) the authority to lease the lands of the Cape to anyone who would improve them under conditions specified by the Town Commissioners; b) the authority to col-

---

[68] See the Survey of Lewes done by Robert Shankland in 1723, Shankland's Surveys and Warrants, 1718: 222.

[69] Sussex County Deed Record, AL-34, 323-326.

[70] 14 *Laws of Delaware* 126 (1871). Wilson Report, Exhibit BX. Cf., 14 *Laws of Delaware* 588 (1873). Wilson Report, Exhibit BZ.

[71] Ibid.

lect quit rents from those individuals who had assumed possession of the lands of the Cape without right; c) powers to assess and levy taxes on the lands of the Cape; and finally, the power to exercise the same measure of control over the lands of the Cape as the Commissioners exercised over the inhabitants and geographical area included within the corporate limits of the town. [72] The above enumeration of powers was again greatly expanded on April 11, 1907, when the General Assembly passed an act which delegated expanded authority to the Town Commissioners over all of the public lands. Section 7 of this act read in part:

> All the public and vacant lands lying within the corporate limits of said Town of Lewes, and all the public or vacant lands contiguous to but outside the corporate limits of said town and fronting on the Bay between the point of Cape Henlopen and the South and Veasey's inlet on the north, shall be vested in the commissioners of Lewes and the said commissioners shall have jurisdiction over the same. [73]

---

[72] The various acts are: the Act of January 28, 1831 in 8 *Laws of Delaware* 102 (1831), Sections 2 and 3 and Wilson Report, Exhibit BT; the Act of March 2, 1871, 14 *Laws of Delaware* 126 (1871), Section 9 and Wilson Report, Exhibit BX; the Act of March 31, 1873, 14 *Laws of Delaware* 585 (1873), Section 3 and Wilson Report, Exhibit BY): the Amendment of March 31, 1873 to the Act of March 1871, 14 *Laws of Delaware* 588 (1873), Section 9 and Wilson Report, Exhibit BZ); the Act of February 19, 1885, 17 *Laws of Delaware* 813 (1885),Section 1 and Wilson Report, Exhibit CF); the Act of April 5, 1889, 18 *Laws of Delaware* 839 (1889), Section 1 and Wilson Report, Exhibit CG); the Act of March 7, 1901, 22 *Laws of Delaware* 447 (1901) and Wilson Report, Exhibit CK); another Act of March 7, 1901, 22 *Laws of Delaware* 448 (1901) and Wilson Report, Exhibit CL); and the Act of April 18, 1905, 23 *Laws of Delaware* 391 (1905), Section 1 and Wilson Report, Exhibit CQ).

[73] 24 *Laws of Delaware* 594 (1907). Wilson Report, Exhibit CR. See also the Act of March 28, 1921, in 32 *Laws of Delaware* 419 (1921). Wilson Report, Exhibit CW.

It is through this authority that all ordinances subsequently adopted by the Commissioners which would affect the public lands outside the town limits were to have the same force and effect with regards to the described public lands as within the town limits. Also authorized by the act of 1907 was the provision to lease "to persons who will improve or agree to improve the same such portion of said public lands for such time and upon such terms as they, the said commissioners, may deem proper for the interest and benefit of said town." [74]

By virtue of the 1907 legislation, the Town of Lewes had perfected its claim over the public lands and subsequently began to issue numerous leases to these lands. This is evidenced today by the many homes along the bay shore known as Lewes Beach, as well as the many newer developments near the Cape along the bay shore. [75]

When the town was reincorporated by an act of the General Assembly on May 21, 1941, the powers of the Town of Lewes over the public lands remained substantially the same as the provision enumerated in 1907, as amended by the Act of April 2, 1925, which allowed the commissioners "to sell sand and gravel by measure or otherwise,

---

[74] Ibid.

[75] The areas along Delaware Bay near Cape Henlopen where present day residential communities are situated were formerly the site of menhaden processing factories and other industrial pursuits.

[76] 34 *Laws of Delaware* 362 (1925). Wilson Report, Exhibit DB. The case, *Lewes Sand Co. v. Commissioners of Lewes* (1937), involving a lease to certain lands of the Cape did not really question the right of the commissioners to lease any of these lands. It should also be noted that Judge J. Rodney delivered an opinion in *Lewes Sand Co. v Graves, et al.*, (1939) involving the claimed rights and privileges of certain parties holding "Lewes Leases" on the Cape. In his statement of facts Rodney said, "the State of Delaware held a large tract of vacant land contiguous to the Town of Lewes and reaching the seashore, on which land were large deposits of sand in the form of sand hills or dunes." Moreover, C.J. Layton in his concurring opinion stated, "the lands in question, belonging to the State with a certain jurisdiction over them vested by statute in the municipality of Lewes, contain large deposits of sand in the form of hills or dunes." See Wilson Report, Part 4, 106-109.

wherever the same may be located within the limits of the vested lands of the Town of Lewes." [76]

The United States Government's Interest 1791 - 1941

As the story opened in the beginning of this chapter, the Federal government's interest in Cape Henlopen as a coastal defense installation began in earnest during the summer of 1940. This was prompted by surveys undertaken by the U.S. Army Corps of Engineers of nationally owned land that had been acquired on Cape Henlopen in the past. The history of Federal ownership began in 1791, when the first parcel of the original Penn grant was transferred from the State of Delaware to the United States Government. This began a series of transfers that over time would established a strong Federal interest in the Cape that ultimately was to culminate with the acquisition of 1010.8 acres of land in 1941 by the action of the condemnation proceedings.

By statutory action on September 30, 1763, James Hamilton, the Lieutenant Governor of Pennsylvania and the Three Lower Counties under the proprietaries, Thomas and Richard Penn, with the advice of the General Assembly, established the order for the construction of a lighthouse on Cape Henlopen. [77] Within two months the Surveyor General was duly authorized to lay out 200 acres at the Cape for the lighthouse. [78]

After Delaware and Pennsylvania declared their independence from Great Britain, and after Delaware became the "First State" in the United States (in 1787), the new Federal government passed a law for the support of lighthouses, beacons, buoys, and public piers, provided that they were ceded to the United States by the appropriate State.

---

[77] 6 Statutes at Large of Pennsylvania 302-305 (1759-1765). Wilson Report, Exhibit DN. Additionally, the Wilson Report, Part 5, 111 provides the citations to later supplements to this act.

[78] Sussex County Survey Warrants, B-1776, 138 and 384. Wilson Report, Exhibits DO, DP and U. A copy of the survey(s) appears in John W. Beach, *The Cape Henlopen Lighthouse* (Dover: Henlopen Publishing Co., 1970), 17 and 20.

Consequently on January 29, 1791, the General Assembly of the young State of Delaware authorized the execution of a deed that would be the formal conveyance to the Federal government.

> All the right, title, and interest of the Delaware State in and to the lighthouse situate in Sussex County, near the entrance of the Bay of Delaware, ...together with all the lands, tenements, and appurtenances thereunto belonging, with all the necessary jurisdiction over the same. [79]

The next transfer from the State to the Federal government came on July 26, 1871, when 500 feet of the bay shore extending inland 1,000 feet was ceded to the Federal government for the purpose of constructing a pier into the bay. This was to later become known as the *Iron Pier Reservation*, and the total area included approximately 11 ½ acres.[80] On February 5, 1875, a third parcel was conveyed by the State Legislature. This property measured 2,100 feet along the bay shore running to a depth of 3,000 feet (over 140 acres) lying between the *Iron Pier Reservation* and the point of Cape Henlopen. The transfer was made "upon the express condition that defenses, to be built by the United States at the Delaware Breakwater Harbor, shall be constructed thereon." [81] This was to become known as the *United States Fort Reservation*.

The next conveyance to the United States took place on April 12, 1889, when another parcel containing 1,500 feet frontage on the bay and 1,200 feet deep between the Iron Pier Reservation and the Cape

---

[79] 2 *Laws of Delaware* 1018 (1791). Wilson Report, Exhibit DQ.

[80] 14 *Laws of Delaware* 247 (1871). Wilson Report, Exhibit DU. There were two previous attempts to cede the same area, but apparently because of the terms – complicated by the inclusion of the issue of slavery – no action was taken. See Wilson Report, Part 5, 116-117 and Exhibits DS and DT.

[81] Wilson Report, Exhibit DW. A copy of the plot appears in Sussex County Deed Record, No. 84, 448.

was acquired with the proviso that a *Quarantine Station* (also referred to as the *Quarantine Reservation*) be established. [82] Such a facility was later built and maintained for a number of years until 1939 when the station was dismantled and the title to the land was subsequently "reinvested in the State of Delaware." [83] This area was again transferred back to Federal ownership by the Declaration of Taking in 1941 that led to the condemnation proceedings before Judge Southerland.

Immediately south of the original Cape Henlopen tract, the United States acquired an additional one acre parcel on April 1, 1897, which became the site of Coast Guard Station No. 140. [84] Later the General Assembly ceded to the Federal government, on March 29, 1935, the remaining coastline between the Quarantine Reservation and the Cape for an eight-year period. This condition, however, stated that if during this time defense installations were constructed, the grant would extend indefinitely as long as the land was used for defense purposes. [85] In 1945, after the Federal government had acquired title to the 1010.8 acres through the Declaration of Taking and after the initiation of the condemnation proceedings, begun earlier and prior to the issuance of the final judgment on these proceedings in November 1948, the State of Delaware ceded these very same lands to the Federal government.

A postscript to this history of conveyances happened in 1962, when the Federal government announced plans to release a large part of its holdings on the Cape and declare certain lands "excess property." Consequently, over the next several years, much of the land of the now defunct Fort Miles returned to the possession of the State of

---

[82] 18 *Laws of Delaware* 549 (1889). Wilson Report, Exhibit DY.

[83] 42 *Laws of Delaware* 3 (1939). Wilson Report, Exhibit EA. It is interesting to note that the laying out of the Quarantine Reservation overlapped a large portion of the United States Fort Reservation.

[84] Wilson Report, Part 5, 124.

[85] 40 *Laws of Delaware* 11 (1935). Wilson Report, Exhibit EM.

Delaware, which made plans for the establishment of Cape Henlopen State Park. [86]

The Pepper Survey of 1926 Defines the Public Lands

It is perhaps a reasonable assumption that the reader has been somewhat perplexed as to the physical boundary lines of the public lands. The Shankland Survey of 1736 clearly defines the extent of the Great and Beach Marshes northwest of the town. But this still leaves the question of what is the actual extent of "all public and vacant lands contiguous to but outside the corporate limits of said town and fronting on the bay between the point of Cape Henlopen on the South and Veasey's Inlet on the north?" [87] This, of course, would ultimately delimit what has historically been set aside and considered as the public commons.

In the act of 1907, the General Assembly extended the boundary of Lewes to include all of Cape Henlopen to the northwest as far as the Broadkill Creek. This would include that area known as Veasey's Inlet which was cut between Lewes Creek (also referred to in colonial times as Lewes River) and the bay, and where the Broadkill and Lewes Creek meet. (Remember, what historically was called "Lewes Creek" or "Lewes River" is now the Lewes and Rehoboth Canal.)

Veasey's Inlet was in use prior to the completion of the Roosevelt Inlet in 1937 at the juncture of Canary Creek and Lewes Creek (River). There is nothing in the wording of the Act of 1907 (as well as subsequent statutes) which determines if the General Assembly intended to include the Great and Beach Marshes southwest of Lewes River and

---

[86] See Delaware State Planning Office, *A Plan for the Public Utilization of Cape Henlopen*, (Dover, 1963).

[87] It was later held that although the legislation described the geographic boundaries of the vested lands as "fronting on the Bay," etc., the judicial construction of the term "Fronting" also means adjoining. Thus "fronting" does not necessarily mean at the immediate edge of the Bay." *Opinions of the Delaware Attorney General 1969* (Opinion 69-139) "Sand Dunes Protection at Lewes," 324.

northwest of Canary Creek. Also, whether or not they are to be included in the vested lands of the town, outside of its corporate limits, cannot be said with any degree of certainty. [88] Houston Wilson found the same dilemma and drew the following analysis:

> Looking down the Cape towards its point or tip, one runs into equal difficulties in comprehending exactly what lands are intended by the statute(s). We know that the public or vacant lands referred to must be contiguous to but outside of the corporate limits of the town. We know that they must front on the Bay. We know that they extend to the point of Cape Henlopen on the south. One difficulty here is that the point of Cape Henlopen is not on the south of the corporate limits of Lewes, the traveler would have to go in a northeast direction. If the traveler went south from any point within the corporate limits of the Town of Lewes, or southeast or southwest therefrom, he would be going in the opposite direction from the point of Cape Henlopen. However, if we assume that the statute intended to mean those public or vacant lands contiguous to the corporate limits, extending from the corporate limits and fronting on the bay to the waters of the Atlantic Ocean to the east, one still has the difficulty of defining the southern boundary line of those lands. Under this theory, at first blush, one would say that they included all of the lands and marshes of Cape Henlopen. This theory does not work out in practice, however, because the Commissioners of Lewes have never claimed jurisdiction, control or

---

[88] Wilson Report, Part 4, 105.

authority over all of Cape Henlopen to the east of the corporate limits of the town. [89]

The essence of Wilson's argument is, of course, based upon a keen sense of logical deduction from known facts. Yet, what he could not take into consideration – simply because the knowledge was not available to him at the time – was the pattern of coastal geologic change that has occurred in and around Cape Henlopen over the last several hundred years. This phenomenon, based on the early research findings of Professor John C. Kraft of the University of Delaware, concerning the changing land morphology of Cape Henlopen (as discussed in Chapter 2), offers scientific evidence as to why there has been difficulty in making any exact determination of where the public lands (commons) lie.

Returning to efforts to describe the public lands, we find that on April 2, 1913, the General Assembly passed an act which established a Public Lands Commission and authorized it "to ascertain the location of the public lands of the State of Delaware and to have the same surveyed and plotted and to have general supervision over said public lands." [90] Pursuant to this provision, the Commission ordered the public lands adjoining the Atlantic seaboard from the State of Maryland to Cape Henlopen to be surveyed. The survey was finally undertaken in 1926 by Thomas B. Pepper, and subsequently filed in the office of the Recorder of Deeds in Sussex County. [91]

Apparently, when Pepper surveyed these lands, he found himself in a bit of a quandary when he reached Cape Henlopen. He no doubt

---

[89] Wilson Report, Part 4, 105-106. Cf., a description of the lands in question from physiological and other sources in the Wilson Report, Part 2, 34-37 and Exhibits G to U.

[90] 27 *Laws of Delaware* 9 (1913). Wilson Report, Exhibit EW. The Public Lands Commission was the precursor of the Delaware State Highway Department created in 1929.

[91] The plot that concerns this discussion was designated "public lands north of Rehoboth to Henlopen Light House Lands," in plot filing case No. 1. Office of the Recorder of Deeds, Georgetown, Delaware.

knew that the Commissioners of Lewes had supervision and vested control over the Cape Commons. In order to complete his work, he decided to define the northern boundary line of the public lands of the State in the following manner:

> ...by a line starting at a point along the border line of the waters of the Atlantic Ocean at the eastern-most point of the southeastern boundary line of the Henlopen Lighthouse reservation: thence in a southwesterly direction, along with the southeastern boundary line of said reservation, and as the same may be extended, to a point where the said line, if so extended, would intersect the course of Lewes River (or Creek). [92]

The Outcome: Judge Southerland's Decision in 1943

Returning to the court held before the Special Master in 1943 to resolve questions of title to the lands of Cape Henlopen that had been previously condemned by the Federal government, Judge Southerland, in issuing his opinion on the boundaries of the public lands offered a reasoned conclusion.

> Surely failure to specify a number of acres is of no consequence. The lands are identified as 'public and vacant lands' (Not public or private lands,...); as contiguous to the corporate limits; and as fronting on the Bay between Cape Henlopen and Veasey's Inlet. The error in compass direction I think of no moment. As counsel for the town correctly observe, the eastern shore line of the United States runs in a generally north-south direction; and an error of this sort is readily understood. There is no doubt about the

---

[92] Wilson Report, Part 7, 136.

actual location of either Cape Henlopen or Veasey's Inlet. [93]

Although the several acts of the General Assembly affecting the Charter of Lewes have not fixed the southern boundary of the lands under the town's jurisdiction, the line drawn in the Pepper survey had been accepted since 1926. Southerland again: "It is sufficient for the present purpose to show that an actual line, apparently acceptable to both bodies, [the Town of Lewes and the State Highway Department] has been adopted as the southerly boundary of the town jurisdiction, and all uncertainty of boundary thereby removed." [94] The Report of the Special Master included several "findings of fact" as follows:

1. Fee simple title to the lands described in the petition of the United States filed in this cause July 7, 1941, (hereinafter called 'the condemned lands') was at and immediately before the time of taking thereof by the United States vested in the State of Delaware, subject to use or trust hereinafter described.

2. All of the condemned lands were, at the time of the taking thereof, subject to a certain charitable use or trust for the benefit of the inhabitants of the Town of Lewes and County of Sussex, created by a certain proprietary grant of the Court for the County of Sussex, made at the session thereof held on January 9, 10, and 11, 1682/3.

3. Commissioners of Lewes, a municipal corporation of the State of Delaware, was at the said time of the taking of the condemned lands...vested with full exclusive authority, control and jurisdiction

---

[93] Southerland Report, 43.

[94] Ibid., 44 and 49. Southerland also concluded that "the description of the 'vested lands' is not void for uncertainty."

over said lands, as trustee or agent designated by
the State of Delaware in and

4. by virtue of the act of the General Assembly of the
State of Delaware approved May 21, 1941. [95]

Following from his "findings of fact," and based upon all evidence presented, Southerland drew several "conclusions of law."

1. The grant of the court for the County of Sussex to
Edmond Warner at a session thereof held on January
9, 10 and 11, 1682/3, created a valid charitable use
or trust in respect of the lands therein described for
the benefit of the inhabitants of the Town of Lewes
and County of Sussex.

2. The Warner Grant of a right of common for the
benefit of the inhabitants of the Town of Lewes
and County of Sussex is not a reservation from or
exception to the grant to Edmond Warner, and its
validity and effect is not to be determined by the
rules of law respecting reservations and exceptions
in deeds to real property.

3. The Warner Grant of a right of common for the
benefit of the inhabitants of the Town of Lewes
and County of Sussex is not void because for the
benefit [sic] of an indefinite or fluctuating class of
persons.

4. At and before the time of the making of the
Warner Grant, William Penn, as proprietary of
the Counties of New Castle, Kent and Sussex,

---

[95] Ibid., 51-52. Southerland listed ten additional findings of fact pertaining to several
parties holding "valid leaseholds" on the condemned lands, refuting the claim of
Sussex County to any rights on the condemned lands, and dismissing any claim
to adverse possession by any party to the condemned lands.

was seized and possessed of seigniorial rights and powers of government over the lands of the said counties.

5. The several acts of the General Assembly of the State of Delaware relating to the control and administration of the 'lands of the Cape,' were enacted in exercise of the powers of the General Assembly as *Parens Patriae,* and are valid and constitutional.

6. The act of the General Assembly of the State of Delaware approved May 21, 1941, is not violate of the provisions of Section 16 of Article II of the Constitution of the State of Delaware.

7. The description of the so-called 'vested lands' contained in the said act approved May 21, 1941, is not so vague or indefinite as to be meaningless or unenforceable. [96]

The Report of the Special Master as later adopted by the Federal District Court in the case *United States v. 1010.8 Acres*, emphasized that the Warner Grant of 1682, which created unrestricted rights of common in the people of Lewes and of Sussex County, constituted a charitable use or trust. The court further concluded that the series of legislative acts giving recognition to the Warner Grant – including the existing statute vesting jurisdiction over the Cape lands in the town commissioners – are valid and constitutional.

---

[96] Ibid., 54-55. One additional conclusion of law indicated that none of the several acts of the General Assembly had transferred any control or jurisdiction of the condemned lands to the State Highway Department.

A Final Word

The claim of a public commons is a unique claim, not just for the people of Lewes or Sussex County, but for all of us who treasure the bounties of nature. And the claim should rightly be protected by all of us—the people, or their delegated authority—for our mutual enjoyment and pleasure in a world so much threatened with the destruction of what should be recognized as a basic human responsibility.

The later history of the common or public lands was destined to be continually involved in controversy as to how the land should be used—or not used. Yet, the underlying philosophical and moral theme remains for us today and future generations. Here is a unique historical heritage of a public trust—a trust that should not be compromised by individual or personal prerogative.

EPILOGUE

The advancement of our society oftentimes has taken or unleashed a wrathful vengeance against that which has passed before—that we may think of as the progress of a previous age. The basic nature of man has perhaps not changed in millions of years. We accepted the attitude of apathy and many times stood by as actions of destruction have taken their toll on our historic and cultural fabric. If the attitude cannot be re-fashioned, and the continual actions cannot be stopped, then both the powerful and the lowly will unwittingly share the fate of a sterile society.

If we have sensed the pattern of different cultures through philosophical ideals, unique lifestyles, and what events have occurred through changing times, we will, in large measure, have a basis to build upon. The future awaits today's commitment.

To merely document historical happenings, to uncover archaeological finds, or to preserve the physical remains of our predecessors, only provides an awareness. Yet, the real challenge is the demand placed upon the present generation to harness both the spiritual and material resources to prevent a future scarred by cultural obliteration.

Almost four centuries have come and gone since those earliest Europeans arrived in the place that they called Swanendael, a land extolled "because of its excellence and fruitfulness before the very best of New Netherland." We have recounted their successes and their failures and we have momentarily re-lived their foresight and shortcomings.

Appendix 1

The Duke of York Patents
on Pilottown Road

The original land titles in Delaware are contained in what is known as the *Duke of York Record* that was first published in 1903. David Marine made a study of these records as they pertain to Lewes and published his results in 1955. What follows is the work of Marine as he wrote it. [1] The present author has not disturbed the essential content of Marine's work (that at times is awkward to read) other than to re-arrange source citations and to make clarifying notations where appropriate.

Documented data of land grants and patents on the Western shore of Delaware Bay and River prior to the English occupation in 1664 are fragmentary; and the *Duke of York Record*—a transcription of land titles and patents made from the records in New York under the direction of Thomas McKean and the authority of a law enacted by the Colonial Legislature of Delaware in 1770—is incomplete. This incompleteness may be due (1) in part to partial destruction of the transcript by the British when New Castle was captured during the Revolutionary War, and (2) to overlooked or lost records of the Colonial Governors' office in New York.

---

[1] *Archeolog* 7 (September 1955): 1-4.

In the course of some historical work [conducted under the auspices] of the Sussex Archaeological Association—particularly in connection with (1) a dike across Pagan Creek and (2) a nearby trading post possibly of the Dutch West India Company, it seemed possible that in locating the [Duke of York] patents in this area, (historically Delaware's first square mile), and studying their sales and transfers, some information might be obtained bearing on these problems. This study has established the fact that both the dike and the trading post were located on the 'West India Fort' or 'The Company's Fort' Tract. [2]

Eight Duke of York patents have been located in this area and these eight patents account for all the frontage on Pilottown Road northwest of Shipcarpenter Street. The original town site of Lewes also was probably an old Dutch grant as Robert Shankland in his official survey of the town in 1723 states that 'The land of the town was first taken up or claimed by one Dyreits Paten.'

Patent No. 1.

No permanent land mark was found from which we could positively locate a corner of any of the eight patents. Hence it seemed safest to begin with boundaries of the town of Lewes as surveyed in 1723 by Robert Shankland.[3] He stated that Front Street which parallels Lewes Creek (now the Lewes and Rehoboth Canal) extended the full width of the town from South Street (Savannah Road) on the southeast to Shipcarpenter Street on the northwest and gave its length as 80 Perches[4] or 1320 feet. Measured today with a 100 ft. steel tape by the straightest line we get 1290 ft. This seems to be a close enough check if one remembers that the street has less curves now than in Shankland's time.

---

[2] The theory of a "Dutch Trading Post" existing prior to the Swanendael settlement in 1631 has been discounted based on existing archeological and historical evidence and has been discussed in Chapter 2.

[3] *Shankland's Warrants and Surveys, 1713 – 1728*, 222.

[4] A perch or rod is an old form of measuring land and equals approximately 15 ½ feet.

Shipcarpenter Street, therefore, seemed not to have shifted much in 231 years and served as our fixed starting point. Also of importance was the statement by Shankland that a Duke of York patent to Helmanus F. Wiltback abutted on the northwest side of Shipcarpenter Street, but he does not further identify the patent. Since 'Hermanus Woolbanch' owned three of the eight Duke of York patents we are here concerned with, the question arises which one of these patents was bounded on the southeast by Shipcarpenter Street. Two of these three patents, or, their mention of other bounding lands which place them definitely farther down Lewes Creek, while one (that of July 7, 1675) makes no mention of adjoining patents or lands.[5] This patent was therefore designated No. 1 in the series, and located as adjoining Shipcarpenter Street. It has 67 perches frontage on Lewes Creek and parallel southwest lines of 320 perches each, back to Pagan Creek (Canary Creek) with a total of 134 acres. Portions of this tract remained in the Wiltbank family for three generations. This grant was previously owned by Anthony Pieters (see Patent No. 2).

Patent No. 2

Title to this patent was confirmed to Dirch Pieters, brother of Anthony, May 25, 1670, and had previously been made over to Dirch Pieters by Abraham Clementie.[6] It fronted on Lewes Creek 105 rods, Dutch measure, (a Dutch rod equals 11 ft.) and extended southwest about a mile to a kill (Pagan Creek) (most of the patents expressly state the southwest distance to be 320 perches) and was bounded on the northwest side by William Claesen's land, and on the south side by Anthony Pieters' land. Dirch Pieters assigned this patent to Hermanus Wiltbanck.[7]

---

[5] *Duke of York*, 53.

[6] Ibid., 145.

[7] Sussex County Deed Book, GN7, 291.

Patent No. 3

This patent was granted to Simon Parling (also spelled Palaing, Palling, Pawloing, Pallen) on January 24, 1675. He was elected to the office of Constable at the Horekill January 4, 1676.

This patent is not recorded in the Duke of York Record, but full details are given in a deed of sale dated November 3, 1714.[8] Here it states that Parling assigned the patent to Nathaniel Walker on September 9, 1697, who, in turn, assigned it to William Clark on June 14, 1681, etc. The land is defined as follows: Whereas there is a certain tract of land on the west side of Delaware Bay near the town of Lewes called 'New Hall', beginning at a bounded pine tree (this pine will also figure in the next patent – No. 4) and running in breadth 30 perches to a bounded red oak standing by the kill; thence, southwest 320 perches to the first bounded pine standing by the Whorekill Creek, containing and laid out for 50 acres – the which land was granted by patent, under the hand and seal of Edmund Andros, Governor of N.Y. etc, bearing date January 24, 1675, unto Simon Pawling.

It was bought at the estate sale in 1714 by Thomas Bedwell and wife, Honor, (a daughter of William Clark). William Clark served as clerk and as a Magistrate at the Horekill under both the Duke of York and William Penn.

This tract was also surveyed for 50 acres on Oct. 3, 1670, by the Maryland Colony for William Clauson (Claesen).[9] It is evident from several documents that William Klaesen owned this tract prior to the Duke of York patent to Simon Parling.

---

[8] Ibid., FG, 246-247.

[9] Skirven, P.S., Maryland Historical Magazine 25 (1930), 162. This is the only information about this citation from Marine's original work.

Patent No. 4

This Duke of York patent for 150 acres was granted to Hermanus Woolbanck, July 2, 1672, but is not recorded in the Duke of York Record. This tract was also surveyed for 150 acres by the Somerset County Land Office of the Maryland Colony (Francis Jenkins) for William Clauson (Claesen) and entered as follows: 'Rent three shillings for 150 acres, The Company's Fort surveyed October 3, 1670 for Hellmans Frederick Wilbank on Chesterfield Creek at the marked tree of William Clauson (Claesen).' [10]

The Duke of York Patent for this tract is quoted at length in the deed from Joseph Claypoole to Samuel Rowland, who came from Philadelphia and settled in Lewes in 1696, dated August 5, 1703, at the price of 50 pounds sterling as follows: 'Whereas Francis Lovelace, Governor of N.Y. etc., by his grant or patent under his hand and seal of the province bearing date ye second day of July 1672 did grant and confirm unto Hermanus Frederick Wiltbank all that piece of land at the Whorekill, (since called Lewis) in Delaware Bay, bounded on the south side with a marked pine tree next to the land of William Claesen; on the northwest next to ye land of ye heirs of Jan Jardyns, a Frenchman, containing in breadth 114 rods, each rod being 11 English feet, stretching northeast and southwest into the woods to ye hindmost kill which piece of land is called ye West India Fort to hold ye Hermanus F. Wiltbank his heirs and assigns forever and by ye said Hermanus Wiltbank these lands and patent were assigned over unto Norton Claypoole of Philadelphia, PA., in 1682.' .[11]

Norton Claypoole sold it to his brother James—a merchant of Philadelphia. It passed by will to his youngest son, Joseph.

The two important facts which locate this patent are (1) the "bounded pine tree of William Claesen" (or Clausen) is mentioned

---

[10] *Debt Book or Rent Roll For Kent and Cecil County Maryland* 2: 349.

[11] Sussex County Deed Book, C-3, 80-82.

in both the Maryland survey and the later Duke of York patent, and (2) that William Claesen's land formed the southeast boundary of the 'West India Fort' or 'The Company Fort.'

Patent No. 5

This Duke of York Patent was granted to William Tom July 7, 1675, and definitely defines the tract as containing 132 acres and formerly belonging to Peter Alrick.[12] Luke Watson obtained this tract from the estate of Wm,. Tom. He in turn sold it to Dr. Thomas Wynn of Philadelphia April 4, 1687. It passed to his son, Jonathan Wynn of Blockley Township, County of Philadelphia, who sold it to Samuel Roland.[13] Dr. Thomas Wynne died in 1692. It is bounded on the south-east by Hermanus Woolbanck's land (patent No. 4) and on the northwest by the land of Alexander Molestedy (Patent No. 6). It had a frontage of 66 perches on Lewes Creek.

An earlier confirmation dated August 3, 1668, probably is for the same tract of land, although specific metes, bounds and acreage are not given.[14] However, it does state that the land 'stretches southeast by ye land formerly belonging to ye Frenchman deceased' just as the patent (No. 4) of 1672 to Woodbank is bounded on the northwest by 'ye land of ye heirs of Jan Jardyns, a Frenchmen.' Apparently prior to the English occupation in 1664 the Frenchman's estate was included in the Dutch grant to Peter Alrick (Peter Alrick was a nephew of Jacob Alrick who died in New Amstead [Amsterdam] in 1659) which was confiscated by the English and patented to William Tom.

---

[12] *Duke of York*, 53 and 54.

[13] Sussex County Deed Book, D-4, 252.

[14] *Duke of York*, 135.

Patent No. 6.

This patent for 80 acres was granted to Alexander Molestedy dated July 7, 1675, and is bounded on the southeast by the land of William Tom (Patent No. 5) and on the northwest by the land of John Kiphaven. It has a frontage of 40 rods on Lewes Creek.[15]

Patent No. 7

This patent was confirmed to John Kiphaven January 15, 1675, and is bounded on the southeast by the land of Alexander Molestedy. The metes and bounds as given in Duke of York Record do not meet the requirements for a 60 acre tract.[16] [Moreover, a further] description of this patent gives 23 perches instead of 320 perches [that] checks with the total of 69 acres given in both transcriptions of this patent. Hence, there is an error in the metes and bounds as given in the Duke of York transcript. Also, 320 perches for breadth on the Whorekill would exceed greatly the available distance that could be allotted to the patent, while 23 perches for breadth fits in well with the available distance. John Kiphaven assigned this patent to Wm. Clark Feb. 9, 1680, and he assigned it to Capt. Nathaniel Walker on April 12, 1681.[17]

Patent No. 8

This undated patent calling for 112 acres and a frontage of 78 perches on Lewes Creek was granted to Cornelius Verhoofe.[18] It is triangular in shape. It was called 'Carpenters' Yard and was situated upon the Whorekill Creek at the mouth of the said kill.' The Verhoofe estate sold this land to William Clark in 1683 and in 1685 it became part

---

[15] Ibid., 52.
[16] Ibid., 95.
[17] Sussex County Deed Book, C-3, 209.
[18] *Duke of York*, 178.

of Jonathan Bayley's (Bailey) larger land holdings which included the 'ancient cemetery' that Bailey unsuccessfully tried to appropriate.[19]

Reference to the map will show that seven of the eight patents are roughly rectangular in shape with the northeast ends formed by the bank of Lewes Creek and the southwest ends by Pagan Creek or a branch of it. These natural boundaries made it simple enough to determine the general location of the patents, but we have not been able to locate a single specific monument or boundary except possibly Shipcarpenter Street.

The eight grants [patents], therefore, have been laid off from this starting point. They account for all the land between Shipcarpenter Street and the Great Marsh, and call for a total of 7424 ft. on Lewes Creek. Measured on Pilottown Road this would be approximately 1.14 miles, or 6019 ft. to (the) De Vries Monument and 0.26 mile, or 1405 ft., beyond and extending into the edge of the Great Marsh. The Kiphaven patent, according to these measurements, extends 118 ft. (northwest) beyond the Monument and therefore would include its site, as well as the site of the 'ancient cemetery'.

It should be pointed out that the size (the largest is 150 and the smallest is 50 acres) of these patents is far below the average for Duke of York patents in this (territory) and, together with their parallel lateral lines further suggest that they are not the first surveys of these lands, but rather that they followed lines of older surveys and grants (Dutch) made prior to the British occupation (1664). Two of the Duke of York patents (Nos. 2 and 4) use Dutch rods in describing the metes and bounds, and there is a documentary evidence that at least five of these patents (Nos. 1,2,3,4, and 5) and probably more were of Dutch origin, including the original town site of Lewes.

This view is further supported by the action taken by Richard Nicolls – first English governor after the occupation in 1664 – who

---

[19] Bailey's "ancient cemetery" or burying ground" is discussed in Chapter 7 concerning the public commons claim over the Great and Marshes.

was sent from Fort James, N.Y. on Oct. 4, 1664. He directed that all the old Dutch land grants must be reconfirmed or reviewed under the English rule, and, in addition, that Peter Alrick be allowed to continue his right to trade with the Indians from Boomties (Bombay) Hook to Cape Henlopen, which right had been granted by Alexander d'Hinojossa and Wilhelm Beeckman acting for the West India Co. in 1660. [20]

---

[20] *N.Y. Colonial Documents* 12: 454.

Appendix 2

Public Commons Documents

The following documents have been referred to in Chapter 7, The Story of the Public Commons, and appear here as key source material.

Extracts from
"An act for the Effectual Establishment and Confirmation of the Freeholders of This Province and Territories, Their Heirs and Assigns, in Their Lands and Tenements."
1700 [1]

Whereas at the first laying out and settling of lands in this province of Pennsylvania and territories thereunto belonging, many great neglects and errors have been committed, through the want of experience and care both in officers and the people, as well to the wrong of the proprietary, as the insecurity of the said people, and the great inconveniency of both: For remedy whereof, and for the safety of the said province and territories, in general, and that the inhabitants may be completely and absolutely settled, and fully secured in their rights and titles to land, and all occasions of difference and contest... may forever

---

[1] Chapter 10, a. 12 William III, A.D. 1700. Wilson Report, Exhibit. F.

hereafter be prevented and removed. Be it enacted by the Proprietary and Governor, by and with the advice and consent of the freemen of this province and territories, in General Assembly met, and by the authority of the same, That all tracts and parcels of land taken up within this province and territories, and duly seated by virtue of letters patents or warrants, obtained from Governors or lawful Commissioners, under the crown of England, before the King's grant of the Proprietary and Governor for this province (except the same was held by fraud or deceit) shall be quietly enjoyed by the actual possessors, their heirs and assigns. And that all lands and tracts of land, duly taken up by virtue of warrants obtained pursuant to purchases made and had from the proprietary and by the Proprietary to any other person (except as before excepted, and except where the same does interfere with other persons just rights and claims) shall be quietly and peaceably enjoyed by, and confirmed to the possessor (according to the said warrants) his heirs and assigns forever, and although no patent hath been granted, yet, if peaceable entry and possession hath been obtained, by warrants, or otherwise as aforesaid, and thereupon quiet possession hath been held during the space of seven years, or more, such possession, or entry as aforesaid shall give an unquestionable title to all such lands, according to the quantity they were taken up for, and shall be deemed and held good, and be confirmed by the Proprietary to the senters [sic] or possessors thereof, their heirs and assigns, forever.

And be it further enacted by the authority aforesaid, that all grants for lands from the proprietary, shall be henceforth under the Great Seal of this province and territories; which grants shall give the respective grantees an absolute title for all the lands therein to be granted or confirmed, be they more or less then laid out for, and shall never more thereafter be subject or liable to any further survey.

Proprietary warrant from Thomas Penn to Simon Kollock, Jacob Kollock and Rives Holt for certain marsh lands
June 23 1739 [2]

Whereas a certain Tract or quantity of Marsh lying on the side of the Delaware Bay between the Broad Creek and the Canary, at Pagan Creek in the County of Sussex Hath been for several years Past by some Expectation Given by our late father to the inhabitants of the Town of Lewes Deemed and taken to belong to the said Town as a Common or pasture for the said Inhabitants But no regular survey been formally made on the same yet by our Permission at the request of Simon Kollock, Jacob Kollock and Rives Holt Three of the Principal Inhabitants of the Town of Lewes aforesaid the said Marsh hath been lately surveyed and circumscribed as appears by a draught thereof new exhibited and thereupon the said Simon Kollock Jacob Kollock and Rives Holt on behalf of themselves and the other inhabitants of the said Town request that we would be pleased to Grant our Warrant in order that the Survey made on the said Marsh may be duly returned and Established these are therefore to authorize and require thee to accept and receive the Survey of the said Marsh and made Return thereof unto our Secretary's Office in Order for Confirmation to the said Simon Kollock Jacob Kollock and Rives Holt in Trust and for the use and Behoove of the Inhabitants of the Town of Lewes aforesaid and their Successors to be holden of us our heirs and successors under the yearly quit rent of one penny sterling for every acre thereof to be duly paid by the said Inhabitants for and toward the support of a school to be kept within the said Town.

---

[2] Sussex County Surveys C-1776, . 379. Wilson Report Exhibit AQ.

To Benjamin Eastburn, Surveyor General.
Caleb Rodney, Esq. v. William Russel
1797 [3]

Caveat. Aug. 18th Cont. Nov. 11th Cont. Feby 23rd 1797 Cont. April 13th Cont. on rule peremtory Trial at the Setting of the Commissioners in July Next, And now to with July 19th 1797 the parties to this Caveat appeared before the Board of Commissioners and by their attorneys laid before them their Respective Claims to the Lands in question all which being heard Examined and Maturely Considered by the Commissioners they do order Judge and determine that agreeable to the laws of the State of Delaware it is considered that the said William Russel take nothing by his said warrant, and that the said William Russel shall not be permitted to hold the Land contained in his said survey, and thereupon the Defendant prays an appeal from the Judgment and determination of the said Commissioners to the High Court of Errors and Appeals of the said State which is granted.

Petition from sixty-nine citizens of Lewes to the General Assembly
of the State of Delaware.
January 6, 1817 [4]

The Petition of the Subscribers, Citizens of Lewes, respectfully represents:that the Lands and Marshes on the North East side of Lewes Creek called Cape Henlopen." were granted to them as a Common in the year 1682 the validity of which was not questioned until after the passage of "An Act to Open and Establish a Land Office" in the year 1793. Soon after said Act was passed six or eight of the most influential men of the County, among whom were two lawyers procured Land

---

[3] Houston Wilson wrote in his Report the following: "This transcribed Caveat Docket is now on file in the Office of the Recorder of Deeds, in and for Sussex County. The author [Wilson] has made a true and exact copy of pages 249 and 250 of this transcribed Caveat Docket: which copies are hereto appended and designated as Exhibit AL." Wilson Report, Part 3, 57.

[4] The original of this document is in the Hall of Records. Wilson Report. Exhibit AN.

Warrants and laid them on said lands and Marshes, these Warrants were Caveated by the Inhabitants and decisions were had before the Board of Commissioners, the Supreme Court, and the High Court of Errors and Appeals, all of which established the validity of the Grant to the inhabitants as a common. In this Grant an indefeasible Right to the timber and food is given to the inhabitants as commoners. Notwithstanding the rights of your Petitioners has been thus established and at a considerable expense in carrying on the law suits for the protection of those rights, yet they perceive with regret a Law passed Feby. 15th, 1814, Entitled "An Act Authorizing the Court of General Sessions of the Peace and Goal delivery of the State of Delaware to appoint Trustees to take charge of and secure the rents of the land and marsh commonly called Cape Henlopen for the use of the County of Sussex" which prohibits them from the enjoyments of their rights of Common in the [aforesaid] Lands and Marshes.

Your petitioners believe that exclusive of their Constitutional rights in Common with all other citizens to the protection of their property, that the law above recited has had no beneficial effect whatsoever, while on the other hand it makes a sinecure for three Trustees, Subjects innocent individuals to the expense and trouble of carrying on Lawsuits in defense of their just rights while those quits are carried on against them at the public expense, and violates two great principles of Constitutional and natural rights by preventing people from using their rights as commoners, and by making it penal to turn out cattle to Roam over and feed on a place which has no enclosure.

Your Petitioners therefore pray your Honors to Repeal the Act above recited that was passed Feby. 15th, 1814.

Three letters concerning the grant to Edmond Warner addressed to Governor John Hunn from James C. Beebe
1901 [5]

(1) November 30, 1901

Hon. Sir. According to 82d Chap. (620, 621, 622, 624 pages) Revised Code of Delaware, I hereby inform you that the lands of the Cape Commonly called Cape Henlopen was granted to Edmond Warner in 1682; And that Said Edmond Warner died without any Known heirs or Kindred to Claim the Land, hence it Escheats to the State of Delaware, Subject to the privilege granted to any or all the inhabitants of Sussex County. The timber, feed, of said land and Marshes thereunto belonging be and forever hereafter lye in Common for the inhabitants of Lewes and Sussex County &c. The Beach is not Feed or timber or Marshes, therefore it escheats to the State, and should be done at the earliest possible moment, as the Beach is now in demand and no one has an equitable right to Sell or Convey it. Please inform the Escheater of Sussex County, as I stand ready to procure the necessary evidence to substantiate the title of the State to the Same.

(2) December 4, 1901

Hon. Sir. I hereby inform you this fourth day of December, A.D. 1901, that the Lands of the Cape Commonly Called Cape Henlopen was Granted to Edmond Warner in 1682, and that said Edmond Warner died interstate without any known heirs or kindred to claim the Land hence it Escheats to the State of Delaware, subject to the privileges (timber feed and gather Berries) granted to any or all the Inhabitants of Sussex County, and as the said Land has been buffeted about by the legislature (and the State never did own a foot of it) it has been under trustees appointed by the Levy Court and now under the Commissioners of Lewes neither of which had an equitable right to said land, and cannot Sell it or give a title to it, and as said Land is

---

[5] Executive Correspondence Files, Hall of Records. Wilson Report, Part 3, 62-65.

now in demand provided a good Fee Simple Deed could be given for it. Therefore I stand ready to procure evidence to Substantiate the title of the State to the Same, in accordance to law.

(3) December 9, 1901

Hon. Sir. Hoping that the necessity of the case will be sufficient apology of me again intruding on your time and patience; I received yours of the 5t inst. Wherein you state that the attention of the Legislature will be called to the Cape Henlopen Matter; I wish to state that I think the Legislature has done all it possibly can do in the Case, when it passed the Law for Escheats, authorizing the Governor to appoint an escheated in each County, therefore I do most respectfully ask of you to appoint Charles H. Maull of Lewes Delaware as Escheater for Sussex County; believing that Mr. Maull has the ability and would honestly and truly attend to the Matter of Escheating Cape Henlopen to the State of Delaware; And the Governor be thus able to Grant the said Lands to the purchasers thereof, To hold to him or them their heirs and assigns forever, as the Said Law of Escheats directs, hoping this may receive your most favorable Consideration.

Excerpts from the petition signed by fifty-eight citizens of Lewes to the General Assembly of the State of Delaware seeking a Charter of Incorporation for the Town of Lewes.
January 11, 1810[6]

Your Petitioners further represent that whereas a large quantity of marsh lying to the North West of Lewes called the Great Marsh, and formerly granted to the town for the purpose of erecting and maintaining a school, and also the land and marsh on the North East of Lewes Creek called the Cape all which was granted to the aforesaid town as a common are now and have ever been useless to the great majority of its citizens, one part of the said marsh and land affords a considerable

---

[6] Wilson Report, Exhibit BP.

degree of profit to a few individuals who live in its vicinity while the other exposes a bait that may entrap the unwary & every induce the penurious, in attempting to engross to themselves every advantage that can possibly be derived from the land thus appropriated, & to infringe the Laws of the State. To Prevent for the future so partial an enjoyment of a general benefit which under the present existing circumstances will ever be the result, to remove every the slightest inducement to violate the Law, & especially to extend, encourage and promote the sciences the firm and durable basis of every free government, Your Petitioners deem it prudent & a duty which they owe to themselves and to posterity to pray your honors to invest in the commissioners of the Town (when appointed) with authority to dispose of the property above specified and all vacant property within the bounds of Lewes and considered as belonging to the town in such manner as shall best conduce to the establishing a fund to defray the expense of erecting & supporting in the town of Lewes an academy in which may be taught the various branches of useful literature and of such other general improvement as the commissioners shall deem advantageous to the town.

*The petition from forty-four citizens of Sussex County
in reply to the petition from the citizens of Lewes
c. 1810*[7]

The petition of sundry inhabitants of Sussex County respectively showed that from a variety of sources they have been informed at a petition of the inhabitants of the Town of Lewes has been presented to the honorable body of the Legislature containing requests derogatory to the rights of the citizens of the State and County invading the private privileges of the inhabitants of the Town of Lewes - in its immediate consequence abridging the liberty of the Citizens and tending to deprive the poorer Class of these useful and necessary immunities claimed by grant and exercised from the first settlements of that party

---

[7] Wilson Report, Exhibit BQ

of the County. Not to oppose a measure so pretentious of inconvenience and injury by every legal and honorable method we should deem a dereliction of that duty we owe to ourselves to unborn ages and to humanity.

That your Petitioners, convinced from Experience, the best guide in human Transactions, view an incorporation of the Town of Lewes as an Omen of all the Inconveniences that will arise from an abridgement of that liberty the Citizens have heretofore enjoyed and all the evils that will flow from individual property being rendered less secure by a Legislative Authority being turned from its proper channel and left in the hands of Commissioners as Authority that may possibly become the Engine of injustice and Oppression.

And your Petitioners further Represent that it is with no small degree of regret and astonishment they look upon that part of the Petition which contains a prayer to your honors requesting that you may by Legislative act vest in the commissioners a Power to dispose of the Great Marsh and of the Land and Marsh called the Cape and all vacant property within the bounds of Lewes. This grasping request amounts to a demand that the Legislative body of this State may infringe whose contracts that exist between the Proprietary and the Original Grantees that your Honors may invade the almost immemorial rights of your Petitioners. And as if poverty was not in itself sufficiently distressing deprive the poorest inhabitants of the Town of one rightful source of support. It is a notorious fact scarcely disputable that the Great Marsh and Cape was granted by a Proprietary Warrant for the express use of the said Town and County as a common of pasturage. This grant invested the Citizens with a complete and indefeasible title that cannot consistently with the Constitution be divested or suffer any modification unless the consent of a majority of the inhabitants of the County is first obtained nor can the vacant property situate within the limits of the Town of Lewes be regulated in many manner so as to become more generally useful. A fortuitous and happy concurrence of circumstances connected with a few salutary laws have rendered it of general utility and the most politic regulations that effect a change could not produce the smallest benefit to the Town collectively without sacrificing the Property and Ease of a number of our most respectable and honest citizens. Actuated by these impressions and guided by the Dictates of fellow feelings, the impulse of which it is honorable to obey, Your Petitioners pray not without the strongest reasons that Justice, Policy and Humanity can afford that the request contained in the above named petition may be rejected in extense with the manly intelligence that has ever marked the course of this Legislative body.

The following "Memorial" was signed by twenty-one citizens of Lewes in reply to the statement of the citizens of Sussex County
c 1810 [8]

That your memorialists perceive with regret that a number of the inhabitants of Lewes, and the County of Sussex, are signing remonstrances against the enacting of a Law for incorporating commissioners for the Town of Lewes but as we are well informed that the opposition is almost entirely excited either by pernicious individuals from the mercenary interested views, or by others who are misinformed as to facts, and therefore join the opposition, your memorialists deem it their duty to state explicitly some of the material circumstances which have led to the opposition.

1st. From South Street to the lower end of Pilot Town along the edge of the Bank there are twenty four houses erected. The owners of eight of them have petitioned in favor of Incorporating the Town - the owners of Nine of them have signed the remonstrances against it, the remainder of the houses are owned by women non-residents and Negroes.

2d. The Marsh to the North West of the Town although granted to the Inhabitants of the Town of Lewes specifically for a school is nevertheless claimed by a number [of people] as having a right of com-

---

[8] Wilson Report, Exhibit BR.

mon therein this has induced many to sign the remonstrances some of whom have declared that if this marsh was left out of the Act, they would sign the Petition for Incorporation.

3d. There are others who keep teams and follow hauling of wood from off the Cape, for sale, and some who cut the timber for the purpose of making salt, together with a few who have part of the public grounds enclosed, nearly all of whom join in the opposition.

4th. It has been represented to the People of the county adjacent to Lewes that it was the intention of the petitioners to debar them from the privilege of pasturing their cattle on the Cape, this together with the erroneous impression that the Great Marsh was granted for a common we believe is the entire cause of their having signed the remonstrance.

It will be perceived that the petitioners in favor of incorporating the Town are residents therein, many others might have been obtained from the adjacent County but that it was deemed improper for such to interfere in the internal regulation of the place.

Your Memorialists further state that notwithstanding the opposition that has been made the petitions in favor of the incorporation are signed by a majority of the inhabitants residing within the limits of the Town, and who possess more that two thirds of the property, on the other hand if we take off from those who reside in the town and even own houses that stand on Public ground, those who are Trespassers on the Cape, together with such as have acted from an erroneous opinion with regard to the Great Marsh, it is believed there would not be a dozen names left thereon, and nearly all of the few left, are such as have no sentiment of their own on the subject, and have only signed at the instance of the others. Your memorialists further create serious apprehensions that if measures conductive to their security are not speedily entered into the Marshes on the Cape will soon be overflowed with sand, and the Creek so choked up, as to impede the navigation thereof, these effects it is believed are now in part and soon will be entirely produced bye the Injurious manner of cutting the timber, those persons before mentioned who cut and haul of so much of the timber take that which is nearest the Sand Hills which gives room for the sand to advance while from experience it is proven that if the timber is suffered to remain on the hills it holds the sand together.

Your memorialists therefore hope that the evils suffered by the Inhabitants of Lewes together with the advantages resulting from good regulations & the establishing of a seminary of learning will be deemed by the Honorable Legislature sufficient consideration for the enacting the law prayed for by the petitioners.

Excerpts from an Act to Improve the Navigation of Lewes Creek, to Survey and Regulate the Streets of the Town of Lewes, and for Other Purposes February 2, 1818 [9]

Section 4. And be it enacted, That it shall be the duty of the trustees of the town of Lewes, and they are hereby invested with full and ample powers therefore, to cause all the streets lanes and alleys and other public lands within the said town to be opened and repaired, as they may judge necessary, except where buildings are erected thereon, and in that case to levy a ground rent, which shall not exceed one fourth part of the sum that the buildings and ground so occupied would usually rent for, which said rents, together with such voluntary donations as can be obtained, shall be exclusively appropriated towards cleaning out and deepening the channel of Lewes Creek and in such works as may be useful to prevent injury and obstructions to the said channel by the drifting of sand therein from the cape.

Section 9. And be it enacted, That the said town of Lewes shall begin at the north corner of Robert West's land, where it intersects the line of William Russel's land on the road or street leading to Pilot town, thence running in a southwest direction parallel with Ship-Carpenter's street to Canary Creek or branch, thence up Canary Creek to a place two hundred feet higher up said branch than South street, thence in

---

[9] 5 *Laws of Delaware* 309 (1818). Wilson Report, Exhibit BS.

a north east direction parallel with South street keeping two hundred feet distance to a place where a north west course from the intersection of the road leading from Lewes to Rehoboth with the road leading to William Wolfe's will intersect with this line, thence northwest across the Rehoboth road aforesaid and two hundred feet up the road leading to William Wolfe's, then in a northeast direction keeping two hundred feet distance from said Rehoboth road until it intersects with a line drawn parallel with South Street and one quarter of a mile southeasterly of the same, thence with said line northeasterly across Lewes creek to the edge of the cape, then along the edge of the cape until it intersects a northeast line from the first boundary, thence running across Lewes creek southwesterly home to the place of beginning.

Excerpts from an Act to Incorporate the Town of Lewes
and for Other Purposes
March 2, 1871 [10]

Section 3. That the limits and bounds of Lewes shall be as follows: Commencing at the mouth of Canary Creek, thence up Canary Creek and Lenter's Branch to the road leading from Paynter's Mill to Shepard P. Houston's; thence around said road to the road leading from Lewes to Rehoboth; thence down said road to Wolfe's lane; thence down said lane to Edward Burton's farm; thence down the Gills' neck road to the road leading to Restore B. Lamb's farm, including said roads; thence in a northeasterly course parallel with South Street to the low water mark on the Delaware Bay shore; thence in a northwesterly direction along said bay shore to a place northeast of the mouth of Canary Creek; thence in a southwesterly direction across the beach to the mouth of the said Canary Creek and the place of beginning.

Section 9. And be it further enacted as aforesaid, That all the public and vacant lands lying within the corporate limits of the said town shall, from and after the passing of this act, be vested in the Town

---

[10] 14 *Laws of Delaware* 126 (1871). Wilson Report, Exhibit BX.

of Lewes, and the commissioners of said town shall have jurisdiction over the same, and are hereby authorized to lease (to persons who will improve or agree to improve the same), such portions of said lands upon such time and terms as they may deem proper for the interest and benefit of said town; and if hereafter any person or persons shall, without the permission and consent of the commissioners of said town, build upon or enclose any of the said public lands, he or they shall forfeit such improvements or buildings to the said town; and the said commissioners may assess a ground rent on persons having buildings now erected on any of the public lands which shall not exceed two dollars on the one hundred dollars of the assessed value of said buildings, and may assess any person or persons having enclosed or claiming the use or privilege of any of the said public grounds a tax not exceeding six per cent of the assessed value of said lot or lots so enclosed or claimed. The said Commissioners of the Town of Lewes are hereby invested with full and exclusive authority and control over the Great and Beach Marshes, Cape and Cape Marshes, near Lewes, and may sell and dispose of the grass and hay thereof in the month of July, in each and every year, at public sale, giving notice by advertisements, posted in three of the most public places in Lewes and Rehoboth hundred ten days before the day of sale, to the highest bidder or bidders for the same; the notices shall specify the place when and there the grass or hay will be sold; and are further authorized to sell the wood and timber on the Cape and Cape Marshes at any time that it may be necessary or desired to any improvement made in or near said town by and with the concurrence of a majority of said commissioners; and the proceeds arising from the sale of the grass, hay, wood and timber shall be paid over to the treasurer of the town, to be applied by the said commissioners to such improvements of the Town of Lewes as they may deem proper. If any person or persons, without first obtaining permission from the commissioners, shall fall, cut, cart or convey any green timber or wood, or any timber on or from said Cape for any private use whatsoever, except wood cut from dead timber for fuel, he or they shall forfeit and pay any sum not exceeding fifty dollars, with costs, to be recovered by the commissioners, for the use of the town, in the same manner as debts of that amount are recoverable; or the said commissioners may seize any timber or wood so cut from any person or persons so offending, and may dispose of the same to the highest bidder for the use of said town, and may pass any rules, regulations and ordinances regarding the cutting said timber they may deem proper for the interest of said town: Provided that nothing in this section or act shall authorize the said commissioners to pass any ordinance to prevent any citizen of said Town of Lewes or State of Delaware from fishing along said Delaware Bay shore, or from grazing cattle on said Cape or Beach or Cape Marshes.

Bibliography of Works Cited

The following includes all of the principal works cited in the text, including primary and secondary source material. Individual author bibliographic entries have not been made for many original publications by historic figures previously cited. For example, excerpts from de Vries' Journal, *Korte Historiael Ende Journaels Aenteyckeninge, 1630-1633, 1643* have been translated over the years by G. Troost (1841), Henry C. Murphy (1857), A.J.F. Van Laer (1908), and H.T. Colenbrander (1911), each of which is cited here.

Court cases, various deed records, land warrants, survey documentation, *Laws of Delaware*, and other official records referenced throughout the text, have been omitted from the following listing since complete citations are provided in the appropriate footnotes.

Albertson, B.S., Jr. *Picturesque and Historic Lewes, Delaware* (Milford, 1929).

American Archives, 4th Ser. (1846).

Beach, John W. *The Cape Henlopen Lighthouse* (Henlopen Publishing Co.: Dover, 1970).

Bennett, George Fletcher. *Early Architecture of Delaware* (New York: Historical Press, Inc., 1932).

_____. Interview with author May 23, 1969.

Beverly, Robert. *The History of Virginia* (reprinted from the London Edition of 1722 in 1855).

Blaker, Margaret C. "Pottery Types from the Townsend Site; Lewes, Delaware," *Eastern States Archaeological Federation Bulletin* No. 9 (July 1950).

Bonine, Chesleigh A. "Archaeological Investigation of the Dutch 'Swanendael' Settlement Under DeVries, 1631-1632," *The Archeolog, The Sussex Society of Archeology and History* 8 (December 1956).

_____. "The South Bastion of the DeVries Palisade of 1631," *The Archeolog,*

The Sussex Society of Archeology and History 16 (1964).

Boyd, John. *Delaware State Directory* (Wilmington, 1859-1860).

Britton, D.G. *The Lenape and Their Legends* (1885).

Brodhead, J. Romeyn. *History of the State of New York* (New York, 1874).

Byron, Gilbert. "The Challenge of the 'de Braak'" *Delaware Today* 8 (August-September 1969).

Chandler, Alfred N. *Land Title Origins* (New York: Robert Schalkenback Foundation, 1945).

Chapelle, Howard I. and M.E.S. Laws. "H.M.S. deBraak: 'The Stories of a Treasure Ship'" *The Smithsonian Journal of History* 5 (Winter 1967-1968).

Clark, William Bell. "The Battle in the Delaware," *Year Book* (New Jersey Society of Pennsylvania, 1930).

_____.ed., *Naval Documents of the American Revolution* 5 vols. (Washington, D.C.: U.S. Government Printing Office, 1960-1969).

Cohen, William J. and George Nocito. *"The Changing Lewes and Rehoboth Canal,"* *Delaware Conservationist* 21 (Summer 1977).

Colenbrander, H.T., ed. [de Vries Journal] *Korte Historiael ende Journaels Aenteyckeninge* ('s-Gravenhage, 1911).

Condon, Thomas J. *New York Beginnings: The Commercial Origins of New Netherland* (New York: New York University Press, 1968).

Connor, William H. and Leon de Valinger, Jr. *Delaware's Role in World War II,* 2 vols. (Dover: Public Archives Commission, 1955).

Crozier, Archibald. "The Nanticokes of the Delmarva Peninsula," *Bulletin, The The Archeolog, The Sussex Society of Archeology and Historical Society of Delaware* 1 (October 1934).

Cullen, Virginia. *History of Lewis, Delaware* (Lewis: Colonel David Hall Chapter, Daughters of the American Revolution, 1956).

Delaware State Planning Office. *A Plan for the Public Utilization of Cape Henlopen* (Dover, 1963).

_____. *Information Supplement To A Plan for the Public Utilization of Cape Henlopen* (Dover, 1963).

Denton, Daniel. "A Brief Description of New York" [1670], in William Gowan *Bibliotheca Americana* (New York, 1845).

de Valinger, Leon, Jr. "Indian Land Sales in Delaware," *Bulletin, The , The Archeolog, The Sussex Society of Archeology and Historical Society of Delaware* 3 (February, 1940).

_____."The Burning of the Whorekill, 1673," *Pa. Magazine,* 74 (October 1950).

Dunlap, A.R. "A Bibliographical Discussion of the Indian Language of the Delmarva Peninsula," *Bulletin, The Archeolog, The Sussex Society of Archeology and Historical* 4 (January 1942).

_____. *Dutch and Swedish Place-Names in Delaware* (Newark: University of Delaware Press, 1956).

Dunlap, A.R. and C.A. Weslager. *Indian Place-names in Delaware* (Wilmington:

The Archaeological Society of Delaware, 1950).

_____. "Dutch and Swedish Land Records Relating to Delaware," *Delaware History* 6 (March 1954).

_____. "Toponymy of the Delaware Valley as Revealed by an Early

Seventeenth-Century Dutch Map," *Bulletin, The Archaeological Society of*

New Jersey Nos. 15-16 (November 1958).

Eberlein, Harold Donald and Cortlandt V.D. Hubbard. *Historic Houses and*

Buildings of Delaware (Dover: Public Archives Commission, 1963).

Evans, William and Thomas Evans, eds. "Memoirs of the Life of William Penn," *The Friends Library* 12 Vols. (Philadelphia, 1841).

Fernow, B., ed. *Documents Relating to the Colonial History of the State of New York,* Vol. 12 (Albany, 1877).

Fox, J. [Rijksarchivaris, the Hague]. Personal communication to the author, June 29, 1970.

Gipson, Lawrence Henry. *Lewis Evans* (Philadelphia: The Historical Society of Pennsylvania, 1939).

Grubb, Ignatius C. "The Colonial and State Judiciary of Delaware," *Historical and Biographical Papers, Historical Society of Delaware* *17* (1897).

Hancock, Harold B. "A Calendar of English Microfilms Relating to Delaware and Delawareans," TMs (typewritten manuscript, no date) on file in the Morris Library, University of Delaware.

_____. *The Delaware Loyalists* (Wilmington: The Historical Society of Delaware, 1940).

Harder, Leland. "Plockhoy and His Settlement at Zwaanendael," *Delaware History* 3 (March 1949).

Harder, Leland and Marvin Harder. *Plockhoy from Zurik-zee*, (Newton: Mennonite Historical Series, 1952).

Hart, Simon. *The Prehistory of the New Netherland Company: Amsterdam Notorial Records of the First Dutch Voyages to the Hudson* (Amsterdam: City of Amsterdam Press, 1959).

Hazard, Samuel. *Annals of Pennsylvania From the Discovery of the Delaware 1609-1682* (Philadelphia, 1850).

Heckewelder, John. *An Account of the History, Manners, etc.*, Historical Society of Pennsylvania Memoirs (Philadelphia 1876).

Higgins, Anthony. "The Swamp Where They Mined Cypress," *The Baltimore Sun*, April 1, 1932.

Houston, John W. "Address on the History of Boundaries of the State of Delaware," *Historical and Biographical Papers, Historical Society of Delaware* 2 (1879).

Hugg, David S. "How Many Survived the 1631 Lewes Massacre?" *Delaware Today* (June-July, 1963).

Jameson, J. Franklin. *Narratives of New Netherland 1609 – 1664* (New York: Charles Scribner's Sons, 1909)

Johnson, Amandus. *The Swedish Settlements on the Delaware*, 2 vols. (New York, 1911)

Jordan, Francis. "Remains of an Aboriginal Encampment at Rehoboth, Delaware" (1866).

_____. "Aboriginal Fishing Stations on the Coast of the Middle Atlantic States" (1906).

Kensman, F.J. and George Gray. "Landing of the deVries Colony at Lewes, Delaware," *Historical and Biographical Papers, Historical Society of Delaware* 54 (1909).

Kingsburg, Susan Myra. *The Records of the Virginia Company of London*, 2 vols. (Washington, D.C., 1906)

Kraft, John C. *A Guide to the Geology of Delaware's Coastal Environment* (Newark: University of Delaware, 1971).

_____."Sedimentary Facies Patterns and Geologic History of Holocene Marine Transgression," *Geological Society of America Bulletin* 82 (August 1971).

Leidy, Joseph. "Report on Kitchen Middens at Cape Henlopen," Academy of Natural Sciences (1866).

Leupe, P.A. *Inventaris der Verzameling Kaarten berustende in het Ryks Archief* ('s Gravenhage, 1867).

Lewis, William D. "University of Delaware: Ancestors, Friends, Neighbors," *Delaware Notes* 34 (University of Delaware, 1961).

Lossing, Benson J. *The Pictorial Field Book of the War of 1812* (New York, 1869).

Lunt, Dudley. *The Bounds of Delaware* (Wilmington: Star Publishing Company, 1947).

_____. *Tales of the Delaware Bench and Bar* (Newark: University of Delaware Press, 1963)

Marine, David. "The Woolbank (Wiltbank) Grant and the Russell Site," *The Archeolog, The Sussex Society of Archeology and History* 4 (July 1951).

_____. "Examination of the Pagan Creek Dike," *The Archeolog, The Sussex Society of Archeology and History* 7 (June 1955).

_____. "The Duke of York Patents on Pilottown Road," *The Archeolog, The Sussex Society of Archeology and History* 7 (September 1955).

_____. "Report on the Russell Site," *The Archeolog, The Sussex Society of Archeology and History* 9 (May 1967).

Marine, David, et al. "Preliminary Report on a Shell Deposit in the Wolfe's Neck Archaeological Complex," *The Archeolog, The Sussex Society of Archeology and History* 17 (1965).

_____, S. Bryn, R.R. Bell. "Further Work on a Shell Deposit in the Wolfe's Neck Archaeology Complex (7-S-D10)," *The Archeolog, The Sussex Society of Archeology and History* 18 (1966).

Marine, William M. "The Bombardment of Lewes by the British," *Historical and Biographical Papers, Historical Society of Delaware* 33 (1901).

Marvil, James E. *Pilots of the Bay and River Delaware*, (Laurel: The Sussex Press, 1965).

_____. *Sailing Rams: A History of Sailing Ships Built in and Near Sussex County, Delaware* 2nd ed. (Lewes: The Sussex Press, 1974).

_____, ed. *A Pictorial History of Lewes, Delaware 1609-1985* (Lewes, Del.: Lewes Historical Society, 1985).

Marvine, William M. "Pirates and Privateers in the Delaware Bay and River," *The Pennsylvania Magazine of History and Biography* 32 (1908).

McCauley, William H. "Junction and Breakwater Railroad Primarily a Sussex County Project," *The Archeolog, The Sussex Society of Archeology and History* 2 (July 1959).

Munroe, John A. *Federalist Delaware*, (New Brunswick: Rutgers University Press, 1954).

_____. *The University of Delaware: A History* (Newark: University of Delaware, 1986).

Mayre, William B. "Indian Paths of the Del-Mar-Va Peninsula," *Bulletin, The The Archeolog, The Sussex Society of Archeology and History* 2, Nos. 3-6 (March 1936 through June, 1938).

Murphy, Henry C. ed. [de Vries Journal] *Korte Historiael ende Journaels Aenteyckeninge, Collections of the New York Historical Society*, sec. ser. 3 (1857).

Mustard, Virginia L. "Lewes Schools" and "The Genesis of Education in Lewes" *Notebooks* deposited in the Hall of Records, Division of Archives and Cultural Affairs, Department of State, Dover, Delaware.

Myers, A.C., ed. *Narratives of Early Pennsylvania, West New Jersey and Delaware, 1630-1707* (New York, 1909).

Neill, Edward D. "Matthew Wilson, D.D. of Lewes, Delaware," *The Pennsylvania Magazine of History and Biography* 8 (1884).

Newcomb, William W. Jr. "The Culture and Acculturation of the Delaware Indians," *Anthropological Papers* No. 10 (Ann Arbor: University of Michigan, 1956).

Nissenson, S.G. *The Patroon's System* (New York: Columbia University Press, 1937).

Nocito, George. *The Future of the Past.* Proceedings of a Symposium sponsored by the Lewes Historical Society, May 28, 1975.

O'Callaghan, E.B. *History of New Netherland Or New York Under the Dutch*, 2 Vols. (New York, 1855).

_____. *Documents Relative to the Colonial History of the State of New York,* vols. 1 and 2 (Albany, 1856).

Omwake, H. Geiger. "For the Record," *The Archeolog, The Sussex Society of Archeology and History* 1 (September 1948).

_____. "Preliminary Comments on the Ritter Site near Lewes, Delaware," *The Archeolog, The Sussex Society of Archeology and History* 4 (July 1951).

_____. "A Report of the Archaeological Investigation of the Ritter Site #2 Near Lewes, Delaware," *Bulletin, The Archeolog, The Sussex Society of Archeology and History* 6 (April 1954).

_____. "A Report on the Miller-Toms Site, Lewes, Delaware," *The Archeolog, The Sussex Society of Archeology and History* 6 (June 1954).

_____. "A Report of the Excavations at the Ritter Site #2 near Lewes, Delaware," *The Archeolog, The Sussex Society of Archeology and History* 6 (December 1954).

_____. "Did the Indians Construct the Dike Across Canary Creek and a Causeway Over One of Its Branches?" *Bulletin, The Archeological Society of Delaware* 9 (March 1958).

_____. "The Lighthouse Site, 7-S-D22, Cape Henlopen, Lewes, Delaware," *Bulletin, The Archeological Society of Delaware* 4 new ser. (Spring 1965).

Omwake, H. Geiger and T.D. Stewart, eds. "The Townsend Site Near Lewes, Delaware," *The Archeolog, The Sussex Society of Archeology and History* 15 (1963).

"Papers Relating to the Provincial Affairs of Pennsylvania," *Pennsylvania Archives* 2nd ser. (1878).

Parr, Charles McKew. *The Voyages of David DeVries* (New York: Thomas Y. Crowell Company, 1969).

Peets, O.H. ed. "Aboriginal Evidence from the Grounds of the Lewes School*," The Archeolog, The Sussex Society of Archeology and History* 3 (May 1951).

_____. "The Caldron," *The Archeolog, The Sussex Society of Archeology and History* 3 (May 1951).

_____. "Examination and Report," *The Archeolog, The Sussex Society of Archeology and History* 3 (November 1951).

_____. "DeVries and the Old Cemetery in Pilot Town," *The Archeolog, The Sussex Society of Archeology and History* 4 (February 1952).

_____,ed. "The Derrickson Site 'Worked Conchs,'" *The Archeolog, The Sussex Society of Archeology and History* 4 (February1952).

_____. "How Was the Stockade Built?" *The Archeolog, The Sussex Society of Archeology and History* 4 (November 1952).

_____. "Site 7-S-D10 Should Be Restudied," *The Archeolog, The Sussex Society of Archeology and History* 13 (October 1961).

Potter, Helene C. "Facts vs. Fiction," *The Archeolog, The Sussex Society of Archeology and History* 4 (November 1952), unpaged.

Powell, Walter A. *A History of Delaware* (Boston: The Christopher Publishing House, 1928).

_____."Fight of a Century Between the Penns and the Calverts Over the 'Three Lower Counties on Delaware'" TMs (typewritten manuscript, 1932).

"Proceedings of the Council of Maryland 1667-1687/8," *Archives of Maryland* 5 (1887).

Public Archives Commission. *Delaware Archives* 5 Vols. (Wilmington, 1919).

_____. *Governor's Register State of Delaware* (Dover, 1926).

Pusey, Pennock. "History of Lewes, Delaware," *Historical and Biographical Papers, Historical Society of Delaware* 38 (1903).

Reps, John W. *The Making of Urban America: A History of City Planning in the United States* (Princeton: Princeton University Press, 1965).

Rodney, Richard, S. "The End of the Penns' Claim to Delaware," *The Pennsylvania Magazine of History and Biography* 61 (April 1937).

Ryden, George H. "The Relation of the Newark Academy of Delaware to the Presbyterian Church and to Higher Education in the American Colonies," *Delaware Notes* 9th ser. (University of Delaware, 1935).

Sabine, George H. *A History of Political Theory* (New York: Holt, Rinehart, and Winston, 1962),

Salwen, Bert. "Archaeological Survey of the Hercules Powder Company Properties Near Lewes, Delaware," *Bulletin, The Archeological Society of Delaware* 4 new ser. (Spring 1965).

Scharf, J. Thomas. *History of Delaware, 1609-1888,* 2 vols. (Philadelphia, 1888).

Schenk, W. *The Concern for Social Justice in the Puritan Revolution* (New York: Longman's, Green & Co., 1948).

Schomette, Donald G. *Hunt for H.M.S. Debraak: Legend and Legacy* (Durham: Carolina Academic Press, 1993).

Semmes, Raphael. *Captains and Mariners of Early Maryland* (Baltimore: Johns Hopkins University Press, 1937).

Snow, Edward Rowe, *Famous Lighthouses of America* (New York: Dodd, Mead & Company, 1955).

Spears, John R. "Sand-waves at Cape Henlopen and Hatteras," *Scribners Magazine* (October 1890).

Speck, Frank G. "Indians of the Eastern Shore of Maryland," (Baltimore: Eastern Shore Society of Baltimore City, 1922).

Stith, William. *History of the First Discovery and Settlement of Virginia* (1747).

Stokes, I.P.N. *The Iconography of Manhattan Island* 6 vols. (New York: R.H. Dodd, 1915-1928).

Sweeney, Jeremiah, "Early Delaware Land Grants, Plantations & Families," TMs [typewritten manuscript, Farnhurst, Del.: 1958].

"The Calvert Papers" no. 2 (Selections from Correspondence), *The Maryland Historical Society: Fund Publications* (1894).

Thomas, Ronald, A. Personal communication to the author September 30, 1969.

_____. Personal communication to the author October 22, 1970.

Troost, G. ed. [de Vries Journal] *Korte Historiael ende Journaels Aenteyckeninge, Collections of the New York Historical Society*, sec. ser. vol. 1 (1841).

Turner, C.H.B. *Some Records of Sussex County, Delaware* (Philadelphia, 1909).

_____. *Rodney's Dairy and Other Delaware Records* (Philadelphia, 1911).

Tyler, David B. "The Cape Henlopen Lighthouse," *Estuarine Bulletin* 2 (University of Delaware, August 1956)

Van Laer, A.J.F., ed. *Van Renneslaer Bowier Manuscripts* (Albany, 1908).

Vincent, Francis. *A History of the State of Delaware* (Philadelphia, 1870).

Wabeke, Bertus Harry. *Dutch Emigration to North America 1624-1860* (New York: The Netherlands Information Bureau, 1944).

Wainwright, Nicholas B. "The Missing Evidence: Penn v. Baltimore," *Pennsylvania Magazine of History and Biography* 80 (April 1956).

Ward, Christopher L. *The Delaware Continentals, 1776-1783* (Wilmington: The Historical Society of Delaware, 1941),

Weslager, C.A. "An Aboriginal Shell Heap Near Lewes, Delaware," *Bulletin, The Archeological Society of Delaware* 3 (October 1939).

_____. "Indian Tribes of the Delmarva Peninsula," *Bulletin, The Archeological Society of Delaware* 3 (May1942).

_____. *Delaware's Forgotten Folk* (Philadelphia: University of Pennsylvania Press, 1943).

_____. "The Anthropological Position of the Indian Tribes of the Delmarva Peninsula," *Bulletin, The Archeological Society of Delaware* 4 (November 1947).

_____. *The Nanticoke Indians: A Refugee Tribal Group of Pennsylvania* (Harrisburg: The Pennsylvania Historical and Museum Commission, 1948).

_____. "The Indians of Lewes, Delaware and an Unpublished Indian Deed Dated June 7, 1659," *Bulletin, The Archeological Society of Delaware* 4 (January, 1949).

_____. "Robert Evelyn's Indian Tribes and Place-names of New Albion," *Bulletin, Archaeological Society of New Jersey* No. 9 (November 1954).

_____. "An Early American Name Puzzle," *Names* 2 (December 1954).

_____in collaboration with A.R. Dunlap. *Dutch Explorers, Traders and Settlers in the Delaware Valley 1609-1664* (Philadelphia: University of Pennsylvania Press, 1961).

_____. "Who Survived the Indian Massacre at Swanendael?" *de Halve Maen* 40 (October 1965).

_____. *The English on the Delaware: 1610-1682* (New Brunswick: Rutgers University Press, 1967).

_____.*Delaware's Buried Past,* rev. ed. (New Brunswick: Rutgers University Press, 1968).

_____. Written comments provided to the author on draft manuscript February 1971.

_____. *The Nanticoke Indians—Past and Present* (Newark: University of Delaware Press, 1983).

Wickersham, James Pyle. *A History of Education in Pennsylvania: Private and Public, Elementary and Higher* (Lancaster, Pa. 1886).

Wilson, Houston. "Cape Henlopen," [the Wilson Report] 2 vols. TMs (typewritten manuscript, 1942).

Wilson, W. Emerson. *Forgotten Heroes of Delaware* (Cambridge, Md.: Deltos Publishing Company, 1969).

Wiltsee, Jerome. *A Genealogical and Psychological Memoir of Philippe Maton Wiltsee and His Descendents* (Atchison, Kansas: G.W. Myers, 1908).

Year Book of the Holland Society of New York (1914).

Zeisberger, David. *History of the North American Indian*, A.B. Hulbert and W.N. Schwarze, eds., (Columbus, Ohio 1910).

Index

Russell, William 154, 155

S

Salwen, Bert 18
sand dunes 2, 19, 119, 120, 139
Seymour, Howard xvii
Shankland, Rhoads, Jr. 154
Shankland, William 159
Shankland Survey 160, 174
Sharpe, Governor Horatio 91
shell heaps (Indian) 2, 3, 4, 5, 11
Ship Building 126, 127, 130
Siconese Indians 21, 23, 25, 26. *See also* Lenape Indians
Society of Friends 122
Sockum, Levin 132
Southerland, Judge Clarence A. 141, 142, 148, 152, 153, 156, 173, 177, 178, 179
South River. *See* Delaware River
Speck, Frank 22
St. Albans 106
St. George's A.M.E. Church 130
St. Peter's Episcopal Church 58
Stango, Mayor Alfred A. xvii
State of Delaware v. Griffith 157
State of Delaware v. Levin Sockum 132
Stewart, T.D. 23
Stuyvesant, Peter 65
Sub-Sal, Inc. 108
Sussex Archeological Association. *See* Sussex Society for Archeology and History
Sussex Society for Archaeology and History 6, 14, 57, 61
Swanendael xv, xxii, xxiv, xxv, xxvi, xxviii, xxix, 26, 29–67, 81, 83, 93, 94, 105, 120, 183. *See also* de Vries (?) sketch
  archeology of remains 54
  palisades 40, 42, 57
  survivors 45, 46, 47, 48

T

This book was typeset
by Angela Werner
in Adobe Garamond and Emigré Mrs. Eaves
on Macintosh equipment.

237